BLACK'S N

BIRDS
OF BRITAIN AND EUROPE

Volker Dierschke

A&C BLACK
LONDON

Contents

Species

How to use this book

Unless otherwise indicated, the main photograph on each page shows a male bird with breeding plumage. The captions highlight key identifying features and other illustrations show significant details or alert you to similar species. You can refer to the texts, photographs and maps in the margin that includes additional information about habitat and breeding habits. General information is available in the main description of each species. If a whole page is devoted to a single bird, you can also find a **'Birder's tip'** or a **'Did you know?'** box. Last but not least, you can easily identify many birds by referring to the brief description of their call or song.

Size
Body size: Length from head to tail
Wingspan (WSp): Distance between wing tips of spread wings

General information
You will find fascinating details on behaviour, feeding habits and much more.

Wh
Motac.
L 18 cm

The Wh to the w deeply constar and hur along w bobbing places th flies like darker Pi the Britis numbers

Characteristic plumage
This section lists key features to help you identify different species.

Plumage variations
These illustrations show different plumages that vary with sex (♂, ♀), age (juvenile, adult) or season (e.g. winter eclipse plumage, summer alternate plumage). Key identifying features are marked with captions.

light-coloured f

winter plumage

Distribution map
Distinctive colours highlight where the birds can be observed during the breeding season, in their hibernation habitat and during migration.

Red
Present in summer

Green
Present all year round

Yellow
Present on migration

Blue
Present in winter

Yellow stripes
Main migration areas

Similar species
If not explained else-where, the illustrations show similar birds (names underlined) and captions highlighting their key identifying features.

flank blacki

Common name
Scientific name
Family

Migration habit
Does the bird stay in one geographical area all year round or migrate?

gtail
ails and pipits)
Short/Medium distance migrant

nmistakeable due
displays a
ht, is almost
long tail
attering
head
and around
ads of little
pats. The
arrellii) lives on
breeds in smaller
nt's North Sea coast.

long tail

white wing patches

Habitat Lives in villages and suburbs as well as in open and partly open country, preferably near water.

Breeding season April–August
5–6 light grey eggs with fine spots
2 broods per year

Habitat
An image of the bird in its natural habitat, with accompanying caption describing its habitat preferences.

Flight outlines
Shows a bird in flight. Note that in this position sex and age differences are not always visible.

ead black-and-white

back of head grey

3

back grey

♀

29

Breeding information
Details about season (from the start of egg-laying until the last brood fledges), clutch size, colour of eggs and number of broods per year.

Distribution map
(see p. 4 below).

Colour code
Each of the six bird groups is colour-coded (see also p. 1).

Silhouette
The bird's silhouette allows a more accurate distinction of the six bird groups (also see p.1).

juvenile

black sub-moustachial stripe

ied Wagtail

Voice Calls 'tchizzick' or 'tchik'; inconspicuous twittering song with jaunty calls.

Birder's tip
If a predator is approaching from the air the White Wagtail behaves in a very conspicuous way. If it flies everywhere, loudly twittering in alarm, then it won't be long before a Carrion Crow (p. 87), a Sparrowhawk (p. 148) or even a Kestrel (p. 149) will be seen overhead or nearby.

Song
A description of calls and song.

Birder's tip
Here you will find tips on where and how you can watch a bird's interesting habits. For some species, a **'Did you know?'** box highlights interesting general facts and other details.

Identifying features

A bird's plumage colour is often a telltale feature for identification purposes, but the following aspects also play a crucial role: a bird's **size**, **shape**, its movement and **habits**. If you see a bird you cannot identify, it often helps to compare the bird to other species you are familiar with. The next sections provide a few handy hints that are intended to make it easier for you to concentrate on gathering information about appropriate identifying features.

Almost all bird species display different plumages. Often there are differences between male and **female** birds as well as between the **adults** and **juveniles**. Birds frequently have a more colourful **breeding plumage** and a less conspicuous, camouflage-coloured **winter plumage**. While the winter plumage is mostly seen in winter, the breeding plumage tends to be mainly displayed in spring and summer during the mating and breeding season. The mating season for ducks starts in early winter and the male birds show their colourful plumage much earlier than other birds.

Note that during the **moult** or the change from one plumage to another, several transitional stages are always observed. Some species also obtain their alternate plumage without moulting: colourful plumage appears when the plain coloured, worn-down wing tips disappear.

Finding the species

Over 440 species are listed in this book. You are therefore likely to find almost every bird that you can see in Europe, either as a breeding, migrant or hibernating bird. The species are mostly described by family and in consecutive order, according to family relation. In most cases, similar species are included on adjacent pages in order to make comparisons easier.

Firecrest markings

Lateral crown stripe
Supercilium (eyebrow)
Crown stripe
Eye ring
Lore
Moustachial stripe

Topography and plumage of a male Yellowhammer

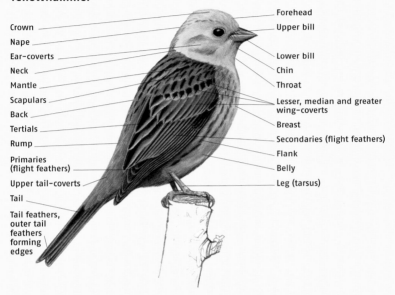

Crown

Nape

Ear-coverts

Neck

Mantle

Scapulars

Back

Tertials

Rump

Primaries (flight feathers)

Upper tail-coverts

Tail

Tail feathers, outer tail feathers forming edges

Forehead

Upper bill

Lower bill

Chin

Throat

Lesser, median and greater wing-coverts

Breast

Secondaries (flight feathers)

Flank

Belly

Leg (tarsus)

Plumage of a female Mallard

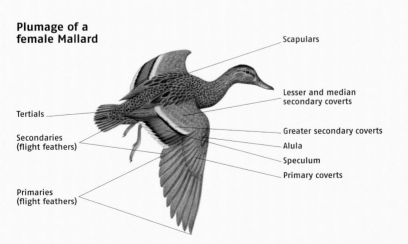

Tertials

Secondaries (flight feathers)

Primaries (flight feathers)

Scapulars

Lesser and median secondary coverts

Greater secondary coverts

Alula

Speculum

Primary coverts

Size

From Wren and Goldcrest to Crane and White-tailed Eagle - birds come in a variety of shapes and sizes. Noting the finer distinctions between similar species is essential for identification purposes. A black-and-white feathered bird with long red legs and a long red bill may either be an Oystercatcher or a White Stork. You might also notice other differences and looking closely at a bird's size can help avoid confusion. Even slight differences in size must be taken into account. Consider the black-and-white woodpeckers – the Great, Middle and Lesser Spotted Woodpeckers, or the small-sized Chiffchaff and marginally larger Willow Warbler (p. 53). Quite a few waders (pp. 176–192) are seen out and about in early autumn on mudflats. Most birds have grey or brown feathers, for instance, the Little Stint or Curlew, however, make sure you check noticeable differences in size.

A precise estimate of a bird's size is not always easy. As a rule, a bird always appears slightly larger from a distance than when you are close up. The length (from head to tail) should help you classify a bird's size in comparison to other, familiar birds. Note that in a crouching position or with drawn-in neck, a bird can appear smaller than it really is. Birds' wingspan in flight is more striking than body length. Therefore, you will find additional information on the distance between each wing tip when fully outstretched.

Similar coloured woodpecker species differ in size.

The Oystercatcher and White Stork have the same colours but different patterns and sizes.

Shape

A bird's shape is governed by the size ratios of its different body parts. Body shape may vary from slender to stout, but the length of the neck, legs and tail stands out. The overall impression is completed by details such as the length of the bill and wings. Despite its long bill, the Snipe appears rather plump with its stout body and short legs and neck. In contrast, the Curlew with its long neck and long legs appears very slender – an impression that is reinforced by the long, thin bill.

If we compare very similar species, noting these kind of details may be crucial. For example, the

Slender Curlew and plump Snipe.

longer wings of the Lesser Black-Backed Gull reach further over the tail than the wings of the short-winged Great Black-Backed Gull. Thus the Lesser Black-Backed Gull appears as considerably more slender. In many cases, tail and wing shape can also help you identify a bird. The Sparrowhawk's wings are shorter and more rounded at the tips than those of the falcons (pp 149-153). In turn, falcons' wings look narrower and longer as well as more pointed. The Black and Red Kite (p. 143) have a forked tail, whereas other birds of prey do not.

Longer wings give the Lesser Black-Backed Gull a more slender appearance.

Another very helpful identifying feature is the shape of the bill. Among the songbirds, buntings (pp. 105–111), finches (pp. 94–104) and sparrows (pp. 91–93) are easily identified because of their thick bill, which they use to crack seeds. Insect-eaters, on the other hand, have finer bills. Take a closer look at the sandpiper family and your efforts will pay off: the Dunlin's bill is slightly curved, whereas the Little Stint's bill is shorter, not decurved. The Curlew Sandpiper has a longer and even more curved bill.

Slight differences in the shape of the bill help identify sandpipers.

9

Colours and Patterns

Colourful birds, such as the Kingfisher (p. 122), the Bluethroat (p. 61) and the Golden Oriole (p. 90) are usually easy to identify straight away because of their conspicuously coloured plumage. You can identify many other species if you remember the colouring of key plumage features, especially the head, wings, rump, tail and bare parts (legs and bill). It is fairly easy to identify a small songbird with yellow belly, green rump and black-and-white head as a Great Tit (p. 76).

the underside. When the bird is in flight you should pay attention to the colour of the tail (some species' tails have white outer margins) and wings. Also, the colour of the rump can help identify a bird. When a mixed flock of finches takes off, a Brambling will immediately stand out because of the white rump, whereas the Chaffinch's rump is inconspicuously green-coloured. Apart from plumage colours, the colours of the bill and legs are also often important.

The male Tree Sparrow is distinguished from the House Sparrow by the black mark on its cheek.

We frequently see birds with inconspicuous plumage colours that are basically brown or green. Since these birds are camouflaged quite well, they are difficult for us to identify. Therefore details like patterns or specific conspicuous features are vital. The House Sparrow and Tree Sparrow are generally quite similar, but the Tree Sparrow can always be identified by the black spot on the cheek – this is always missing on the House Sparrow. Plumage elements are frequently a good clue for identification, for instance, the stripes on the head and wing patches and marks or stripes on

Finches in flight can often be identified by their rump colours.

Flight

All European birds can fly – but their flight styles may differ considerably and thus provide another clue for identification. Ducks and waders beat their wings constantly when in flight and therefore have a straight flight path and are very fast. Many songbirds alternate between short flaps of their wings and brief rest periods, so their flight is more of an up-and-down path; their flight speed, most of the time, is lower. Many birds can fly over longer distances without once flapping their wings. Birds of prey and storks prefer soaring upward, cruising on the streams of warm air (thermal currents). Shearwaters and many other sea birds use the air drafts between waves to glide over the sea for hours on end and without a single flap of their wings.

Many birds of prey sail through the air with out-spread wings.

Migrating cranes can be identified from a considerable distance because of their flight pattern – phases of slow wing flaps change intermittently with gliding phases. Geese, which fly in V formations like cranes, flap their wings constantly and much faster.

Apart from their different shapes, their flight also helps differentiate the House Martin from the Swift soaring high up in the sky. Swifts fly tremendously fast, with powerful and rapid flaps of their wings and often with long gliding phases; in contrast, the House Martin's flight appears much more fluttering and gliding phases are much shorter.

Swifts and house martins can be identified by their flight styles.

Some birds of prey, especially the Kestrel frequently display a special way of flying: to search for their prey in flight, they hover above the ground with rapidly fluttering wings. This so-called '(wind)hovering' can also be seen in terns (pp. 203–207).

Kestrel hovering.

Behaviour

When you are out watching birds, you will soon discover how their movement and behaviour provide vital clues to help you identify them quickly. The best time to observe birds is often as they forage for food. How they search usually helps you narrow down the number of species to

Woodpeckers, treecreepers and nuthatches climb tree-trunks.

consider. For example, there are only a few birds that climb up a tree trunk and pick insects from the bark. Woodpeckers, treecreepers and also nuthatches do this. Ducks usually search for food in the water, some collect it from the surface or only immerse their heads and necks (Mallard and similar species), others dive underwater to feed and are briefly out of sight (e.g. Tufted Duck and Pochard). In these instances, you can only identify the species by carefully checking distinctive features of their plumage.

Other behavioural patterns that may help with identifying species are, for example, courtship display and, especially during migration, also flock formation. During active migratory flight as well as resting phases, some species form huge swarms, whereas others are loners or only congregate in small groups.

Distribution

The area where you see a bird may help you to identify it, as different species occupy distinct geographical regions. Distribution maps should show you at a glance whether or not a bird regularly occurs in a particular area. However note that individual birds may stray to areas that have not been marked for their species on maps. Within the general region they occupy, many birds will only be found in particular habitat types. Many species can only be found in the forest, on lake or coastal shores or in the open countryside. Here you also have to consider that migratory birds do not always find their preferred habitat and may therefore have to rest in unfamiliar terrain.

Reed Warblers only live in reeds.

Song

Apart from their colourful plumage, we are usually most attracted by birds' songs. Almost every species has its own call and song repertoire, so this feature also becomes a major part of the identification puzzle. In the species information, you will find a short description of a bird's song or voice. Sound recordings are widely available as an additional identification guide. Taking part in birdsong excursions is also highly recommended. Many nature conservation societies or adult education centres host these events. If you are patient, however, you also have the option of learning about birdsong patterns on your own, by listening to birds sing and memorizing the combination of their voice and appearance. Birdsong varies and may be complex and melodious or (to our

The River Warbler sings hidden away in thick shrubs.

ears) very simple and tuneless. For many species, only males produce song, although in a few cases the females sing as well. In general, birds sing for two reasons: to delineate their breeding territory acoustically from neighbours of the same species; and to attract a mate. Often, the male bird

presents itself in an elevated position, on top of a shrub or on protruding branches of a tree, to show off its colourful plumage. Especially in the open countryside, some species display song-flights, performing their song high up in the air. Other species only sing when hidden away in thick shrubs.

Birds of the same species keep in some sort of contact by using their different calls. Migrating birds, in particular, can be heard from far off. Often they

The Bluethroat presents its colourful front when singing.

attract attention by sounding warning calls to alert others to the presence of predators nearby, such as birds of prey or cats. They can also threaten a neighbour intruding on their territory.

The Tree Pipit's song-flight starts from the top of a tree.

Purpose

Many European bird species are migratory. Since they cannot find food in their winter breeding areas, they fly south in autumn, spending the winter where food supplies are more easily found. They only return the following spring. Seedeaters find food almost everywhere in winter and therefore do not migrate far, or not at all. Insect-eaters, on the other hand, are almost always migratory birds. Some stay in western Europe or the Mediterranean, while others cross the 3,000 km Sahara and reach as far as central or southern Africa.

Distribution

The Green Woodpecker is a typical resident bird that does not leave its breeding habitat and only roams about a little farther in winter. The Fieldfare belongs to the group of short distance migrants and shifts its distribution area in winter a little southwards, but only within Europe. Some wader species, as well as many songbirds, belong to the group of long distance migrants. For example, the Curlew Sandpiper breeds in the northern Siberian Arctic and only crosses Europe on its way to west and South Africa, where it winters.

'Fuel'

To survive their long journeys, migratory birds have to store the right amount of energy before they start out. For several weeks they consume a lot of food, storing up large fat supplies and generally fattening up. These supplies serve as 'fuel' for the flight. Normally, migratory birds have to stop between flights and 're-fuel'. They need resting areas, which provide a rich variety of food. For many ducks, geese and waders, mudflats on the coastlines of Germany, Denmark and the Netherlands serve as crucial fuelling stations, before their departure for Africa in the autumn or Siberia in springtime.

As a resident bird, the Green Woodpecker winters in its own breeding territory.

The short distance migrant Fieldfare can winter in Europe with berries as winter food.

As a long distance migrant, the Curlew Sandpiper crosses Europe en route from Siberia to South Africa.

Migration

Birds migrate in the daytime (diurnal) as well as during the night (nocturnally). The direction and duration of their migration is as innate to these birds as their orientation mechanism. Depending on the species, the bird relies on an inner compass, which follows the position of the sun, stars, the earth's magnetic field, or a combination of all three. Many birds therefore migrate in a sweeping front, i.e. they fly on a direct route from the breeding area to their winter home.

Some birds navigate using visual landmarks, which serve as 'guidelines', such as a coastline or river course. Birds of prey and storks migrate in soaring flight. To reach the necessary altitude, they use thermal updrafts. But because these updrafts only form over land, if possible, the birds avoid flying over large stretches of water like expansive sea areas. Instead of crossing the Mediterranean, migrating flocks of birds of prey and storks make for the Straits of Gibraltar and the Bosporus and to a lesser extent also for the straits between Tunisia and Sicily.

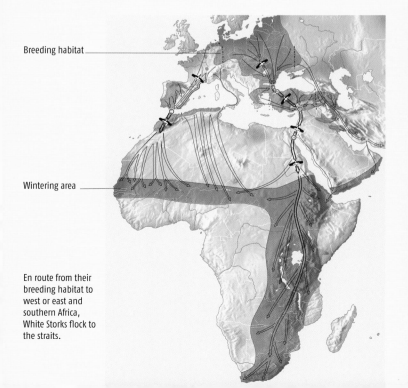

Breeding habitat

Wintering area

En route from their breeding habitat to west or east and southern Africa, White Storks flock to the straits.

Sand Martin

Riparia riparia (swallows and martins)

L 12 cm   WSp 27–29 cm   Long distance migrant

Habitat *Always nests in steep sandstone rock faces, mostly on shores or banks. It catches flying insects in the surrounding countryside.*

> **Breeding season April–September**
> **4–6 pure white eggs**
> **1–2 broods per year**

The Sand Martin breeds mostly in colonies. It builds its nesting tunnels in the few existing steep cliff faces there are in the countryside. For instance, a few thousand Sand Martin pairs inhabit the biggest colonies on steep banks along the Baltic Sea coast. This breeding method has the advantage of preventing predators like badgers or foxes from reaching the nesting sites. On the other hand the broods are constantly endangered by sand slides. The Sand Martin is gregarious at all times, even when migratory and in its African winter habitat.

throat white

brown breast patch

top uniform brown

tail slightly forked

breeding colony

Voice *Hard, purring calls ('tchrrip') during flight. Twittering, inconspicuous song.*

Did you know?

The male bird digs a nesting tunnel up to 90 cm deep in sand pits using its claws. This takes one to two weeks and after finishing this job, it pads the hole with grass and feathers. Both parents share breeding and feeding responsibilities.

18

Swallow

Hirundo rustica (swallows and martins)
L 17–19 cm   WSp 32–34 cm   Long distance migrant

The Swallow usually breeds in caves but can nowadays be seen attaching its nest, which consists of compressed clay and stalks, to open buildings (like stables) or under low bridges. Old nests are likely to be reused. The female bird detects a male's suitability as a mate from the length of his tail streamers. This is important because males with longer tails take part in breeding activity with greater enthusiasm, start early with breeding, and therefore sometimes manage another one or two broods within the same year.

nest with almost fully-fledged young

Habitat Breeds mostly in villages; hawks for insects over grassland and wetlands.

> Breeding season April–September
> 3–6 white eggs with brownish spots
> 1–3 broods per year

Voice Often calls 'tswit' during flight, also repeatedly; twittering song that sometimes ends with a warble.

19

adult

top shimmering blue

throat and forehead rufous

long forked tail

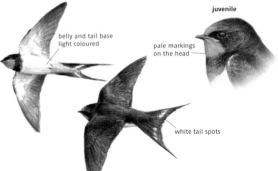

juvenile

belly and tail base light coloured

pale markings on the head

white tail spots

Did you know?

The Swallow is one of the most familiar migratory birds among European songbirds. Apart from a few birds that stay in the Mediterranean, over winter, the Swallow remains in areas south of the Sahara, down to the most southerly point of the continent.

Red-rumped Swallow

Cecropis daurica (swallows and martins)
L 16–17 cm   WSp 32–34 cm   Long distance migrant

breast with light dotted lines

tail base black

tail deeply forked

This bird is very similar to the the Swallow (p. 19) in all ways. However, it nests on natural rock faces more frequently than the Swallow does. The nest, which is completed in one or two weeks, is built with glued-together little lumps of clay and straw, with a narrow pipe-shaped entrance.

Habitat *Breeds either in rocky gorges or in settlements; foraging in open countryside.*

> *Breeding season April–September*
> *3–5 pure white eggs*
> *1–3 broods per year*

nape rufous

throat light-coloured

rufous rump spot

nest with pipe-shaped entrance

Voice *Similar to the Swallow's, but calls softer. The chattering song is lower and shorter.*

Crag Martin

Ptyonoprogne rupestris (swallows and martins)
L 15 cm   WSp 32–34 cm   Resident bird/Short distance migrant

Habitat *Nests in mountains on sunny, exposed rock faces but also inhabits urban landscapes; likes to hunt above waters.*

> *Breeding season May–October*
> *2–5 red-white spotted eggs*
> *1–2 broods per year*

In contrast to other European swallows, the Crag Martin does not breed in colonies – it even defends its breeding territory against others in its family. It builds its nest in cavities or beneath overhanging rocks, but its broods can also be found on buildings and below bridges. As a mountain bird, the species is prepared for the cold and only spends a few weeks away from its breeding sites.

Voice *Utters a quiet, chattering song during flight. Calls with a purring or hard 'prrit'.*

top uniform brown

white tail spots

brownish underparts

wing base dark

tail not forked

House Martin
Delichon urbicum (swallows and martins)
L 13 cm   WSp 26–29 cm   Long distance migrant

The House Martin mostly hunts for little insects high up in the air. It can often be spotted flying alongside swifts (p. 120–121) and thus flies in distinctly higher regions than the Swallow (p. 19). It mixes the insects caught during flight with saliva and feeds its young with the sticky mixture. During cold and wet spells, when food is scarce, the juvenile birds may enter a torpid state, induced by the cold. Consequently their growth is interrupted for the duration of the cold weather and so the nesting period can vary from three to five weeks.

nest

Habitat Originally an inhabitant of rock faces, now most birds nest in towns and villages.

> *Breeding season May–September*
> *3–5 white eggs*
> *1–2 broods per year*

21

Voice Call is a hoarse 'tchirrip', song a soft twitter.

back black with bluish shimmer

pure white below

leg white-feathered

tail lightly forked

large, glowing white area on rump

Birder's tip
The House Martin rarely lands on the ground, except when it is preparing to build its nest, when it collects mud as building material from puddles. Then, you can observe how little lumps of mud are used to build a nest underneath projecting roofs.

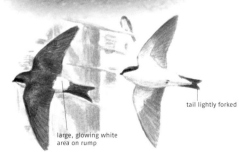

Crested Lark
Galerida cristata (larks)
L 17 cm   WSp 29–38 cm   Resident bird

Habitat *Lives in dry, open spaces; also along streets, in parking lots and fallow sites.*

> **Breeding season April–September**
> **3–5 whitish eggs with grey spots**
> **2–3 broods per year**

The Crested Lark prefers arid and barren habitats. During periods of warm climate conditions (in the 16th and 18th centuries) the species spread across Europe, but withdrew further south during cooler periods (in the 17th century). Over the past 100 years, additional habitats have developed with the increasing agricultural use of large areas, but over time, they have become too overgrown and are no longer suitable as nesting habitats. However, increased temperatures due to global warming favour this species, though the accompanying higher rainfall does not.

secondaries tinged rufous

Did you know?
The Thekla Lark (G. theklae), which is very similar to the Crested Lark, lives in Spain and north-west Africa. It prefers even drier and more barren habitats and can be best identified by streaks on its breast and its shorter, stouter bill.

Thekla Lark

bill relatively short and thick

strong streaks on breast

spike-like crest

bill long, slightly decurved

thin streaks on breast

Voice *Loud, warbling song delivered during flight or from ground perch. Calls resemble melancholy whistling.*

Skylark
Aluda arvensis (larks)
L 18–19 cm   WSp 30–36 cm   Short distance migrant

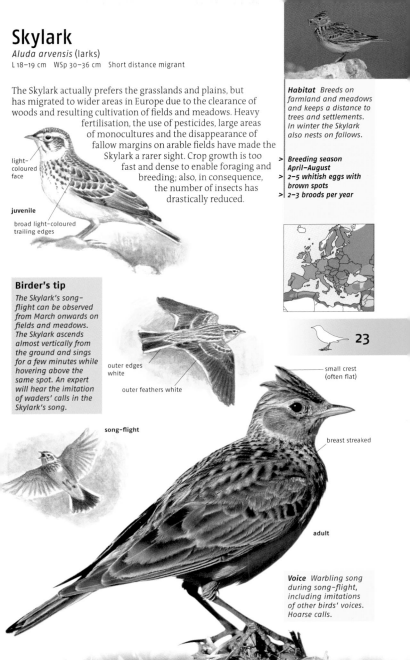

The Skylark actually prefers the grasslands and plains, but has migrated to wider areas in Europe due to the clearance of woods and resulting cultivation of fields and meadows. Heavy fertilisation, the use of pesticides, large areas of monocultures and the disappearance of fallow margins on arable fields have made the Skylark a rarer sight. Crop growth is too fast and dense to enable foraging and breeding; also, in consequence, the number of insects has drastically reduced.

light-coloured face

juvenile

broad light-coloured trailing edges

Habitat *Breeds on farmland and meadows and keeps a distance to trees and settlements. In winter the Skylark also nests on fallows.*

> *Breeding season April–August*
> *2–5 whitish eggs with brown spots*
> *2–3 broods per year*

23

Birder's tip
The Skylark's song-flight can be observed from March onwards on fields and meadows. The Skylark ascends almost vertically from the ground and sings for a few minutes while hovering above the same spot. An expert will hear the imitation of waders' calls in the Skylark's song.

outer edges white

outer feathers white

song-flight

small crest (often flat)

breast streaked

adult

Voice *Warbling song during song-flight, including imitations of other birds' voices. Hoarse calls.*

Woodlark
Lullula arborea (larks)
L 15 cm   WSp 27–30 cm   Short distance migrant

white marks on upper wings

short tail

Habitat *Prefers sandy, fairly open country: heaths, woods with clearings or the periphery of woods, but also seen foraging on farmland.*

> **Breeding season March–July**
> **3–6 whitish eggs with brown dots**
> **1–2 broods per year**

thin bill

During song-flight the Woodlark spirals upwards, sometimes from treetops. But generally, the Woodlark is a ground-roaming bird that looks for insects in barren areas. It also nests on the ground. The nest is well hidden among tufts of grass. Juvenile birds leave the nest before they are fully fledged.

rufous cheeks

supercilium stripes meet on back of head

Voice *Song has melodious, cascading, flute-like phrases. Calls with a yodelling 'lit-loo-eet'*

24

Short-toed Lark
Calandrella brachydactyla (larks)
L 13–14 cm   WSp 25–30 cm   Short/Medium distance migrant

Lesser Short-toed Lark

bill thick

breast streaked

primaries protruding from beneath tertials

Habitat *Inhabits dry, open land: partial deserts, arid grassland and barren arable land.*

> **Breeding season April–July**
> **3–5 whitish eggs with dark spots**
> **2 broods per year**

The Short-toed Lark's song is more monotonous than the Skylark's (p. 23), but the song-flight's path, with its wavelike ups-and-downs and flapping phases, is much more varied. The Lesser Short-toed Lark (*C. rufescens*), native to Spain and the Ukraine, looks very similar to the Short-toed Lark.

long wing-tips are almost fully cloaked by tertials

bill strong and sharp

breast mostly without streaks

no pale trailing edge to wing

Voice *Song-flight with monotonous phrases, also imitating other birds' voices. Calls with a sharp 'tchi-tchirrup'.*

Shore Lark
Eremophila alpestris (larks)
L 14–17 cm WSp 30–35 cm   Short/Medium distance migrant

white outer tail feathers

The Shore Lark prefers to winter along seashores. The species is mainly seen at the edges of the shoreline, where large amounts of plant seeds from salt marshes are washed ashore and can be collected more easily here than anywhere else. The birds will come back to good spots for many years in succession.

Voice *Thin, whistling 'tsee-sirrp' call. Song consists of twittering phrases with high-pitched tones.*

black thin 'horns' above the eyes

black and yellow head marks

♂

♀

juvenile
head pattern pale

Habitat *Nests in barren, stony habitats; in winter on seashores as well as on salt marshes and arable fields.*

> *Breeding Season April–July*
> *3–5 yellow-brown eggs with dots or spots*
> *1–2 broods per year*

---

underwings blackish

Calandra Lark
Melanocorypha calandra (larks)
L 18–19 cm WSp 34–42 cm   Resident bird/Short distance migrant

The Calandra Lark hovers in the air during its song-flight, like the Skylark, but flaps its wing surprisingly slowly in comparison. In summer it feeds on insects, which it sometimes digs out of parched ground in its breeding habitat, by using its heavy bill. In winter the Calandra Lark feeds on grains and uses its bill to separate the grain from the seed capsule.

white stripe above and behind eye

bill thick, yellowish

black patch on neck sides

Voice *Deep, melodious song that is performed during flight and contains imitations. Chirping calls during flight.*

Habitat *Originally inhabits dry plains and grassland, meadows and fallows but is nowadays also often seen on cornfields.*

> *Breeding season April–July*
> *4–5 reddish or bluish, dotted eggs*
> *1–2 broods per year*

Tawny Pipit
Anthus campestris (wagtails and pipits)
L 17 cm WSp 25–28 cm Long distance migrant

juvenile
dark spot in front of eye
breast with streaks

adult
light-coloured area in front of the eye

Richard's Pipit
breast with streaks
long-legged

back almost monochrome

breast without streaks

Habitat *The Tawny Pipit inhabits dry, sparsely overgrown areas on sandy grounds like heaths, fallow areas and clearings.*

> **Breeding season May–August**
> **4–5 white to brownish, dotted eggs**
> **1–2 broods per year**

The Tawny Pipit needs barren regions to exist. With the climate becoming more and more humid, the increased use of fertilisers in agriculture and the destruction of large heath and marshland areas in central Europe, litttle suitable habitat remains. As a consequence the population is rapidly decreasing. Every autumn a few Richard's Pipits (*A. richardi*) from Siberia reach Europe.

Voice *Song of repetitious disyllabic elements. Flight call similar to the House Sparrow's 'chirrup'.*

Red-throated Pipit
Anthus cervinus (wagtails and pipits)
L 15 cm WSp 25–27 cm Long distance migrant

winter plumage
long cream-coloured stripes on the back

breast and flank are heavily marked with dotted lines

Habitat *Nests in open marshlands (Tundra, bogs); when migrating and in winter the bird prefers wet grassland.*

> **Breeding season June–August**
> **5–6 dotted eggs, basic colour varies**
> **1 brood per year**

The colouring of the Red-throated Pipit's front area frequently varies in spring. The larger the proportion of rusty-red colouring on head and breast, the fewer dark streaks there are. Despite the fact that the Red-throated Pipit is a very common breeding bird in northern Scandinavia, it is rarely seen as a migrant bird in central Europe, because most of the birds take a south-easterly route and stay in east Africa over winter.

head and breast rufous

flank with black dotted lines

breeding plumage

Voice *Thin, drawn-out flight call that is also reflected in song, similar to the Meadow Pipit's.*

Tree Pipit

Anthus trivialis (wagtails and pipits)
L 15 cm   WSp 25–27 cm   Long distance migrant

song-flight

As conspicuously as the Tree Pipit behaves during its song-flight, it remains hidden while foraging for food. It picks up little insects from the ground, protected by dense vegetation. The Tree Pipit covers the distance between breeding habitat and its African wintering grounds by flying in the mornings; the rest of the day is spent looking for food and filling up its energy reserves.

longish head profile

strong brown streaks on cream-coloured breast

finely streaked on flanks

Voice *Blaring song that is uttered during flight, right after ascent to treetops; flight call is a hoarse 'teez' or 'steeze'.*

Habitat *Breeds at edges of woods and in clearings as well as in fairly open country with few trees.*

> *Breeding season April–August*
> *3–6 spotted eggs, basic colour varies*
> *1–2 broods per year*

Meadow Pipit

Anthus pratensis (wagtails and pipits)
L 14 cm   WSp 22–25 cm, Short/Medium distance migrant

thin wing patches

white outer tail feathers

Apart from its conspicuous song-flight the Meadow Pipit is hardly noticeable in its breeding habitat. It inhabits open country, but hides its nest in dense grass and also stays hidden during its search for food. Because of the large breeding populations in Scandinavia, the Meadow Pipit is more often seen out as a migrant, especially because it migrates during the day and calls constantly.

round head profile

equally strong dotted lines on breast and flanks

Habitat *Inhabits open country, from marshlands, heath and tundra to meadows and fields.*

> *Breeding season March–August*
> *4–6 pale eggs with dark spots*
> *1–2 broods per year*

Voice *Calls 'seep' or 'weesk', often repeatedly. Varied song is performed during down-gliding flight.*

Water Pipit
Anthus spinoletta (wagtails and pipits)
L 17 cm   WSp 24–29 cm   Short distance migrant

white outer
tail feathers

Habitat *Breeds above the tree line in mountainous grasslands; in winter it breeds on plains, meadows, banks and shores.*

> **Breeding season May–August**
> 3–6 grey or brown eggs with strong marks
> 1–2 broods per year

The Water Pipit shows a strong inclination to migrate to lower altitudes in autumn, which is typical for many mountain birds. It migrates for example from the Alps to the lowlands and the Baltic Sea. The Water Pipit finally returns to the mountainous breeding habitat while there is still snow. When choosing its nesting site the bird looks for natural stony canopies, which protect from further snowfall.

Voice *Call 'feest', a little longer than Meadow Pipit's (p. 27); song also similar but with many trills.*

winter plumage

basic colouring
greyish-brown

distinct
supercilium

white
wing
patch

head grey
with
whitish
supercilium

pinkish
breast

**breeding
plumage**

legs dark

Rock Pipit
Anthus petrosus (wagtails and pipits)
L 17 cm   WSp 23–28 cm   Short distance migrant

grey outer
tail feathers

Habitat *Breeds and hibernates on rocky shores; in winter also in salt marshes and hard mud coasts.*

> **Breeding season May–August**
> 4–6 grey or brown eggs with strong marks
> 1–2 broods per year

The Rock Pipit's speciality as a maritime bird is finding food in rocky and muddy tidal areas. In winter it feeds on seaweed flies, little crayfish, woodlice and smaller snails. In summer, it mainly feeds on insects. There is a considerable difference between the breeding plumages of the British Isles and Scandinavian breeding birds.

British Isles
upperparts
blackish-grey

winter plumage

base colour
olive

supercilium blurred
upperpart grey

**breeding
plumages**

pinkish breast

Scandinavia

Voice *Call and song both as for Water Pipit.*

blurry streaks on
buff underparts

legs dark

White Wagtail

Motacilla alba (wagtails and pipits)
L 18 cm   WSp 25–30 cm   Short/Medium distance migrant

The White Wagtail is unmistakeable due to the way it moves. It displays a deeply undulating flight, is almost constantly wagging its long tail and hunts insects by pattering along with exaggerated head bobbing, preferably in and around places that attract myriads of little flies like puddles or cowpats. The darker Pied Wagtail (*M. yarrellii*) lives on the British Isles and also breeds in smaller numbers on the continent's North Sea coast.

long tail

white wing patches

Habitat Lives in villages and suburbs as well as in open and partly open country, preferably near water.

> *Breeding season* April–August
> 5–6 light grey eggs with fine spots
> 2 broods per year

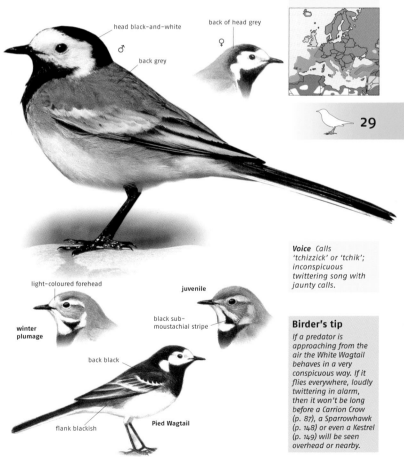

head black-and-white

♂

back grey

back of head grey

♀

29

Voice Calls 'tchizzick' or 'tchik'; inconspicuous twittering song with jaunty calls.

light-coloured forehead

winter plumage

juvenile

black sub-moustachial stripe

back black

flank blackish

Pied Wagtail

Birder's tip

If a predator is approaching from the air the White Wagtail behaves in a very conspicuous way. If it flies everywhere, loudly twittering in alarm, then it won't be long before a Carrion Crow (p. 87), a Sparrowhawk (p. 148) or even a Kestrel (p. 149) will be seen overhead or nearby.

Grey Wagtail
Motacilla cinerea (wagtails and pipits)
L 18–19 cm   WSp 25–27 cm   Resident bird/long distance migrant

Habitat Lives near fresh water, only occasionally also in dry areas.

> Breeding season March–August
> 4–6 lightly marked grey eggs
> 2 broods per year

The Grey Wagtail builds its nest close to water, very often underneath tree roots or between stones but also beneath bridges. Because the birds always forage close to water, wintering Grey Wagtail populations may suffer heavy losses during longer periods of frost. The similar looking Citrine Wagtail (*M. citreola*) lives in eastern Europe. It mainly lives in wet grasslands and stays in India and south east Asia over the winter but appears every year in small numbers in central Europe.

rump yellowish-green

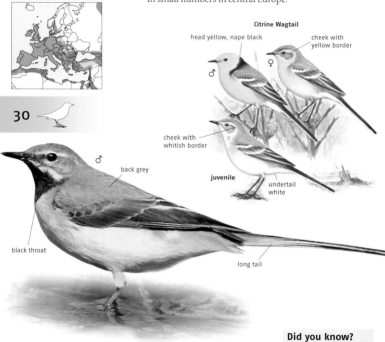

Citrine Wagtail

head yellow, nape black

cheek with yellow border

♂   ♀

cheek with whitish border

juvenile

undertail white

back grey

♂

black throat

long tail

Voice Calls higher and more clipped than White Wagtail (p. 29). Song is an unmelodious string of tones similar to calls.

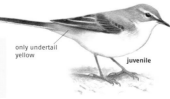

only undertail yellow

juvenile

Did you know?
Swiss researchers discovered that rearing their young is quite a feat for the Grey Wagtail. For one brood, the parents need 30,000–45,000 insects, which they feed to the juveniles with about 4,500 visits to the nest.

Yellow Wagtail

Motacilla flava (wagtails and pipits)
L 17 cm   WSp 23–27 cm   Long distance migrants

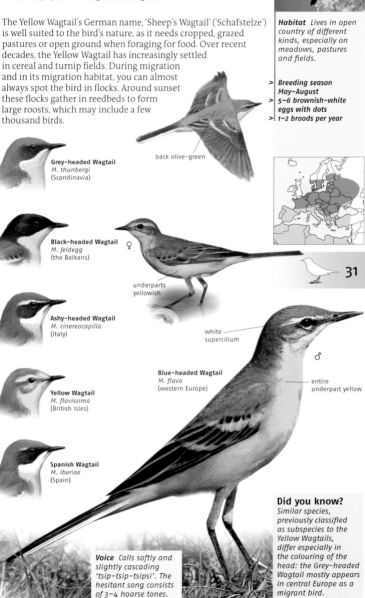

The Yellow Wagtail's German name, 'Sheep's Wagtail' ('Schafstelze') is well suited to the bird's nature, as it needs cropped, grazed pastures or open ground when foraging for food. Over recent decades, the Yellow Wagtail has increasingly settled in cereal and turnip fields. During migration and in its migration habitat, you can almost always spot the bird in flocks. Around sunset these flocks gather in reedbeds to form large roosts, which may include a few thousand birds.

Habitat Lives in open country of different kinds, especially on meadows, pastures and fields.

> **Breeding season** May–August
> 5–6 brownish-white eggs with dots
> 1–2 broods per year

back olive-green

Grey-headed Wagtail
M. thunbergi
(Scandinavia)

Black-headed Wagtail
M. feldegg
(the Balkans) ♀

underparts yellowish

Ashy-headed Wagtail
M. cinereocapilla
(Italy)

white supercilium

Blue-headed Wagtail
M. flava
(western Europe)

♂

entire underpart yellow

Yellow Wagtail
M. flavissima
(British Isles)

Spanish Wagtail
M. iberiae
(Spain)

Did you know?
Similar species, previously classified as subspecies to the Yellow Wagtails, differ especially in the colouring of the head: the Grey-headed Wagtail mostly appears in central Europe as a migrant bird.

Voice *Calls softly and slightly cascading 'tsip-tsip-tsipsi'. The hesitant song consists of 3–4 hoarse tones.*

Waxwing

Bombycilla garrulus (waxwings)
L 18 cm WSp 32–35 cm Resident bird/Short distance migrant

yellow wing patch

star-shaped flight profile

Habitat *Nests in coniferous and birch woods in taiga; in winter in open woodlands, parks and gardens.*

> *Breeding season May–August*
> *4–6 bluish-grey eggs with black dots*
> *1 brood per year*

During the breeding season the Waxwing feeds on insects. Its migratory behaviour, however, depends on the availability of rowan berries in Scandinavia. In a good year, most of the birds stay close to the breeding habitat. If there are not enough fruits, the Waxwing arrives in central Europe in droves where, apart from various berries, it also eats apples.

red 'spikes' on primaries

primaries with strong pattern

juvenile

primaries with pale pattern

throat and eye-stripe black

winter flock

Voice *Calls 'zhree" in high and whirring pattern; song consists of long sequences of calls and similar noises.*

Dipper

Cinclus cinclus (dipper)
L 18 cm WSp 26–30 cm
Resident bird/Short distance migrant

belly blackish-brown, in northern Europe

Habitat *Only lives close to fast-flowing streams and rivers.*

> *Breeding season February–July*
> *4–6 whitish or light cream-coloured eggs*
> *1–2 broods per year*

The Dipper is the only songbird able to plunge into fast-flowing water. It does this frequently to collect grubs, sand hoppers and other small water insects from the stream bed. Swimming also plays a role in mating rituals. The Dipper builds its globular nest next to water, in a hollow to protect it from splashes.

adult

throat and breast white

tail short

juvenile

upperparts grey

belly rufous

belly mottled dusky and white

Voice *Clear song that consists of whistling to tinkling notes that are often drowned by the sound of rushing water.*

Wren

Troglodytes troglodytes (wrens)

L 9–10 cm   WSp 13–17 cm   Resident bird/Short distance migrant

Despite the male Wren's minuscule size, its song is one of the loudest and most conspicuous bird sounds in Britain and Europe. Its voice can be heard throughout the entire year. It not only uses it to mark the boundaries of its breeding territory, but also its feeding territory. Looking for insects and spiders, the Wren forages through thick undergrowth but draws attention to itself by uttering its harsh warning calls. It can be observed best when it changes its position on whirring wings.

light-coloured supercilium

short, often cocked tail

short wings

Habitat *Lives in woods, parks and gardens that are rich in undergrowth and bigger bushes.*

> *Breeding season April–August*
> *5–7 white eggs with brown spots*
> *2 broods per year*

33

Voice Powerful, strident, fairly musical son; calls with a harsh 'tit-tit-tit' and a 'churr'.

Did you know?

The male builds the outer structure of several globular nests and the female then chooses one for breeding. That nest's construction is then completed. Many males have two, sometimes up to four mates. Birds also use the nest overnight.

fledgling young

Dunnock
Prunella modularis (accentors)
L 14 cm   WSp 19–21 cm   Resident bird/Short distance migrant

Habitat *Coppices, shrubs on fields, hedgerows, parks and gardens.*

> **Breeding season April–August**
> 4–6 turquoise eggs
> 2–3 broods per year

The Dunnock often attracts attention with its loud song, but otherwise it roams the undergrowth where it keeps itself well hidden. Males and females maintain independent territories during the breeding season. Depending on how much these territories overlap, one male can keep several females and one female up to two males as mates.

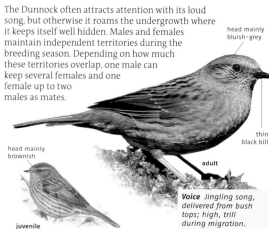

head mainly bluish-grey

thin black bill

adult

head mainly brownish

juvenile

Voice *Jingling song, delivered from bush tops; high, trill during migration.*

34

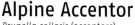

Alpine Accentor
Prunella collaris (accentors)
L 18 cm   WSp 30–32 cm   Resident bird/Short distance migrant

wings with white spots

Habitat *Lives on rocky and short-grassed mountain slopes up to the snow line; in winter it also inhabits lowlands.*

> **Breeding season May–August**
> 3–5 turquoise eggs
> 1–2 broods per year

The female Alpine Accentor chooses a suitable nesting site in a rock face or beneath rocks and builds her nest alone. Often female birds form groups with up to five members to breed together and support each other with their broods. This usually results in successful breeding.

throat has black and white pattern

flanks with chestnut streaks

breeding plumage in autumn

Voice *Rapid song with harsh trills, delivered from cliff tops. Most frequent call 'churrg'.*

Blackbird
Turdus merula (thrushes)
L 24–25 cm   WSp 34–39 cm   Resident bird/Short distance migrant

The Blackbird gradually migrated from forests to gardens and other urban habitats around 150 years ago. In these locations, it found suitable nesting sites in shrubs and trees as well good conditions when foraging for food in cropped meadows. Today the Blackbird with its estimated 40–80 million pairs is one of the most abundant European breeding bird species. While many northern European birds migrate to the south-west in autumn, in most cases, the central European Blackbird population remains in its breeding habitat.

Habitat Dense forests and small wood piles, frequents residential and inner-city areas.

> *Breeding season February–August*
> *4–5 bluish eggs, often with brown markings*
> *2–4 broods per year*

35

upper- and underwing dark

juvenile

long tail

mottled light brown above

dark bill

darkly mottled below

♀

plumage dark brown

Voice Melodious, whistling warble, delivered from vantage points; loud, scolding 'chink' when alarmed.

yellow bill

♂

plumage black

Birder's tip
The Blackbird's song is audible especially during early mornings or at dusk. If you listen carefully, you will hear several imitations of other voices or noises, for instance, in residential areas the Blackbird often imitates people whistling or telephone ring tones.

Ring Ouzel
Turdus torquatus (thrushes)
L 23–24 cm WSp 38–42 cm Short/Medium distance migrant

upper wing more lightly coloured than Blackbird's

Habitat *Nests in open coniferous forests in mountainous regions, in Scandinavia also on rocky fells and in Birch woods.*

> *Breeding season April–July*
> *3–6 greenish-brown spotted eggs*
> *1–2 broods per year*

Like the Blackbird, the Ring Ouzel feeds mostly on earthworms, which are best found in short cropped grass or sparsely overgrown ground. Its diet is rather more vegetarian once fruits become available during summer. In winter the Ring Ouzel stays in the Mediterranean region and especially in north-western Africa.

northern/western Europe
plumage black

central/southern Europe
belly heavily scaled

white crescent
belly lightly scaled

plumage dark brown
♀
light crescent

Voice *Blackbird (p. 35), song is more harsh and monotonous and calls throatier.*

Fieldfare
Turdus pilaris (thrushes)
L 26 cm WSp 39–42 cm Short distance migrant

underwing with white flashes

Habitat *Nests in undergrowth on fields, in parks and larger gardens; searches for food preferably on grassland and arable fields.*

> *Breeding season April–July*
> *5–6 pale blue, reddish spotted eggs*
> *1–2 broods per year*

The Fieldfare prefers to breed in small colonies. Invading crows or birds of prey are attacked by groups of Fieldfares and driven away by splashes of excrement. However the Fieldfare is also markedly gregarious outside of the breeding season. It is always seen out in bigger groups or flocks when migrating or foraging for food.

head grey

grey rump

nest

breast beige with dark spots

Voice *Hoarse, chuckling calls; song squeaky and croaking, often delivered during flight.*

Song Thrush
Turdus philomelos (thrushes)
L 23 cm   WSp 33–36 cm   Resident bird/Middle distance migrant

Even though its loud song cannot be ignored, the Song Thrush is the most secretive member of the thrush family. Its breeding behaviour is very discreet, as it usually builds its nest well hidden in conifers. Also while foraging for food, the Song Thrush likes to stay protected by undergrowth where it is often only detected because of rustling leaves. When looking for food on the ground it prefers snails, earthworms and insects. During migration it also eats berries, such as the Elderberry.

broken snail shells surround a Song Thrush 'anvil'

underwing yellowish-brown

Habitat *Nests in forests, parks and gardens with trees; during migration and in winter, also in open country.*

> **Breeding season March–August**
> **4–6 greenish-blue eggs with dark spots**
> **2 broods per year**

37

upperparts warm brown

breast spotted on brownish ground

Birder's tip
So-called thrush anvils can often be found in the Song Thrush's habitat. The bird uses suitable stones or stony surfaces like stone steps as an anvil to crack open the snail shells that it holds in its beak. The soft content is then eaten.

Voice *Loud song with shorter phrases that are repeated 2–3 times; call a sharp 'tsip'.*

Redwing
Turdus iliacus (thrushes)
L 21cm WSp 33–35 cm Short/Middle distance migrant

underwing rufous

Habitat *Nests in deciduous, mixed and coniferous forests; outside the breeding season, frequently on meadows and pasture land.*

> **Breeding season April–August**
> **4–6 greenish eggs with brown spots**
> **1–2 broods per year**

Generally, the Redwing builds well-hidden nests among conifers. However, birds breeding in the far north of Europe will make do with nesting sites on the ground. During migration and in its winter home the Redwing mostly appears gregariously in flocks and is frequently accompanied by the Fieldfare.

creamy supercilium

Voice *Song clipped, fairly unmelodious; flight calls sharp, drawn-out 'seeze'.*

darkly mottled whitish breast

flanks rufous

38

Mistle Thrush
Turdus viscivorus (thrushes)
L 27cm WSp 42–47 cm Resident bird/Short distance migrant

underwing white

white outer tail feathers

Habitat *Nests in tall trees, in parks and villages; also forages for food on meadows and fields.*

> **Breeding season February–August**
> **4 greenish eggs with reddish spots**
> **1–2 broods per year**

face lightly coloured

In summer, the largest European thrush feeds on worms and insects and in winter mainly on berries. The sticky fruits of the Mistletoe, a tree parasite, often stick to the bird's bill. Thus the Mistle Thrush transports Mistletoe seeds from one tree to the next and the parasite is given the chance to spread.

upperparts greyish-brown

round blotchy dots on white breast

Voice *Song similar to the Blackbird's (p. 35) with extremely short phrases; long, rasping call.*

Cetti's Warbler

Cettia cetti (warblers)
L 14 cm   WSp 15–19 cm   Resident bird

underparts grey
throat white

The Cetti's Warbler is, unlike the similar looking reed warbler family (pp. 41–44), not a migratory bird and stays in its breeding territory all year round. In winter it continues to sing loudly. The Cetti's forages for food inconspicuously and usually remains well hidden in dense undergrowth. It sometimes appears with twitching tail and wing movements in alarm.

upperparts reddish-brown

flanks rufous

Habitat Overgrown ditches with thick shrubs, reeds and stinging nettles; occasionally also in dry copses.

> **Breeding season April–August**
> 3–5 reddish-brown eggs
> 1–2 broods per year

Voice Fast song, delivered all year round; abrupt beginning, fades out towards the end.

Fan-tailed Warbler

Cisticola juncidis (warblers)
L 10 cm   WSp 12–14 cm   Resident bird

round tail with white patch on tip

In autumn the male establishes its breeding habitat where it builds several nests. Then it attracts the female's attention by song-flights. The male's first mate may start to breed as early as late winter, which does not prevent the male bird looking for another mate. A male Fan-tailed Warbler can have up to nine consecutive mates in one year.

upperparts striped

light-coloured face

Habitat Different terrain in open country, mostly with large grassy areas.

> **Breeding season February–August**
> 4–6 white eggs, partly spotted black
> 2–3 broods per year

Voice Song delivered in undulating flight and in a monotonous series of 'dzeep' calls.

Savi's Warbler

Locustella luscinioides (warblers)
L 14 cm   WSp 18–21 cm   Long distance migrant

under-tail
barely streaked

strong
looking
tail

rufous
upperparts

Habitat *Nests in reeds and bushes in standing water.*

> **Breeding season**
> **April–August**
> 4–6 white, brown-spotted eggs
> 1–2 broods per year

Savi's Warbler skilfully roams reedbeds while foraging for food. Its secretive behaviour and camouflaged plumage make it very hard to see. If alarmed, it behaves like the Bittern (p. 160) and adopts an upright position. The nest is well concealed among reeds, often close to the water's surface where it is safe from predators, albeit constantly threatened by high water.

reddish flanks

Voice *Song is a seemingly endless, insect-like buzzing, but faster and deeper than the Grasshopper Warbler's.*

River Warbler

Locustella fluviatilis (warblers)
L 13 cm   WSp 19–22 cm   Long distance migrant

under-tail coverts
with angled
white tips

Habitat *Bushes and dense undergrowth on wet ground, usually close to water.*

> **Breeding season**
> **May–August**
> 4–6 white, brown mottled eggs
> 1 brood per year

The River Warbler slips almost invisibly to and fro between foliage, stems and leaves, remaining close to the ground, and skilfully balancing on horizontal plant stems. Basically, it can only be spotted when it delivers its song from exposed bush tops. In autumn the River Warbler takes the migratory route via the eastern Mediterranean to South Africa.

breast
with blurred
streaks

upperparts
olive-brown

Voice *Long sustained, monotonous song reminiscent of a sewing-machine's whirring.*

Grasshopper Warbler

Locustella naevia (warblers)
L 13 cm   WSp 15–19 cm   Long distance migrant

under-tail coverts darkly spotted

The Grasshopper Warbler's reeling song consists of two alternating notes produced about 25 times per second. The bird perseveres to achieve this sound and can sustain a single song episode for over an hour. During the mating season, it sings almost incessantly day and night. Like most warblers, it lives well hidden.

Habitat Humid meadows with long grass and fallow areas, often with bushes and hedgerows.

> Breeding season April–August
> 5–6 whitish, rufous spotted eggs
> 1–2 broods per year

upperparts olive-brown with dark mottles

rounded tail-edge

Voice Song a locust-like buzzing that often lasts a few minutes.

Aquatic Warbler

Acrocephalus paludicola (warblers)
L 13 cm   WSp 17–19 cm   Long distance migrant

With less than 20,000 breeding pairs, the Aquatic Warbler is one of Europe's rarest songbirds. Its existence is endangered and habitats have been are being destroyed by draining of wetlands, swamps and heaths. Many birds leave their breeding habitat as early as June and migrate to their western African winter home.

upperparts striped yellowish-brown/ black

Habitat Marshes and meadows with sedge cultures up to 50–70 cm high, sometimes in disused saline meadows.

> Breeding season May–August
> 4–6 brown or brown speckled eggs
> 1–2 broods per year

breast sparsely streaked

pale yellow central crown stripe

pale yellow supercilium

light-coloured around the eyes

Voice Song consists of phrases of rasping and whistling notes with little variation.

Sedge Warbler
Acrocephalus schoenobaenus (warblers)
L 13 cm   WSp 17–21 cm   Long distance migrant

Habitat *Breeds along ditches covered with dense reedbeds, copses, above shallow water.*

> **Breeding season**
> **May–August**
> **4–6 olive-brown eggs**
> **1–2 broods per year**

Did you know?
After the breeding season the Sedge Warbler moves to reedbeds that are heavily infested with greenflies. It feeds on them until it has stored enough body fat to endure the long flight over the Mediterranean and across the Sahara. Afterwards, the Sedge Warbler's ongoing flight to South Africa continues in smaller stages.

The male bird establishes its territory with song-flights. Nest-building and hatching eggs, however, are solely the female's responsibility. The male bird only gets involved again in breeding when feeding the chicks. The similar coloured Moustached Warbler (*A. melanopogin*) nests in reedbeds in the Balkans and Mediterranean. Its song is reminiscent of the Reed Warbler's, but also includes whistling phrases that may be associated with the Nightingale.

blackish edged crown

pale brown supercilium

juvenile

Voice *Song a variety of rasping, whistling notes and often delivered during song-flight.*

rufous upperparts with dark streaks

breast unstreaked

white supercilium

Moustached Warbler

throat white

breast unstreaked

Marsh Warbler

Acrocephalus palustris (warblers)
L 13 cm   WSp 18–21cm   Long distance migrant

The Marsh Warbler is rarely seen as it roams the sedges. It imitates hundreds of other voices that it imports to Europe from its winter home, including calls of many African birds. Blyth's Reed Warbler (*A. dumetorum*), which can also only rarely be observed in its reedbed habitat, looks very similar to the Marsh Warbler and breeds in north-eastern parts of Europe.

upperpart greyish-brown

primaries rich in contrast

legs yellowish-pink

supercilium more distinct than Marsh Warbler's

markedly uniform wings

legs dark greyish-brown

Blyth's Reed Warbler

Habitat Breeds on open land covered with tall shrubs and bushes; also found in crops.

> *Breeding season May–July*
> *3–6 whitish, brown speckled eggs*
> *1 brood per year*

Voice Long song phrases consist almost exclusively of imitations of other calls.

Reed Warbler

Acrocephalus scirpaceus (warblers)
L 13 cm   WSp 17–21cm   Long distance migrant

adult at the nest

indistinct supercilium

The female bird suspends the nest in reeds about half a metre above the water's surface. Since it is often the case that several pairs breed close next to each other, the defended territory is narrowed down to an area by the nesting site that is only left by the birds while they forage for food. The Paddyfield Warbler (*A. agricola*) also breeds in reedbeds, but in regions east of the Black Sea.

fairly long bill

upperparts warm rufous

Habitat Reedbeds; during migration also in bushes.

> *Breeding season May–September*
> *3–5 whitish, brown speckled eggs*
> *1–2 broods per year*

Voice Song of rhythmically phrased harsh notes, interspersed with single whistling sounds.

distinct, darkly outlined supercilium

upperparts pale brown

dark bill-tip

Paddyfield Warbler

Great Reed Warbler

Acrocephalus arundinaceus (warblers)
L 19–20 cm   WSp 25–29 cm   Long distance migrant

adult at nest

Habitat Reedbeds, preferable vegetation near water.

> **Breeding season May–August**
> 4–6 greenish, white, darkly speckled eggs
> 1–2 broods per year

The Great Reed Warbler is by far the largest of the warblers. The male bird neither gets involved in building the nest nor in rearing juvenile birds. Thus, the male sometimes manages to accommodate two females in his territory at the same time and succeeds over rivals. If this is the case the male often only helps the first female with feeding, the second female will have to cope without his support.

stout, thrush-like bill

broad but weakly defined supercilium

Voice Sings 'krik-krik' rhythmically, considerably louder and more slowly than the Reed Warbler (p. 43).

juvenile

strong, dark legs

Booted Warbler

Hippolais caligata (warblers)
L 12 cm   WSp 18–21 cm   Long distance migrant

Habitat Bushes, in regions with marshy meadows or on river-banks.

> **Breeding season May–August**
> 4–6 pink, darkly speckled eggs
> 1 brood per year

The Booted Warbler's appearance, and also its behaviour when foraging for food, is very reminiscent of the leaf warblers (p. 53–55). The Booted Warbler is a skilful climber among bushes and can also often be found hopping about on the ground. In autumn it migrates south-eastwards, towards its winter home in India.

light-coloured supercilium

upperparts light brown

dark bill tip

light outer tail feathers

legs pink

Voice Song a rapid succession of melodious and hoarse sounds; call a clicking 'zett, zett, zett'.

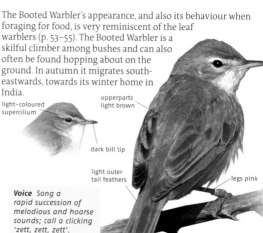

Olivaceous Warbler

Hippolais pallida (warblers)
L 12–13 cm   WSp 18–21 cm   Long distance migrant

The Olivaceous Warbler keeps itself well hidden most of the time and collects insects from leaves. It skilfully climbs up and down the branches, often flicking its tail downwards. In August, it leaves its habitat in the direction of its east African winter home. Southern Spain and north-western Africa are breeding habitats for the similar looking Western Olivaceous Warbler (*H. opaca*).

upperparts brownish-grey

upperparts olive-grey

long bill

Western Olivaceous Warbler

Voice Rapid, chatty song of harsh, choked and fluty notes.

Habitat Trees and copses with thick foliage and also orchards, parks and pine forests.

> *Breeding season May–August*
> 3–4 light grey, black spotted eggs
> 1 brood per year

45

Olive-tree Warbler

Hippolais olivetorum (warblers)
L 16–18 cm   WSp 24–26 cm   Long distance migrant

strong, dagger-like bill

upperparts grey

patch of whitish edges on tertials and inner secondaries

upperparts brownish-grey

juvenile

Like its smaller relatives, this warbler frequently flicks its tail downwards. In alarm or if excited its crown feathers become ruffled. Little information is available on this bird, as it generally keeps well out of sight. What is known, however, is that the Olive-tree Warbler sometimes breeds in loose colonies. Its winter habitat ranges from Kenya to South Africa.

Voice Similar to the Reed Warbler's (p. 41–44), chattering, more raucous song with harsh call.

Habitat Open woodlands, in the Macchian Oak forests and in olive groves.

> *Breeding season May–August*
> 3–4 pink, black spotted eggs
> 1 brood per year

Icterine Warbler
Hippolais icterina (warblers)
L 13 cm   WSp 21–24 cm   Long distance migrant

underparts pale yellow

juvenile

Habitat *Damp forests but also sparse thickets, parks and large gardens.*

> *Breeding season May–August*
> *4–5 pink, black spotted eggs*
> *1 brood per year*

Although the Icterine Warbler is similar in appearance to the leaf warblers (p. 53–55), it leads a much more discreet life. Rather than catching insects in flight, it picks them up from twigs and leaves. It generally attracts our attention with its loud song and equally loud calls. The first Icterine Warblers begin their journey in July to their winter home in the southern half of the African continent.

supercilium only short, in front of eyes

Voice *Rapid song with rasping and screeching sounds, often calls repeatedly 'deederoid' or 'tete-lu-eet'.*

light wing panel

primaries much longer than tertials

legs bluish-grey

adult

Melodious Warbler
Hippolais polyglotta (warblers)
L 13 cm   WSp 18–20 cm   Long distance migrant

Habitat *In clusters of trees and bushes in dry regions.*

> *Breeding season May–August*
> *4–5 pink, darkly spotted eggs*
> *1 brood per year*

The Melodious Warbler is the Icterine Warbler's relative in south-western Europe. Over the last few decades, it has slightly expanded its breeding habitat northwards. Both species sometimes inhabit the same regions, but all in all, the Melodious Warbler prefers drier habitats and hybridisation is generally rare.

juvenile

no pale wing panel

legs brown

primaries not much longer than tertials

underparts pale yellow

Voice *Song reminiscent of the Icterine Warbler's, but softer, faster and without 'deederoid' sound.*

adult

Blackcap
Sylvia attricapilla (warblers)
L 13 cm   WSp 20–23 cm   Short/Long distance migrant

The Blackcap's migratory habits differ depending on the region. While southern European breeding birds are only short distance migrants or do not migrate at all, central European Blackcaps winter at the shores of the Mediterranean. Their northern European relatives migrate to Africa, to regions south of the Sahara. Due to the introduction of garden feeders many central European Blackcaps now stay in England over winter.

often feeds on fruit

black crown

♂

underparts grey

Habitat *Found around trees of all kinds, from dense forests to gardens and parks.*

> **Breeding season April–August**
> 3–6 brownish, darkly mottled eggs
> 1 brood per year

47

Voice *Song starts chattily, grows increasingly louder with harsh fluted ending; calls harsh 'churr'.*

rufous crown

♀

Did you know?
Despite the fact that the Blackcap almost exclusively feeds on insects and larvae during the breeding season it quickly changes to a fruit diet in summer. Then it prefers figs and elderberries to store energy for the migratory flight.

Garden Warbler

Sylvia borin (warblers)
L 14 cm   WSp 20–24 cm   Long distance migrant

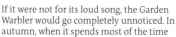

Habitat *Mainly in thickets and copses, in wood clearings and woodland margins.*

> *Breeding season April–August*
> *4–5 whitish, grey speckled eggs*
> *1–2 broods per year*

If it were not for its loud song, the Garden Warbler would go completely unnoticed. In autumn, when it spends most of the time feeding on different kinds of berries to store body fat, it leads an even more inconspicuous existence. On its way southwards from northern Europe, the Garden Warbler constantly gains weight. After the last stop for 'fuel' in northern Africa it crosses the Sahara in one long flight to reach its South African destination.

many Garden Warblers involuntarily also raise young Cuckoos

light grey collar

upperparts brownish–grey

Voice *Monotonous, babbling song with longer sustained phrases than the Blackcap's (p. 47) and without warbling notes.*

Barred Warbler

Sylvia nisoria (warblers)
L 15 cm   WSp 23–27 cm   Long distance migrant

upperparts paler than ♂

♀

underparts less barred with dark crescents

Habitat *Breeds in hedgerows and on commons with shrubberies and single trees.*

> *Breeding season May–August*
> *4–5 grey, olive speckled eggs*
> *1 brood per year*

The Barred Warbler likes to breed near a Red-Backed Shrike's nest. It thus benefits from this powerful bird's defensive behaviour in keeping predators away from the nesting area. Indeed, Barred Warblers that nest close to Red-backed Shrikes are the most successful breeders.

eye light

♂

underparts distinctly barred with crescents

juvenile

light wing-bar

eye dark

only flanks and area under the tail are barred

Voice *Rattling warning call; song shorter, clearer and more distinct in comparison to Garden Warbler's song.*

Whitethroat

Sylvia communis (warblers)

L 14 cm   WSp 19–23 cm   Long distance migrant

Even for the heat-loving Whitethroat, the Sahel zone at the Sahara's southern edge has become too hot and dry. Increasingly inferior living conditions for wintering birds resulted in a considerable decline in species numbers. Clearing hedges and bushes due to modern agricultural methods has also impacted unfavourably on numbers. In Spain and Italy the Spectacled Warbler (*S. conspicillata*), which is similar in colour but much more delicately shaped, nests in bushes near the ground and semi-deserts.

head dark grey

♂

breast pink

♀

Spectacled Warbler

wings rufous

head brownish

♀

Habitat Breeds in open country with bushes or hedgerows; more rare in gardens than some other warblers.

> *Breeding season April–August*
> *3–6 greenish or brownish, darkly mottled eggs*
> *1–2 broods per year*

Voice Song is a loud and hoarse repeat 'whett, whett, whett', often interspersed with quiet, chattering song. Calls varied.

49

song-flight

head grey

♂

throat white

flight feathers conspicuously chestnut-coloured

Birder's tip

The Whitethroat's typical song cannot be missed in areas with shrubberies. The singing male is often spotted on a bush top. Also, you can often observe the bird's song-flight, where ascending flight results in a dancing flight outline.

Lesser Whitethroat
Sylvia curruca (warblers)
L 13 cm   WSp 17–20 cm   Long distance migrant

Habitat *Nests at forest margins, in hedgerows and open country, parks and gardens.*

> **Breeding season April–August**
> **3–7 whitish, grey speckled eggs**
> **1 brood per year**

Out of the scrub warbler family, it is the Lesser Whitethroat that is most frequently spotted inhabiting residential areas in central Europe. It is only noticeable here because of its loud song, since it remains hidden in thick bushes while foraging. In autumn the Lesser Whitethroat migrates in a south-easterly direction towards its winter home, the region between the Sudan and Nigeria.

grey crown and head

upperparts greyish-brown

throat white

Voice *Song of low, barely audible twittering followed by a loud, slightly cascading 'rattling'.*

Orphean Warbler
Sylvia hortensis (warblers)
L 15 cm   WSp 20–25 cm   Middle distance migrant

juvenile

eye dark

♀

eye pale

dull blackish crown

Habitat *Wooded districts and coppices on sunny slopes.*

> **Breeding season April–July**
> **3–5 white, darkly spotted eggs**
> **1 brood per year**

The Orphean Warbler often nests in the same bush as the Woodchat Shrike (p. 82). Both species benefit from the other's skill at detecting predators. The Woodchat Shrike spots predators in open country, while the Orphean Warbler pays attention to the bushes' interior. In the Balkans, this species is represented by the greyer Eastern Orphean Warbler (*S. crassirostris*).

Eastern Orphean Warbler

♂

under-tail mottled

underparts whitish

black crown

♂

Voice *Song repetitive, with differing combinations of sharp and loud notes.*

under-tail white

underparts buff tinted with beige

Dartford Warbler

Sylvia undata (warblers)
L 12 cm WSp 13–18 cm Resident bird/Short distance migrant

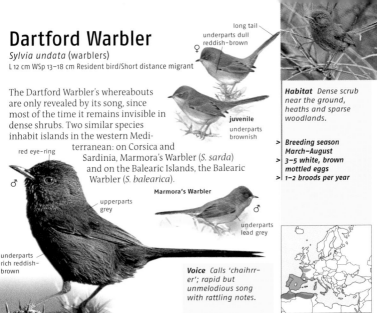

long tail
underparts dull reddish-brown
♀

juvenile
underparts brownish

The Dartford Warbler's whereabouts are only revealed by its song, since most of the time it remains invisible in dense shrubs. Two similar species inhabit islands in the western Mediterranean: on Corsica and Sardinia, Marmora's Warbler (*S. sarda*) and on the Balearic Islands, the Balearic Warbler (*S. balearica*).

red eye-ring
♂

upperparts grey

Marmora's Warbler
♂
underparts lead grey

underparts rich reddish-brown

Habitat Dense scrub near the ground, heaths and sparse woodlands.

> **Breeding season March–August**
> **3–5 white, brown mottled eggs**
> **1–2 broods per year**

Voice Calls 'chaihrr-er'; rapid but unmelodious song with rattling notes.

Subalpine Warbler

Sylvia cantillans (warblers)
L 12 cm WSp 15–19 cm Middle distance migrant

♀
pale head marks
upperparts brownish

The Subalpine Warbler spends most of the time in bush-tops where it is on the lookout for insects and in autumn also for berries. The male birds sometimes especially cross the borders of their Mediterranean breeding habitat on the migratory route back from their winter home in the Sahara. This is why every year single Subalpine Warblers are spotted around the North Sea, for instance, on Helgoland.

white 'moustache'
red eye-ring
♂

Habitat Low bushes and thickets as well as open oak forests.

> **Breeding season April–August**
> **3–5 white, brownish spotted eggs**
> **1–2 broods per year**

throat and chest chestnut-coloured

Voice Song rapid, scratchy twittering, calls include hardish 'teck'.

Sardinian Warbler

Sylvia melanocephala (warblers)
L 14 cm   WSp 15–18 cm   Resident bird/Short distance migrant

Habitat Nests in dense undergrowth and open Oak woods, also in Olive groves.

> **Breeding season March–August**
> **3–5 whitish, darkly mottled eggs**
> **2–3 broods per year**

Voice Rapid, scratching song with longer phrases than the Subalpine Warbler's song; series of rattling calls.

The Sardinian Warbler is a common inhabitant of the Mediterranean. Its call can be heard almost everywhere from dense bushes, yet you almost only spot the bird during song-flight or if it changes its location, always flying near the ground. A breeding pair of Sardinian Warblers will also build their nest close to the ground and hidden in bushes. In Greece or Turkey the pair will often be joined when breeding by the similar, though still distinctive Rüppell's Warbler (*S. rueppelli*).

upperparts brown   ♀ upper head grey

red eye-ring
upper head black
♂
throat white

♂
throat black
white 'moustache'

Rüppell's Warbler

mottled head
♀

Did you know?

The Sardinian Warbler not only feeds on insects and fruits but also on nectar, especially in springtime. It likes to swing beneath almond tree blossom and extract the nectar.

Willow Warbler

Phylloscopus trochilus (warblers)
L 11 cm   WSp 17–22 cm   Long distance migrant

northern Europe

plumage greyer

Willow Warbler males are already singing during migration. The bird migrates surprisingly far. Northern Scandinavian and eastern European breeding birds migrate as far as South Africa, whereas central and western European birds manage to get as far as western and central Africa.

Habitat Open woodlands and countryside with clusters of trees.

> **Breeding season** May–August
> 4–8 whitish, rufous spotted eggs
> 1 brood per year

upperparts greenish-grey

juvenile

breast yellowish

adult

legs brownish

Voice Song subdued, musical cadence with drop in pitch and final loop at end ('Chaffinch in minor key'); call is disyllabic, rising 'hooeet'.

53

Chiffchaff

Phylloscopus collybita (warblers)
L 10–11 cm WSp 15–21 cm Short/Middle distance migrant

juvenile

breast yellowish (less intensely coloured than Willow Warbler)

Unlike the Willow Warbler, its close relative, the Chiffchaff stays in the Mediterranean over winter. It builds its nest on the ground, like the Willow Warbler, and Chiffchaff is spotted more often in bushes and trees while foraging for food. The Iberian Chiffchaff (*P. ibericus*) can only be identified by its song, which consists of three repetitive phrases, and has its breeding habitat in Spain.

Habitat Breeds in woodlands, parks and gardens, preferring thinned out areas.

> **Breeding season** April–August
> 4–6 white, dark brown mottled eggs
> 2 broods per year

Iberian Chiffchaff

generally with greener plumage, but hardly distinguished from the Chiffchaff

Voice Song is a distinctive monotonous 'chiff-chiff-chaff-chiff-chaff'; calls with slightly rising but more monosyllabic 'hweet'.

adult

upperparts greenish-grey, plumage colours variable

legs blackish

Wood Warbler

Phylloscopus sibilatrix (warblers)
L 12 cm   WSp 20–24 cm   Long distance migrant

Habitat Breeds in tall deciduous and coniferous woods.

> **Breeding season** April–July
> 5–8 white, dark brown spotted eggs
> 1 brood per year

At the end of April, only for a few weeks, the Wood Warbler's characteristic song can be heard in the woods. When raising their young, the adult birds disappear into the treetops to search for food and can only be seen when they feed their brood on the ground. In winter the Wood Warbler migrates to rain forests and humid savannahs in central Africa.

adult at the nest

upperparts bright yellowish-green

throat and breast citrus yellow

white belly

Voice Two songs: buzzing 'stip-stip-stip-stip-shreeee' or softly cascading, warbling 'piu-piu-piu'.

upperparts greyer than Bonelli's Warbler

Bonelli's Warbler

Phylloscopus bonelli (warblers)
L 11 cm   WSp 16–18 cm   Long distance migrant

Eastern Bonelli's Warblers

Habitat Breeds in open forests and on sunny slopes in low and high mountain ranges.

> **Breeding season** April–July
> 3–7 white eggs with dark brown mottles
> 1 brood per year

Bonelli's Warbler replaces the Wood Warbler in mountain forests and breeds on the ground, just like its relative. Unlike many other songbirds that start out south of the Sahara, Bonelli's Warbler does not cross the Mediterranean during the spring migration, but follows the coastline. In the Balkans and Turkey its family is represented by the very similar Eastern Bonelli's Warbler (*P. orientalis*).

upperparts greyish olive-brown

wings yellowish-green

underparts white

Voice Song similar to the Wood Warbler's, but less trilling and without starting notes; call a disyllabic 'hou-eet'.

Greenish Warbler

Phylloscopus trochiloides (warblers)
L 10 cm   WSp 15–21 cm   Long distance migrant

pale yellow supercilium as far as forehead

For over 100 years, the Greenish Warbler, whose habitat extends almost throughout Siberia, has ventured further westwards, yet has not established itself as a breeding bird anywhere else apart from in Finland and the Baltic. The Greenish Warbler's winter home is India. The Arctic Warbler (*P. borealis*) is a breeding bird in northern Scandinavia and manages distances of 13,000 km on its migratory route from here as far as south-eastern Asia.

Habitat *Woodlands, especially in clearings and forest margins; prefers steep slopes.*

> **Breeding season June–August**
> **3–7 white eggs**
> **1 brood per year**

pale yellow supercilium ends before bill
large longish head
whitish wing-bar
Arctic Warbler
legs yellowish-brown

plump head
upperparts greyish-green
whitish wing-bar

legs dark grey

Voice *Call similar to White Wagtail (p. 29) with disyllabic 'chee-wee'; song is a succession of rapidly repeated call notes.*

Yellow-browed Warbler

Phylloscopus inornatus (warblers)
L 10 cm WSp 15–20 cm Long distance migrant

supercilium and crown stripe pale yellow
two yellowish wing-bars
lemon yellow wash on rump

Pallas's Warbler

The Yellow-browed Warbler breeds in great numbers in Siberian forests, but it stays in the south-east Asian tropics over winter. Every autumn a few hundred birds, which have taken the wrong route, appear in Europe. A much smaller number of Pallas's Warblers (*P. proregulus*), a relative of the Yellow-browed Warbler that also comes from Siberia, is also seen in Europe every year.

Habitat *Breeds in deciduous and coniferous forests; during migration also in shrubs and bushes.*

> **Breeding season June–August**
> **4–6 white, rufous spotted eggs**
> **1 brood per year**

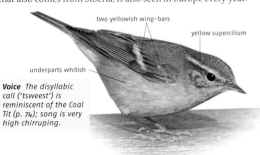

two yellowish wing-bars
yellow supercilium
underparts whitish

Voice *The disyllabic call ('tsweest') is reminiscent of the Coal Tit (p. 74); song is very high chirruping.*

Goldcrest
Regulus regulus (crests)
L 9 cm   WSp 13–15 cm   Short distance migrant

upper head grey

juvenile

Habitat Nests in coniferous forests but also in parks and gardens with conifers; during migration also in deciduous trees and bushes.

> **Breeding season March–August**
> 7–11 whitish, light brown mottled eggs
> 2 broods per year

With a body weight not exceeding five grams, the Goldcrest is Europe's lightest bird. During migration, it is not afraid to cross blustery seas. Generally, however, it prefers to roam in coniferous branches where it ceaselessly slips to and fro between twigs and picks out little insects and spiders.

Voice Rhythmical whispering, high-pitched song with terminal flourish; calls sharply 'sree-sree-sree'.

crown yellowy orange

♂

upperparts greyish-green

crown yellow

♀

whitish wing-bar

Firecrest
Regulus ignicapillus (crests)
L 9 cm   WSp 13–16 cm   Short distance migrant

upper head grey

juvenile

Habitat Nests in coniferous forests and mixed woodland, in south-western Europe also exclusively in deciduous forests and parks with conifers.

> **Breeding season April–August**
> 7–10 rufous, dark brown spotted eggs
> 1–2 broods per year

The Firecrest is generally less partial to conifers than the Goldcrest, yet prefers these as a nesting site. It attaches the globular-shaped nest to the underside of a twig and pads it out with up to 800 feathers. It is the only way to keep the thin-shelled eggs (that weigh only 0.6 grams) intact.

crown yellowish-orange

♂

crown yellow

♀

bold white supercilium contrasting with black eye stripe

upperparts bright greenish-yellow

whitish wing-bar

Voice Rising high-pitched song, more monotonous than the Goldcrest's.

Spotted Flycatcher
Muscicapa striata (flycatchers)
L 15 cm   WSp 23–25 cm   Long distance migrant

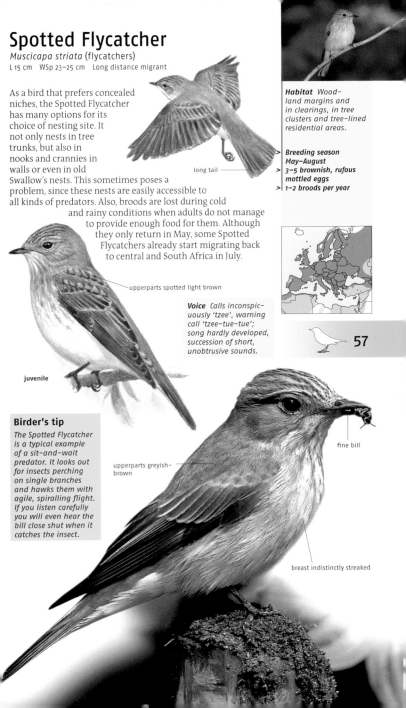

As a bird that prefers concealed niches, the Spotted Flycatcher has many options for its choice of nesting site. It not only nests in tree trunks, but also in nooks and crannies in walls or even in old Swallow's nests. This sometimes poses a problem, since these nests are easily accessible to all kinds of predators. Also, broods are lost during cold and rainy conditions when adults do not manage to provide enough food for them. Although they only return in May, some Spotted Flycatchers already start migrating back to central and South Africa in July.

long tail

Habitat Woodland margins and in clearings, in tree clusters and tree-lined residential areas.

> *Breeding season* May–August
> 3–5 brownish, rufous mottled eggs
> 1–2 broods per year

upperparts spotted light brown

juvenile

Voice Calls inconspicuously 'tzee', warning call 'tzee–tue–tue'; song hardly developed, succession of short, unobtrusive sounds.

57

Birder's tip
The Spotted Flycatcher is a typical example of a sit-and-wait predator. It looks out for insects perching on single branches and hawks them with agile, spiralling flight. If you listen carefully you will even hear the bill close shut when it catches the insect.

fine bill

upperparts greyish-brown

breast indistinctly streaked

Red-breasted Flycatcher

Ficedula parva (flycatchers)
L 11 cm WSp 19–21 cm Long distance migrant

white tail with black 'T'

Habitat *Deciduous forests and mixed woodlands with large, old trees; during migration also in bushes and gardens.*

> **Breeding season** May–August
> 4–7 bluish, rufous marked eggs
> 1 brood per year

The Red-breasted Flycatcher is among the few European breeding birds that stay in regions from India to south-eastern Asia during winter. It only returns to the western edges of its distribution area in May, but is already leaving its breeding areas in August. The Red-breasted Flycatcher stays in the tops of tall trees while foraging for food; it builds its nest in holes in tree trunks.

juvenile
throat brownish
head brown
underparts white
male first year and female

head bluish-grey

rufous throat

at least 2 years old

Voice *Song of clipped single sounds with shorter elements; rasping calls.*

Collared Flycatcher

Ficedula albicollis (flycatchers)
L 13 cm WSp 22–24 cm Long distance migrant

lots of white on wings

rump white

Habitat *Deciduous forests, orchards and field undergrowth with dead trees.*

> **Breeding season** April–July
> 4–7 pale blue eggs
> 1 brood per year

The Collared Flycatcher's distribution range is generally confined to eastern and southern Europe except for two 'outposts' in some regions of southern Germany and eastern France and the Swedish islands of Öland and Gotland. When it comes to occupying and defending the nest, the Collared Flycatcher asserts itself against the Pied Flycatcher (p. 59).

pale nape bar
♀
two bold white wing-bars

white collar
♂
large white patch on forehead

Voice *Song quieter and slower than the Pied Flycatcher's, often with sustained 'eehlp'; calls also include loud 'eehlp'.*

Pied Flycatcher

Ficedula hypoleuca (flycatchers)
L 13 cm   WSp 22–24 cm   Long distance migrant

The male often occupies two breeding territories with one resident female for each. It then has take care of both broods and defend each territory against rivals from its own species and other songbirds. In competition for nesting sites, the Pied Flycatcher has to give way to the Great Tit (p. 76). When it returns from Africa in April, its rival has usually already occupied many suitable nesting sites. In the Balkans, the Pied as well as Collared Flycatchers are replaced by the Semi-Collared Flycatcher.

back consistently dark

Habitat *Breeds in forests, parks and gardens with a sufficient supply of tree trunks (or nesting boxes).*

> **Breeding season May–July**
> **4–8 pale blue eggs**
> **1 brood per year**

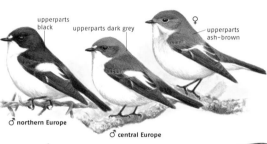

upperparts black

upperparts dark grey

♀ upperparts ash–brown

♂ northern Europe

♂ central Europe

59

Semi-Collared Flycatcher

white nape-bar only

additional white patch on wings

small white patch on forehead

♂

white wing patch

Did you know?

It is proven that many birds return to the same breeding territory every year and this also goes for the Pied Flycatcher. However, in contrast to other species, it also maintains territories in west Africa where it returns every year.

Voice *Song starts with loud, sprightly ('zee-it, zee-it, zee-it') followed by quieter variable twittering.*

Robin
Erithacus rubecula (flycatchers)
L 14 cm   WSp 20–22 cm   Resident bird/Short distance migrant

The Robin usually chooses a slightly elevated position to sing on a branch, but it actually forages on the ground where it looks for small insects and animals, such as, greenfly and earthworms. The female also builds her nest on the ground, preferably beneath tree roots or tufts of grass. She is exclusively responsible for hatching the young, but the male assists with feeding the chicks. Sometimes the female begins her second brood quite early, so that the male is left with the sole responsibility for the first brood.

upperparts pale, mottled

juvenile

breast scaled

adult at nest

Voice *Song is bubbling, cascading in pitch; sharp call 'tic' (often in rapid succession).*

breast and throat reddish–orange with bluish frame

upperparts and tail monochrome brown

Did you know?
The Robins nesting in your garden may not be the same birds visiting your feeders in winter. This is because central European birds migrate to the Mediterranean in winter, whereas northern Scandinavian breeding species move down from the north.

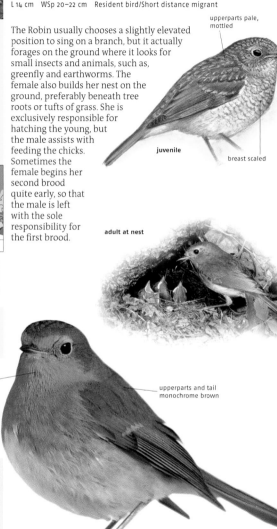

Bluethroat

Luscinia svecica (flycatchers)

L 13–15 cm   WSp 20–22 cm   Medium/Long distance migrant

The Bluethroat's various subspecies differ in their throat colouring. They migrate to different regions in autumn. Red-spotted birds, whose breeding territory reaches from Scandinavia to Siberia and Alaska, mainly stay in India and south-east Asia over winter. Their white-spotted relatives from central and southern Europe, on the other hand, migrate to the African savannah for the winter.

The Bluethroat behaves in a secretive manner wherever it lives and only presents its shiny blue breast patch when it sings.

northern Europe, Alps, the Carpathian mountains

chestnut red-spotted patch

white supercilium

♀

basal chestnut panels on tail, terminal band black

only traces of male's breast marks

central and southern Europe

white

breast band black/white/chestnut

Habitat Swampy thickets and tangled hedgerows with reeds; in Scandinavia in Tundra, marshland and heaths.

> *Breeding season April–August*
> 5–7 olive green eggs
> 1–2 broods per year

61

Did you know?

After a long period of decline numbers, the white-spotted Bluethroat's breeding stocks have now recovered. The bird can now be seen again in many marshy central European areas. The red-spotted subspecies recently settled in the Alps.

Voice Song with increasingly rapid delivery of warbling notes interspersed with imitations of other birds' voices.

Nightingale
Luscinia megarhynchos (flycatchers)
L 16–17 cm   WSp 23–26 cm   Long distance migrant

Habitat *Dense thickets, preferably in damp locations near water.*

> *Breeding season May–July*
> *4–6 yellowish to brown eggs*
> *1–2 broods per year*

Apart from the loud song, secrecy is one of this species' typical characteristics. Even if you stand right in front of the bush where a Nightingale is singing, you rarely manage to sneak a glimpse. Also while foraging for food, the bird stays hidden beneath bushes and shrubs. The winter is spent in a broad belt from western to east Africa.

tail appears a little more rufous than back

upperparts rufous-brown

breast only subtly tinted

Voice *Song loud, mostly delivered at night-time as vehement musical singing and warbling 'sobbing'.*

Thrush Nightingale
Luscinia luscinia (flycatchers)
L 16–17 cm   WSp 24–26 cm   Long distance migrant

Habitat *Prefers damp to moist copses and bushes but also inhabits thickets, parks and gardens.*

> *Breeding season May–July*
> *4–6 yellowish to brown eggs*
> *1 brood per year*

The Thrush Nightingale is the Nightingale's cousin in eastern and northern Europe. It spends the winter in East Africa. The Thrush Nightingale is very similar to the Nightingale in plumage and its secretive behaviour, therefore the two species can only be told apart by more experienced birders. Sometimes the two species meet in narrow intersecting areas, which result in mixed broods.

tail distinctly more rufous than back

breast indistinctly mottled

upperparts dull brown

Voice *Song slower and more clipped than Nightingale's, with rattling phrases but without melodious 'sobbing'.*

Rufous Bush Robin

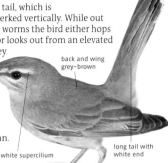

back and wing rufous

Cercotrichas galactotes (flycatchers) **Spain**
L 15 cm WSp 22–27 cm Middle distance migrant

The Rufous Bush Robin's main characteristic is its long tail, which is constantly fanned and jerked vertically. While out foraging for insects and worms the bird either hops around on the ground or looks out from an elevated vantage point for its prey that it will then catch in flight. The Rufous Bush Robin prefers warm climates and crosses the Sahara during its migratory journey south in autumn.

back and wing grey-brown

white supercilium

long tail with white end

The Balkans

Voice Song consists of short phrases with trills and warbles, delivered in flight or perched on a bush; call a hard 'teck teck'.

Habitat Trees and bushes in dry landscape.

> **Breeding season** May–August
> 4–5 whitish eggs with brown mottles
> 2 broods per year

Red-flanked Bluetail

throat white, grey breast band ♀

Tarsiger cyanurus (flycatchers)
L 13–15 cm WSp 21–24 cm Long distance migrant

Only a few breeding pairs get as far as northern Russia and eastern Finland from their original Asian breeding habitat. In autumn they start their long migration to India or even Indochina. Although the Red-flanked Bluetail is not very shy, this magnificent bird is only rarely seen because it spends most of its time hidden in undergrowth.

only tail blue

upperparts metallic blue

♂

Voice Song consists of short stanzas with loud, clear notes; call a string of 'tick-tick' sounds

Habitat Breeds in the taiga's damp coniferous forests; during migration and in winter also in bushes and gardens.

> **Breeding season** May–August
> 5–7 white or lightly mottled eggs
> 1–2 broods per year

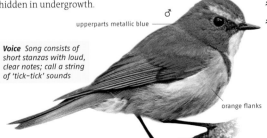

orange flanks

Black Redstart

Phoenicurus ochruros (flycatchers)

L 14–15 cm   WSp 23–27 cm   Short/Middle distance migrant

upper and under-parts grey-brown

Since the 19th century the Black Redstart has gradually migrated to artificial 'rocky landscapes' in residential areas. Instead of holes in rocks, it uses crevices in buildings in which to build its nest. When on the hunt for insects, which it picks up from the ground or catches in flight, the Black Redstart looks for its prey from an elevated position. A typical characteristic of this bird is the flicking of its tail, often with simultaneous bobbing of the body.

♀ and first year ♂

fully-fledged juvenile

back grey

face and breast black

tail rusty orange with dark centre

white wing patch

Birder's tip

You have to be an early bird to experience the Black Redstart's song. In residential areas, this bird is usually the first to start singing in the morning and starts even before dawn.

Voice *Sings from rooftops with a light string of musical notes, interspersed with curious grating and grinding sounds.*

♂ at least 2 years old

Redstart
Phoenicurus phoenicurus (flycatchers)
L 14 cm   WSp 21–25 cm   Long distance migrant

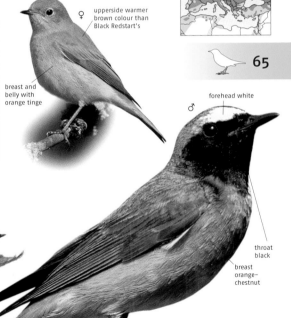

The Redstart prefers to breed in hollows in tree trunks. Throughout Europe, the breeding stock is in serious decline. The loss of old trees, which provide a variety of hollows, could only partly be compensated for by the provision of nesting boxes. Additionally, periods of draught in the Redstart's African winter habitat and the increased use of insecticides also contribute to the decline in numbers. The Redstart forages for food from its perch, but stays close to bushes and trees.

blackish throat

juvenile

Voice Song starts with one high and two low notes ('whee-tic-tic') followed by chattering sounds.

Did you know?
The Redstart and the Black Redstart (p. 64) are not only very similar in appearance, they are also closely related. Occasionally there is some mixed breeding producing birds that master the songs of both species.

Habitat Open forests, parks, gardens and partially open countryside with trees providing nesting holes.

> *Breeding season April–August*
> *5–7 greenish-blue eggs*
> *1–2 broods per year*

65

♀
upperside warmer brown colour than Black Redstart's

breast and belly with orange tinge

forehead white

♂

throat black

breast orange-chestnut

tail orange-chestnut with dark centre

Whinchat

Saxicola rubetra (flycatchers)
L 12–14 cm   WSp 21–24 cm   Long distance migrant

cheeks and crown brown
♀

blackish cheeks and crown
white supercilium
♂

breast pale orange

Habitat *Breeds in damp meadows, pastures and fallow areas; during migration, also in open country.*

> **Breeding season May–August**
> **5–7 greenish-blue eggs**
> **1 brood per year**

The Whinchat can easily be spotted in its preferred habitats. It usually sits perched on a fencing post or tall shrub from where it looks out for insects or sings. The Whinchat avoids habitat without these prominent perches, for example, because of cleared arable land or if meadows are cut very early.

white basal patches on tail, tail-end bar black

wings brown with small white patches

Voice *Song with brief phrases consisting of warbling and scratchy notes; clicking warning call.*

66

Stonechat

Saxicola torquata (flycatchers)
L 13 cm WSp 18–21 cm Resident bird/Short-distance migrant

blackish wings with distinct white patches

Uppertail whitish

Habitat *Open, preferably dry country with bushes, also marshes.*

> **Breeding season March–August**
> **4–6 greenish-blue, subtly mottled eggs**
> **2–3 broods per year**

Although the Stonechat's hunting behaviour is similar to the Whinchat's, its migration habits are different. Many populations are non-migratory, and those that do migrate stay much longer in the breeding habitat (March–October). A vagrant in the regions from Russia to east Asia is the similar-looking Siberian Stonechat (*S. maurus*).

black head
white half-collar

indistinct supercilium
♀

Siberian Stonechat
upper tail-parts creamy-coloured
♀
brownish supercilium
♂
white flanks

upper tail-parts white

♂

breast bright orange

Voice *Song, short with whistling and pressed notes.*

Northern Wheatear

Oenanthe oenanthe (flycatchers)
L 15–17 cm   WSp 26–32 cm   Long distance migrant

The Northern Wheatear, with its conspicuously flashing white tail, is eye-catching in open country. It likes hopping around on the ground and often pauses to look for insects, which it chases, flitting low across the ground or in short flight. The Northern Wheatear preferably breeds in holes beneath larger stones and also in rabbit holes. The breeding habitat of the more palely marked Isabelline Wheatear (*O. isabellinus*), which breeds in holes in the ground, ranges from Bulgaria to the southern Ukraine.

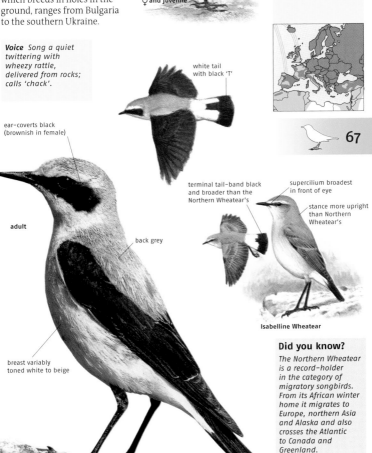

♀ and juvenile

back brown (greyer with older females)

Habitat Breeds in open, sparse country (also in mountains and the tundra); during migration on farmland, meadows and on beaches.

> *Breeding season April–August*
> *4–6 pale blue eggs*
> *1–2 broods per year*

Voice *Song a quiet twittering with wheezy rattle, delivered from rocks; calls 'chack'.*

white tail with black 'T'

ear-coverts black (brownish in female)

adult

back grey

breast variably toned white to beige

terminal tail-band black and broader than the Northern Wheatear's

supercilium broadest in front of eye

stance more upright than Northern Wheatear's

Isabelline Wheatear

67

Did you know?
The Northern Wheatear is a record-holder in the category of migratory songbirds. From its African winter home it migrates to Europe, northern Asia and Alaska and also crosses the Atlantic to Canada and Greenland.

Black-eared Wheatear
Oenanthe hispanica (flycatchers)
L 15 cm   WSp 25–27 cm   Long distance migrant

variations in head marks

68

The Black-eared Wheatear uses its
relatively low body weight to perch
readily on fairly thin plant stems to look
out for insects and spiders. This type of
hunt therefore plays a more important
role than for the heavier Northern
Wheatear (p. 67). The breeding habitat of
the similar looking Eastern Black-eared
Wheatear (*O. melanoleuca*) ranges from
south-eastern Italy to the Balkans and
further east. Until recently, both of these
species were grouped under the same
name of Black-eared Wheatear.

lots of white on
tail and rump

terminal tail–band
black and narrow

crown and back
pale orange

**Eastern
Black-eared Wheatear**

black eye patch

belly, crown and
back chestnut-
orange

Voice *Song with short
stanzas consisting
of hard, sometimes
crackling notes.*

Did you know?
*Male Black-eared and
Eastern Black-eared
Wheatears occur
in two different
plumages: either they
only have a black eye
patch (similar to the
Northern Wheatear)
or a full black face
and throat.*

Black Wheatear
Oenanthe leucura (flycatchers)
L 18 cm   WSp 26–29 cm   Resident bird

♀
plumage brownish-black

In contrast to the other European wheatear species (pp. 67–69) the Black Wheatear is a resident bird. In winter it only moves down from higher mountainous regions to lower regions. It builds its nest in holes in rocks or walls and constructs a platform next to it using hundreds of tiny stones.

♂
plumage dull black

white under-tail

Habitat Inhabits dry, rocky areas like cliffs, gorges or semi-deserts, but also residential areas.

> *Breeding season March–July*
> 3–5 bluish, brown mottled eggs
> 1–2 broods per year

Voice Scratching song with single clear warbling notes, delivered from rock or rooftops.

Pied Wheatear
Oenanthe pleschanka (flycatchers)
L 15–16 cm   WSp 26–28 cm   Long distance migrant

white tail with black 'T'

Pied Wheatears nest very close to each other but every pair has its own breeding territory and the male marks it acoustically by its song delivered from rocks or treetops. During migration to east Africa the species becomes more sociable. Flocks of up to 40 birds have been spotted.

breast grey-brown
♀
♂

Habitat Steppe-like hillsides with occasional rocks; in winter also bushy grasslands.

> *Breeding season May–July*
> 4–6 pale blue eggs with reddish mottles
> 1 brood per year

white crown

paler supercilium

underside orange-coloured

♂ juvenile

black throat

♂

Voice Short, scratchy sounding song; whistling and smacking calls.

Blue Rock Thrush
Monticola solitarius (flycatchers)
L 20–23 cm   WSp 33–37 cm   Resident bird

blackish tail

Habitat *Sunny, rocky slopes, gorges and cliffs along coasts; also breeds among ruins.*

> **Breeding season April–July**
> **4–5 pale blue eggs, sometimes mottled**
> **2 broods per year**

From a distance the Blue Rock Thrush's plumage appears darkly monochrome. When you also consider its song it could be another Blackbird, yet suited to rocky regions. This is the kind of habitat where this shy bird breeds in different kinds of holes. The Blue Rock Thrush is, however, a solitary character and even stays hidden when foraging for small animals and berries on the ground.

upperparts brown ♀

under-side scaled and barred

♂

blue plumage

black wings

Voice *Melodious warbling song, reminiscent of the Blackbird.*

Rock Thrush
Monticola saxatilis (flycatchers)
L 16–19 cm   WSp 33–37 cm   Long distance migrant

white rump

outer tail edges orange

Habitat *Rocky areas in mountain uplands with short grass and sparse shrubs.*

> **Breeding season May–August**
> **4–5 bluish, lightly speckled eggs**
> **1–2 broods per year**

head blue

♂

The Rock Thrush's way of life is generally very similar to the Blue Rock Thrush's, although it mostly spends the breeding season in mountainous regions and is rarely seen below altitudes of 1,500 m. It marks its breeding territory with a show of impressive song flights. Unlike the Blue Rock Thrush, the Rock Thrush migrates to tropical Africa in autumn and stays there over winter in the savannah.

♀

underparts orange-coloured, scaled and barred

breast orange

Voice *Warbling, partly hoarse song with trills, often delivered in flight.*

Bearded Tit

Panurus biarmicus (babblers)
L 13 cm   WSp 16–18 cm   Resident bird/Short-distance migrant

The Bearded Tit is highly sociable. In autumn and winter it lives in association with other birds and even forms loose colonies during the breeding season. Shortly before the egg-laying season the male guards the female every second of the day to prevent impregnation by other males. But this cannot be entirely prevented in the dense, broken reed thickets and so many males from outside the breeding ground rear broods. The Bearded Tit feeds on insects in summer and mostly on reed seeds in winter, swallowing tiny stones in order to help crush the seeds.

♂ juvenile

head orange-brown

black back

♀

Habitat Prefers reeds near water.

> *Breeding season March–August*
> *4–6 brownish, darkly mottled eggs*
> *2–3 broods per year*

71

reed seeds important winter food

head bluish-grey

black 'moustache'

♂ adult

long tail

Did you know?
Bearded Tit pairs often commit to 'long-term marriage' that lasts their whole lifetime when they are only a few weeks old. Sometimes half-siblings from different broods are paired off in this way.

Voice Calls with conspicuous, twanging 'tching'; song consists of three call-like notes, but low and indistinct.

Long-tailed Tit

Aegithalos caudatus (long-tailed tits)
L 14 cm WSp 16–19 cm Resident bird/Short distance migrant

builds globular-shaped nests

Habitat Deciduous and mixed forests, parks and gardens.

> **Breeding season** March–June
> **8–12 whitish, reddish speckled eggs**
> **1 brood per year**

The Long-tailed Tit mostly roams the bushes and trees in association with others, often its own immediate family. In winter 10–20 birds generally get together to defend common feeding territory against neighbouring rival groups. Long-tailed Tits breed in pairs, but adults with unsuccessful broods help to raise related pairs' fledglings.

Voice Repeats high 'see-see-sui' calls and sharp 'tsirrup'; song weak.

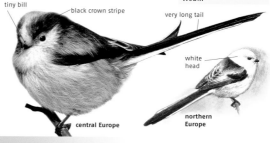

tiny bill

black crown stripe

very long tail

white head

central Europe

northern Europe

Penduline Tit

nest

Remiz pendulinus (penduline tits)
L 11 cm WSp 16–17 cm Resident bird/Middle distance migrant

Habitat Breeds in coppices, often on riverbanks and lake shores; outside of breeding season mostly inhabits reeds.

> **Breeding season** April–August
> **6–8 white eggs**
> **1–2 broods per year**

narrow black 'mask'

The male builds an ovoid nest from woolly plant material and hair, suspended in the twigs of a bush or tree. The female often helps to build the nest, but the actual raising of fledglings usually remains the responsibility of a lone parent. The other then often starts a second brood with a different adult.

♀

head uniform brown

juvenile

broad black 'mask'

fine, pointed bill

♂

Voice Call high-pitched, plaintive ('psui'), slightly weaker and more sustained than the Reed Bunting's (p. 109).

rufous breast

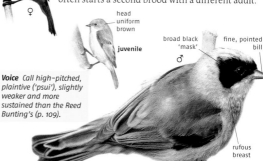

Marsh Tit

Parus palustris (tits)

L 12 cm   WSp 18–19 cm   Resident bird

fully fledged juvenile

The Marsh Tit always chooses tree holes with funnel-shaped entrances or a small nesting area. Thus, it tries to avoid competition with other tits, but there is often not enough space for a whole brood in such nesting holes. Even nests in holes are not safe from predators, because some eggs or chicks are carried off by Great Spotted Woodpeckers, squirrels or martens.

glossy black crown

smaller black bib

Habitat Breeds in deciduous and mixed woodlands; in winter also in gardens.

> *Breeding season April–July*
> 4–12 whitish, rufous mottled eggs
> 1 brood per year

Voice Scolding calls; song is a monotonous succession of 'tchair-tchair-tchair...'.

Willow Tit

Parus montanus (tits)

L 12 cm   WSp 17–20 cm   Resident bird

large black bib

underside bright

Scandinavia

In early spring the Willow Tit looks for a rotten tree and pecks a breeding hole into the decaying wood with its small, but strong bill. This takes one to two weeks. While the female is busy hatching the brood, the male feeds her now and then. If enough plant seeds are available, the Willow Tit hides away some provisions in cracks in the bark for 'a rainy day'.

Habitat Prefers coniferous and deciduous forests in mountainous regions and riverside glades.

> *Breeding season April–July*
> 5–10 whitish, rufous mottled eggs
> 1 brood per year

white wing patch

underside light brown

central and western Europe

Voice Calls reminiscent of the Marsh Tit, but more complacent (loud 'chay-chay-chay'); song a series of cascading warbling notes.

Coal Tit
Parus ater (tits)
L 11 cm WSp 17–21 cm Resident bird/Short distance migrant

visits feeding stations

Habitat *Coniferous forests, but also in gardens and parks with conifer stocks.*

> **Breeding season March–August**
> **5–12 whitish, rufous mottled eggs**
> **1–2 broods per year**

The Coal Tit mostly nests in tree holes, but if there is a shortage of these, it also builds its nest in ground holes, on slopes or even in wall alcoves. Outside the breeding season it lives in groups with other tits, nuthatches and treecreepers. If spruce seeds are rare in Siberia, the resident Coal Tits travel in great numbers to Europe during the autumn.

white patch from rear crown to nape

two white wing-bars

brownish underpart

Voice *Sings monotonously 'seeetoooee'; calls with nasal twang and drawling 'tsui'.*

Sombre Tit
Parus lugubris (tits)
L 13–14 cm WSp 21–23 cm Resident bird

rufous back
rufous flanks

Siberian Tit

Habitat *Open mountain woodlands and rocky slopes with bushes and trees.*

> **Breeding season March–August**
> **5–10 white, reddish mottled eggs**
> **1–2 broods per year**

The Sombre Tit's habitats are in mountainous regions where it builds its nest either in tree holes or small rock crevices. When foraging for insects and seeds, it tends to stay on the ground, although it flies and perches on a twig for the meal, most likely to keep safe from snake attacks. A similar species, the Siberian Tit (*P. cinctus*), lives in the northern Scandinavian taiga.

Voice *Song a monotonous succession of harsh notes; different calls reminiscent of the Great and Blue Tit.*

back dark grey

black throat

whitish belly

Blue Tit
Parus caeruleus (tits)
L 12 cm WSp 18–20 cm Resident bird/Short distance migrant

The Blue Tit feeds its brood with insects. In winter the diet changes mainly to seeds, which the bird opens with its strong bill. Although insects are rare in winter, the Blue Tit need not do without them, as it can use its bill to peck out insects hidden in reeds.

wings and tail blue

green back

juvenile

buff face

underside pale yellow

blue crown

Voice Song is a long trill, opened with 2 to 3 high notes; call scolding ('churrr').

white wing-bar

likes to breed in nesting boxes

underpart yellow

Habitat Breeds in various different forests, parks and gardens, preferably in reeds in winter.

> *Breeding season March–August*
> 6–14 white eggs with rufous mottles
> 1–2 broods per year

Crested Tit
Parus cristatus (tits)
L 12 cm WSp 17–20 cm Resident bird

nest

Crested Tit pairs stay together for an entire lifetime. They also stay in their territory over winter, sometimes in mixed groups with other tit species. Juveniles prefer to choose single, widowed adults as mates. For breeding they prefer self-made tree holes in rotten trees and also woodpeckers' holes or nesting boxes.

pointed black and white speckled crest

upperpart uniform brown

black throat

Habitat Coniferous forests as well as parks and large gardens with conifers.

> *Breeding season March–July*
> 4–8 white, russet mottled eggs
> 1–2 broods per year

Voice Song and calls of high notes and low trills ('seeh–burrurrlt').

Great Tit

Parus major (tits)

L 14 cm   WSp 23–25 cm   Resident bird/Short distance migrant

The Great Tit is a highly versatile and thus
competitive bird. On the one hand, its
superiority is proven when competing for
nesting holes, as it defeats other tits and Pied
Flycatchers. On the other hand, it stays top
of the 'pecking order' with the other
tits, treecreepers and crests that it
prefers to roam about with in winter.
On average, a Great Tit lives up to
two years, although the oldest
known Great Tit reached the
impressive age of 15.

tail and wing
bluish-grey

outer tail edges white

76

♀

narrow black bib
extending down body
centre

underparts yellow

juvenile

triangular
yellowish cheek

black belly
stripe faint

underparts
pale yellow

black head
with white
cheek

♂

underparts bright
yellow

full black bib
extending down
body centre

Birder's tip
*No other bird is
easier to watch in
the garden then
the Great Tit. It likes
to breed in nesting
boxes. In winter it is
a regular visitor to
the bird feeder and
you can marvel at the
skilful way it handles
sunflower seeds.*

Voice *Many different,
partly loud, partly
purring calls; song
with variations, often
'teechew-teechew'.*

Nuthatch

Sitta europaea (nuthatches)
L 14 cm   WSp 23–27 cm   Resident bird

The Nuthatch breeds in tree holes. Unlike the woodpeckers, it does not carve these hollows and, if it finds one, it readily uses an old woodpecker hole. If the entrance hole is too large, it uses mud to reduce the size or if the hole is too small, powerful pecks enlarge the entrance. The Nuthatch collects food stocks throughout the year. In summer it hides insects or nuts and other tree fruits in cracks in the bark. Occasionally, it also buries food in the ground.

upperparts bluish-grey

Habitat Deciduous and mixed forests, parks and gardens with old or tall trees.

> *Breeding season March–June*
> *5–9 whitish, brown mottled eggs*
> *1 brood per year*

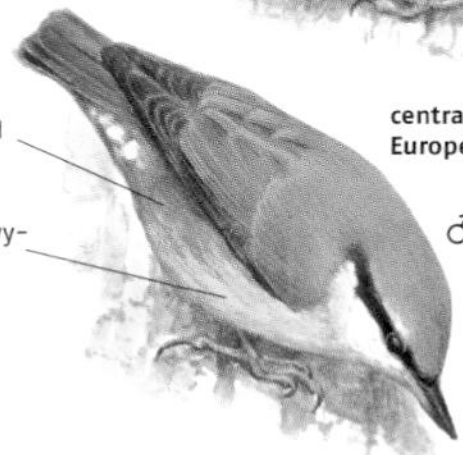

♀

central/southern Europe

upper flanks and vent russet

underside yellowy-orange

♂

77

Voice Calls frequent, loud 'chwit, chwit'; song consists of calls interspersed with warbling elements.

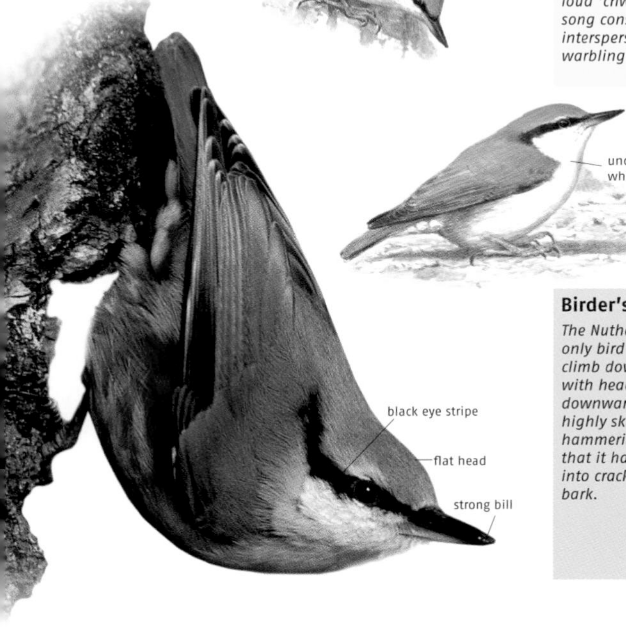

underside white

northern/eastern Europe

Birder's tip

The Nuthatch is the only bird able to climb down trees with head facing downwards. It is highly skilled at hammering open nuts that it has wedged into cracks in tree bark.

black eye stripe

flat head

strong bill

Rock Nuthatch

black crown

Corsican Nuthatch

white supercilium

underpart pale beige

Sitta neumayer (nuthatches)
L 14–15 cm   WSp 23–25 cm   Resident bird

Habitat Rocky landscapes with occasional bushes and trees.

> **Breeding season April–July**
> **8–10 white, reddish-brown mottled eggs**
> **1–2 broods per year**

The Rock Nuthatch chooses crannies or alcoves in rocks for breeding and plasters them almost completely with mud. Thus it forms a 10 cm-long funnel with only a tiny hole remaining open as the entrance. The small Corsican Nuthatch (*S. whiteheadi*) inhabits Corsica's Pine forests and is one of Europe's rarest birds.

long bill

whitish underpart

feeding at the nest

Voice Song a series of long, clear warbling notes gradually descending in pitch.

78

upperwing almost completely red

Wallcreeper

Tichodroma muraria (wallcreepers)
L 17 cm WSp 27–32 cm Resident bird/Short distance migrant

Habitat Stony, rocky areas in high mountains; in winter also in ravines and buildings on lowlands.

> **Breeding season May–August**
> **3–5 white, reddish-brown speckled eggs**
> **1 brood per year**

The Wallcreeper skilfully climbs up and down steep rocky slopes to pick out insects from crevices using its long bill. While doing so, it almost constantly twitches its wings. Sometimes it chases butterflies in flight. The Wallcreeper builds its nest in rock crevices or holes, using moss, lichen or grass, where the female rears the young alone.

bill long and thin

♀

♂

pale grey throat

black throat

Voice Song a succession of up and down warbling notes.

Short-toed Treecreeper

Certhia brachydactyla (treecreepers)
L 13 cm   WSp 17–20 cm   Resident bird

joint sleeping community

rear flanks brown-coloured

back irregularly streaked

Both treecreeper species have a similar plumage and can be best distinguished by their voice. With its relatively short hind claw, the Short-toed Treecreeper preferably climbs trees with furrowed bark. At night treecreepers like to huddle together in groups to store warmth while asleep.

narrow white supercilium

uniform wing-bar without stepped pattern

Voice Calls sharp 'teet'; sings with loud and piercing 'teet, teeteroititt'.

Habitat Deciduous and mixed forests, undergrowth, parks and gardens and also settles in urban greenbelts.

> *Breeding season March–July*
> 5–6 white, reddish-brown mottled eggs
> 1–2 broods per year

79

Treecreeper

Certhia familiaris (treecreepers)
L 13 cm   WSp 18–21 cm   Resident bird/Short distance migrant

broad white supercilium

bill shorter than Short-Toed Treecreeper

Treecreepers climb trees with jerky movements and pick insects from the bark. The Treecreeper is also able to climb slick trunks using its long hind claw. Once it reaches the treetop, it flies to the bottom of the next tree and begins a new ascent. Thus, it covers a climbing distance of up to 3 km per day.

bill thin, decurved

underside white

back speckled white

wing-bar with stepped pattern

Voice Thin song recalling Blue Tit ('tsee-tsee-tsizzi-tsee'); call is Crest-like (high 'tsee' or 'tsit').

Woodpecker-like stiff tail

Habitat Deciduous, coniferous and mixed forests; also in parks, but rarely near residential sites.

> *Breeding season March–August*
> 5–6 white, reddish-brown mottled eggs
> 1–2 broods per year

Red-backed Shrike
Lanius collurio (shrikes)
L 17 cm   WSp 24–27 cm   Long distance migrant

Habitat *Breeds in hedges and bushy commons.*

> **Breeding season May–August**
> **4–7 greenish or reddish, darkly mottled eggs**
> **1 brood per year**

The Red-backed Shrike's nest consists of twigs, stalks and moss and it builds it well hidden in the centre of a thorny bush. These bushes also serve as storage places - extra prey items, like insects or small mammals, are impaled on the thorns for later use. The Red-backed Shrike looks out for its prey from bush tops or other elevated perches. While it catches insects often in flight, it also pounces on other prey, such as mice, as a bird of prey would.

black and white tail pattern

80

head grey-brown ♀

upperpart barred

underside barred

juvenile

black 'mask'

head grey

hooked bill

♂

upperpart reddish-brown

Did you know?
During winter the Red-backed Shrike stays in the southern half of Africa. Its migration route is done in a kind of 'loop': in autumn it crosses Africa on its way south, in spring it takes the route back over east Africa and Arabia.

Voice *Call is a hoarse 'chee-ah' or 'shack' (also in row); quiet chatty song.*

Great Grey Shrike
Lanius excubitor (shrikes)
L 24–25 cm   WSp 30–34 cm   Resident bird/Middle distance migrant

The Great Grey Shrike is a migrant in northern Europe and every breeding season, each bird has to find a new mate. The central European Great Grey Shrike, as a resident bird, stays with its mate its entire life, even if the males and females occupy different territories in winter. A similar bird with slightly darker plumage is native to the dry bush land, steppe regions and semi-deserts of south-western Europe and north Africa. Today these birds are regarded as a species in their own right known as the Southern Grey Shrike (*L. meridionalis*).

Habitat Different kinds of open country with hedgerows, bushes and occasional trees.

Breeding season
April–July
4–7 whitish, brown mottled eggs
1 brood per year

81

upperparts dark grey

juvenile

underparts grey

Southern Grey Shrike

underparts lightly barred

wing black and white

long tail

Did you know?
The Great Grey Shrike is the most fearsome 'bird of prey' among songbirds. With its hooked bill it not only catches insects but also mice and even small birds. In summer as well as winter it impales its prey on thorns to store them.

upperparts pale grey

black 'mask'

strong hooked bill

underparts white

Voice Different hard calls or with nasal twang, sometimes with whistle-like trill; short, metallic sounding song.

Lesser Grey Shrike
Lanius minor (shrikes)
L 20 cm   WSp 32–34 cm   Long distance migrant

wing predominantly black

Habitat *Open, dry countryside with occasional bushes or trees.*

> **Breeding season May–August**
> **4–7 greenish, brown mottled eggs**
> **1 brood per year**

The Lesser Grey Shrike is an eyecatching bird within its habitat. It sights its prey, insects and small mammals, from its perch on electrical wires and catches them after a short flight chase. The Lesser Grey Shrike has been extinct in central Europe for decades because of climate change with increased humidity and the resulting destruction of its habitat.

forehead grey   barred crown

juvenile

forehead black

stout hooked bill

white breast with pinkish glow

Voice *Call is a screeching 'kviell'; quiet, chatty song.*

Woodchat Shrike
Lanius senator (shrikes)
L 18 cm   WSp 26–28 cm   Long distance migrant

white back and rump

Habitat *Dry, sunny habitats with bushes and occasional trees; also orchards.*

> **Breeding season April–August**
> **5–6 greenish eggs with brown mottles**
> **1–2 broods per year**

The male and the female Woodchat Shrike sing as a duet, which strengthens the pair's cohesion. This shrike does not store its prey. The Masked Shrike (*L. nubicus*) breeds in the open woodlands of south-eastern Europe.

♂

chestnut crest and nape

underparts white

upperparts black-white

upperparts brownish

bright scapulars

juvenile

underparts barred

forehead white

black crest

orange flanks

Masked Shrike ♂

Voice *Chatty song, imitating other bird voices; different calls in series.*

Magpie
Pica pica (crows)
L 44–46 cm WSp 52–60 cm Resident bird

very long tail

wings black-white

The Magpie's actual
habitat – varied, partly open
country – has disappeared in many places.
Therefore, as a breeding bird, the Magpie
infiltrated villages and cities and you can spot
them frequently as they look for insects, worms and carrion on
open ground. Occasionally, the Magpie also carries off eggs and
fledglings. Consequently, the Magpie is unpopular, but its
predations do not affect the
numbers of other species. The
smaller Azure-Winged Magpie
(*Cyanopica cyana*) inhabits the
forests of the Iberian Peninsula.

Habitat *Partly open
country with bushes
and trees, residential
areas and parks.*

> *Breeding season
March–August*
> *5–7 greenish, darkly
mottled eggs*
> *1 brood per year*

black crown and cheeks

**Azure-Winged
Magpie**

pale blue tail
and wings

83

head and
breast black

wings and tail
metallic iridescent

belly white

globular nest

Voice *Often calls with a
laughing, loud 'chak-
chak-chak-chak', but
also different notes.*

Birder's tip
*In early springtime 'In
springtime Magpies
are easy to see as they
build their round nests
in the bare treetops.
Sometimes the nesting
place is changed
before breeding starts
and the Magpie takes
its nesting material
with it.*

Jay
Garrulus glandarius (crows)
L 34–35 cm WSp 52–58 cm Resident bird/Short distance migrant

rump white

white wing patch

black 'moustache'

Habitat *Forests, parks and gardens.*

> **Breeding season March–August**
> 4–6 greenish, dark brown mottled eggs
> 1 brood per year

The Jay does eat insects and other little animals, although seeds and fruit form the major part of its diet. In autumn the Jay collects thousands of acorns and buries them as provision for winter and spring. Especially in northern Europe, Jays leave their habitat when food is scarce and migrate in flocks to central Europe.

plumage brownish-pink

black-blue primary coverts

Voice *Warning call is penetrating and raucous; the Buzzard's voice is among many other imitated sounds.*

Nutcracker
Nucifraga caryocatactes (crows)
L 32–33 cm   WSp 52–58 cm   Resident bird

white tail bar

Habitat *Breeds in coniferous and mixed woodland; also in gardens while foraging for food.*

> **Breeding season March–August**
> 3–4 greenish, olive-brown spotted eggs
> 1 brood per year

The Nutcracker feeds on conifer seeds and nuts. When the seeds are ripe it hides up to 100,000 seeds in various places each autumn, and lives off this store for the rest of the year. Seeds that are not found again contribute to the distribution of the respective tree species. The smaller Siberian Jay (*Perisoreus infaustus*) inhabits coniferous woods in northern Europe.

dark brown crest

Siberian Jay

head and upperparts dark brown

under tail-coverts white

orange belly

body plumage spotted white

outer tail feathers rusty red

Voice *Rasping call, harsher and shriller notes than the Jay's.*

Alpine Chough
Pyrrhocorax graculus (crows)
L 38 cm   WSp 75–85 cm   Resident bird

lives mostly in flocks

The Alpine Chough is an artist of the air. It uses thermal currents in the mountains to sail and glide. With wings swept back, it manages speeds of up to 200 km/h as it dives along the rock faces. The Alpine Chough frequents cable car stations and huts to find tit-bits in among the rubbish, although its natural diet is little animals and berries. It breeds in inaccessible rock faces and also on buildings.

yellow bill

round outer tail edge

plumage uniform black

short legs

Voice *Call is a sharp 'krrrree' and metallic whistling.*

Habitat *Cleft rocks in mountain uplands, not normally descending to lowlands.*

> *Breeding season April–August*
> *2–5 whitish, brown mottled eggs*
> *1 brood per year*

Chough
Pyrrhocorax pyrrhocorax (crows)
L 39–40 cm   WSp 73–90 cm   Resident bird

short tail with straight end

The Chough builds its nest in rock crevices from twigs and often uses the nest for many years. A few breeding pairs are frequently together in colonies. While foraging for food, they hop around on the ground, poking about with their bills to find insects and worms. The Chough is sociable and prefers to live in flocks, sometimes even with the Alpine Chough.

Habitat *Mountains and steep coastal cliffs.*

> *Breeding season April–August*
> *3–6 whitish, brown mottled eggs*
> *1 brood per year*

juvenile

bill yellowish

adult

bill red and curved

red legs

Voice *Call reminiscent of the Jackdaw, but brighter ('cheeahh'); also shrill loud calls.*

Jackdaw
Corvus monedula (crows)
L 33–34 cm WSp 67–74 cm Resident bird/Middle distance migrant

wing beat faster and lower than the Crow

Habitat *Breeds in cities and forests; forages on open ground like fields, meadows and lawns.*

> **Breeding season April–July**
> **2–7 bluish, brown mottled eggs**
> **1 brood per year**

The Jackdaw breeds in building alcoves in towns where it fills the air with its typical call. In many places, however, the Jackdaw is also a forest bird and prefers to use deserted Black Woodpecker holes as well as larger nesting boxes to breed. In winter Jackdaws are often seen with Rooks.

deep grey shawl

short bill

bright eyes

nesting hole in tree

Voice *Calls character-istically light 'chak'; song is a quiet twit-ter, only at the nest.*

86

Rook
Corvus frugilegus (crows)
L 44–46 cm WSp 81–99 cm Resident bird/Middle distance migrant

rounded tail-end

Habitat *Breeds in tree clusters, forages in open country.*

> **Breeding season February–July**
> **3–6 blue-green, brown mottled eggs**
> **1 brood per year**

The Rook breeds in big colonies and nests in clusters of trees and often right in the middle of residential areas. It also appears in large groups while foraging for worms, insects and grain. Even larger assemblies of birds occur in winter at roost sites, where up to 150,000 birds flock together at dusk.

steep forehead

juvenile

bill dark

root of bill feathered

bill light-coloured and pointed

root of bill is naked grey skin

breeding colony

Voice *Call is a hoarse 'krraah', longer and hoarser than the Carrion Crow's.*

Carrion Crow

Corvus corone (crows)
L 45–49 cm   WSp 93–104 cm   Resident bird

tail-end almost straight

The Carrion Crow is a fairly unpretentious omnivore and thus very successful nowadays, as plenty of additional food is available, such as refuse or animals killed on the road. The Carrion Crow breeds on trees or posts and often its deserted nests are later taken over by falcons or owls. The Carrion Crow is gregarious when not breeding and flocks to communal roosts in the evening.

flat forehead

strong dark bill

Habitat *Almost all kinds of open or partly open country, avoids dense forests.*

> **Breeding season March–July**
> 3–6 greenish, darkly mottled eggs
> 1 brood per year

Voice Calls loud and hoarse 'krraah', also in a series.

87

Hooded Crow

Corvus cornix (crows)
L 45–47 cm WSp 93–104 cm Resident bird/Short distance migrant

The Hooded Crow replaces the Carrion Crow in northern and eastern Europe. Both species can be found in a small area and they also breed together. The resulting hybrids have less grey in their plumage. The Hooded Crow only starts breeding at the age of three to five years. The male and female usually stay together for life.

underparts greyish black

black head

Habitat *Almost all kinds of open or partly open country, avoids dense forests.*

> **Breeding season March–July**
> 3–6 greenish, darkly mottled eggs
> 1 brood per year

pale grey back and belly

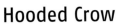

Voice Calls loud and hoarse 'krraah', also in series.

Raven

Corvus corax (crows)
L 64 cm   WSp 120–150 cm   Resident bird

Habitat Breeds in forests and on cliffs; mostly forages in open country.

> *Breeding season February–August*
> *36 blue to green, darkly mottled eggs*
> *1 brood per year*

The Raven breeds in trees and on cliffs and is therefore common in lowlands as well as the mountains. Rock breeders generally tend to build several nests that they use alternately during the year. The Raven is loyal to the same territory throughout its life, where it feeds on carrion and small animals. It also stays loyal to its mate and this can mean a lasting arrangement, as Ravens often live for 20 years or longer.

diamond-shaped tail

feeds on carrion

very strong bill

plumage uniform black

Voice Call is a deep gargling 'koo-rook' but also many other notes in its repertoire.

Birder's tip
The Raven is said to be very playful. This can be observed best in springtime when the pairs perform their aerobatic flight routines: flying closely next to each other, chases, dives and flying upside-down.

Starling

Sturnus vulgaris (starlings)
L 22 cm   WSp 37–42 cm   Resident bird/Middle distance migrant

The Starling raises its young in tree holes and nesting boxes but also in different holes in buildings. Its diet is very varied, apart from bugs and larvae, it also feeds on cherries and berries. On sunny days Starlings athletically pursue and catch flying ants high in the air. In contrast to thrushes (pp. 36–38), which hop, the Starling strides along. The Spotless Starling (*S. unicolor*), which is only lightly mottled, takes the Starling's role on the Iberian Peninsula.

triangular wings

short tail

Habitat *Breeds in forests, field copses, orchards and villages, foraging in open country.*

> **Breeding season**
> *March–July*
> 4–6 greenish-blue eggs
> 1–2 broods per year

Spotless Starling

spotless plumage

blackish bill

brown plumage

juvenile

89

---

winter plumage

blackish bill

head plumage often ruffled

plumage metallic iridescent

underparts mottled white

yellow bill

breeding plumage

Voice *Song a scratchy squeal and whistling with embedded imitation of other bird voices. Calls hoarsely 'err'.*

Birder's tip

Immediately after the departure of the juveniles, starlings form large flocks. While eagerly uttering calls, they search the fields and meadows for food. the sight of thousands swarming around their roost sites is especially impressive.

Rose-coloured Starling

Sturnus roseus (starlings)
L 22 cm   WSp 37–40 cm   Long distance migrant

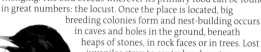

head black

underparts pink

Habitat *Steppes, agricultural land and orchards.*

> **Breeding season May–July**
> **4–6 pale blue eggs**
> **1 brood per year**

The Rose-coloured Starling's habitat is always changing. The bird breeds wherever its primary food can be found in great numbers: the locust. Once the place is located, big breeding colonies form and nest-building occurs in caves and holes in the ground, beneath heaps of stones, in rock faces or in trees. Lost juveniles stray to central and western Europe every summer.

bill pink

pink back

black wings

upperparts pale brown

strong, yellow bill

underparts brownish

juvenile

Voice *Short, hoarse calls, sometimes in series; hoarse, chatty song.*

Golden Oriole

Oriolus oriolus (orioles)
L 24 cm   WSp 44–47 cm   Long distance migrant

wing black

Habitat *Breeds in damp deciduous forests with tall trees, preferably close to water.*

> **Breeding season May–August**
> **2–5 whitish, black mottled eggs**
> **1 brood per year**

Apart from its melodious song the Golden Oriole leads an inconspicuous existence in treetops, where it primarily feeds on fruits and berries and especially caterpillars. The Golden Oriole also breeds well hidden in tree canopies. After five weeks, when the youngsters are fully fledged, the family splits up. The adults and juveniles make their separate ways to their southern African winter home.

♀

upperparts green

underparts whitish, streaked

bill red

body plumage yellow

♂

Voice *Strong, melodious phrases with 3–5 fluted warbles. Hoarse, slightly ascending calls ('waahk').*

House Sparrow

Passer domesticus (sparrows)
L 14–15 cm   WSp 21–25 cm   Resident bird

The House Sparrow's nesting sites are mostly cavities in buildings. A few House Sparrow pairs frequently form little colonies and sometimes even build one communal nest with multiple entrances. When foraging for food, the House Sparrow is also very gregarious and prefers safety in numbers – many eyes help prevent attacks from cats or birds of prey. It primarily feeds on corn and other seeds, although feeds its young exclusively on insects.

grey rump

monochrome tail

Habitat Inhabits cities and villages, also open country while foraging for food.

> *Breeding season March–September*
> *4–6 bluish, white, brown mottled eggs*
> *2–4 broods per year*

pale supercilium

♀

underparts grey

91

dark grey crown

ear-coverts white

pale head marks

brown nape

winter plumage

black throat

♂

Birder's tip

After the breeding season the male House Sparrow moults and changes its entire plumage. Initially, the new crown feathers are pale. The bright colours gradually emerge after a while, so that the plumage is represented in its full splendour in time for the next breeding season.

Voice Different twittering, chirping and grating calls; 'song' consists of a series of slowly repeated 'chirp' calls.

Tree Sparrow
Passer montanus (sparrows)
L 14 cm WSp 20–22 cm Resident bird/Short distance migrant

feeding adult at nest

chocolate brown crown

white collar

black spot on white cheek

Habitat *Villages and gardens; more frequent than the House Sparrow in open country.*

> **Breeding season April–August**
> **3–7 white to greenish, brown mottled eggs**
> **2–3 broods per year**

In comparison to the House Sparrow (p. 91), the Tree Sparrow is a shy bird, although it still breeds in residential areas on the continent where it occupies nesting boxes. It secures breeding holes in autumn, although it initially uses these to sleep in. It is frequently seen with yellowhammers and chaffinches while searching for seeds.

adult

spot on cheek only hinted

juvenile

***Voice** Similar to House Sparrow's, often harder and hoarser calls.*

Spanish Sparrow
Passer hispaniolensis (sparrows)
L 15 cm WSp 23–26 cm Resident bird/Short-distance migrant

brown crown

only throat black

Italian Sparrow

Habitat *Open country and semi-deserts as well as villages; preferably near damp areas.*

> **Breeding season April–August**
> **4–6 whitish, darkly mottled eggs**
> **2–3 broods per year**

The Spanish Sparrow is gregarious and breeds in colonies. However, it is less dependent on human contact than the House Sparrow (p. 91). You can often spot its nesting sites on the foundations of White Storks' nests (p. 165) or birds of prey (p. 136–153). The so-called Italian Sparrow (*P. italiae*) lives in northern Italy and is a hybrid of the House and Spanish Sparrow.

♀

brown crown

♂

resembles House Sparrow, but with stronger streaked lines on flanks

breast densely mottled black

***Voice** 'Chirp' call very similar to the House Sparrow.*

Rock Sparrow

Petronia petronia (sparrows)
L 14 cm   WSp 28–32 cm   Resident bird

The Rock Sparrow likes to breed in deep crannies or rock crevices, less frequently in ruins and also in tree holes. Sometimes the female bird leaves the male in charge of the brood and begins a second brood with another male. The Rock Sparrow was formerly present in southern Germany, although as the climate has become gradually more humid, it has withdrawn to southern Europe.

whitish
supercilium

strong,
two-tone bill

yellow throat
patch

underparts
palely mottled

Habitat Dry, often rocky landscapes and steppes, but also residential areas.

> **Breeding season April–August**
> 4–6 brownish white, brown mottled eggs
> 1–2 broods per year

Voice Calls nasal and ascending 'pey-i'; song is a mixture of calls and buzzing notes, reminiscent of the Greenfinch (p. 96).

93

Snowfinch

Montifringilla nivalis (sparrows)
L 17 cm   WSp 34–38 cm   Resident bird/Short distance migrant

wings black
and white

The Snowfinch can only feed on insects in the mountains in summertime. In winter it finds seeds on ground without snow and is only occasionally forced to venture down to the lowland valleys. It builds its nest on rock faces, under piles of stones as well as on mountain huts or ski-lift pillars.

Habitat Lives above the tree line in rocky mountain areas.

> **Breeding season May–August**
> 3–5 white eggs
> 1 brood per year

grey
head

black throat
and bill

bill yellow

breeding
plumage

winter
plumage

brown back

underparts
white

Voice Song a series of musical notes interspersed with hoarse trills; different light calls.

Chaffinch

Fringilla coelebs (finches)
L 14 cm   WSp 25–28 cm   Resident bird/Middle distance migrant

Habitat *Forests, parks, gardens and other coppices.*

> **Breeding season April–August**
> **3–6 reddish to bluish, mottled eggs**
> **1–2 broods per year**

With an estimated 200 million breeding pairs, the Chaffinch is arguably the most common bird species in Europe. About half of them breed in northern and eastern Europe and, as migrant birds, cross central Europe on their way to/from the southern half of the continent. Many Chaffinches in central Europe are resident birds because they find enough food in winter, like seeds and beechmast. In summer, they primarily feed on insects.

two distinctly white wing-bars

rump olive-green

♀ upperparts greenish-grey

underparts grey

winter plumage

plumage in pale colours

Birder's tip

The male prefers to settle on a protruding branch to deliver its song and proudly present its pink chest. The musical phrases include a cascade of about 12 different notes that often accelerate in tempo and include a range of songs from the repertoire.

Voice *Loud and vigorous, cascading song ending in a flourish; calls include repeated 'chwink' or short 'chwit' and 'chewp' in flight.*

crown and nape blue-grey

breeding plumage

underparts brownish-pink

Brambling
Fringilla montifringilla (finches)
L 14 cm   WSp 25–26 cm   Short/Middle distance migrant

The Brambling's distribution in winter widely fluctuates from year to year and is dependent on a plentiful supply of beechmast – the bird's main food source. Some years the Brambling may completely disappear in certain areas, whereas in other years, when the beeches are exceptionally productive, the Brambling might appear in huge flocks of several 100,000 birds on the continent. In springtime the pale feather tips of the male's winter plumage gradually wear away to reveal a brilliantly colourful new plumage on arrival in its breeding habitat. This occurs entirely without moulting.

♂ **breeding plumage**
bill black

♂ **winter plumage**
head grey-black

♀ head grey

rump white

head and back behind nape black

two narrow white wing-bars

♂

breast orange

belly white

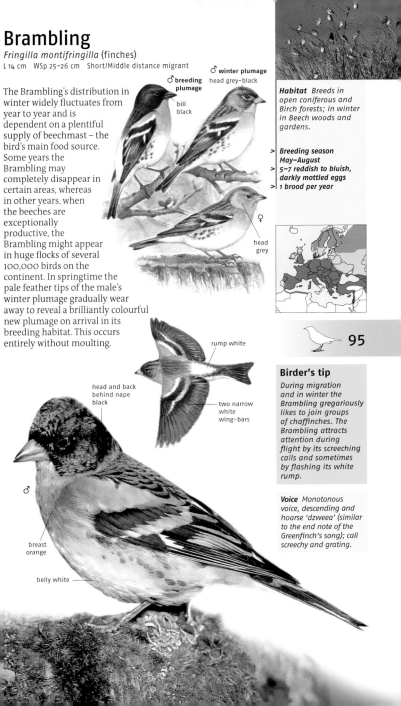

Habitat Breeds in open coniferous and Birch forests; in winter in Beech woods and gardens.

> *Breeding season May–August*
> 5–7 reddish to bluish, darkly mottled eggs
> 1 brood per year

95

Birder's tip
During migration and in winter the Brambling gregariously likes to join groups of chaffinches. The Brambling attracts attention during flight by its screeching calls and sometimes by flashing its white rump.

Voice Monotonous voice, descending and hoarse 'dzweea' (similar to the end note of the Greenfinch's song); call screechy and grating.

Greenfinch
Carduelis chloris (finches)
L 15 cm   WSp 25–27 cm   Resident bird/Short distance migrant

Habitat *Shrubberies, parks and gardens; also residential areas and forest margins.*

> **Breeding season March–August**
> **3–7 bluish white, brown mottled eggs**
> **1–2 broods per year**

Many Greenfinch pairs get together while they are moving around in flocks over the winter. In springtime the female looks for a suitable nesting place in bushes, trees or climbing plants on walls and builds her nest alone. Both parents feed the young birds, initially with greenflies and, afterwards, with seeds they have softened in the crop. After two weeks the fledglings leave the nest for the first time but stay with their family for another few weeks. In summer and autumn the Greenfinch's preferred fodder is the fleshy fruit of the rosehip.

golden basal patch on tail

yellowish-green wing patch

upperparts lightly streaked

juvenile

underparts whitish, streaked

♀
underparts greenish-grey

Birder's tip
In winter the Greenfinch often visits bird feeders where you can watch it eating sunflower seeds. It carefully peels away the skin with its tongue and bill before eating the content.

♂
strong, pinkish-grey bill

underparts yellowish-green

Voice *Clipped sounding song with trilling and twittering elements and long, creaking final note.*

Serin

Serinus serinus (finches)
L 12 cm WSp 20–23 cm Resident bird/Short distance migrant

greenish-yellow rump

The Serin is originally native to the
Mediterranean and has migrated to central
Europe during the past 200 years. While out foraging
for food the Serin is not very conspicuous, yet you can
hear its song far and wide. It sings perched on treetops or aerials
or displays its bat-like song-flight.

Habitat Parks, gardens
and residential sites, in
southern Europe also in
open coniferous woods.

> *Breeding season
> April–August*
> *3–6 bluish, brown
> mottled eggs*
> *2 broods per year*

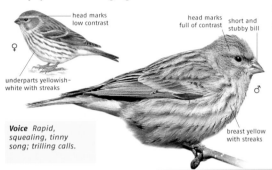

head marks
low contrast

♀

underparts yellowish-
white with streaks

head marks
full of contrast

short and
stubby bill

♂

breast yellow
with streaks

Voice Rapid,
squealing, tinny
song; trilling calls.

97

Citril Finch

broad, yellowish-
green wing-bar

Carduelis citrinella (finches)
L 12 cm WSp 23–24 cm Resident bird/Short distance migrant

In rough, high mountain climates, the Citril Finch builds
its nest on the sheltered side of coniferous tree trunks.
Occasionally when winter returns even in springtime, the Citril
Finch has to interrupt his breeding and start anew
with a second, later brood. The brown-backed
Corsican Finch (*C. corsicanus*) that lives on
Corsica and Sardinia is now regarded as a
species in its own right.

Habitat Margins of
coniferous forests in
mountains.

> *Breeding season
> April–August*
> *2–5 bluish, brown
> mottled eggs*
> *1–2 broods per year*

yellow face
head grey

♂

back grey with streaks

♀

back brown
with streaks

Corsican Finch

underparts
yellowish-green

Voice Calls plaintive
'tsi-i'; song is a rapid,
high twittering but
lower than the Serin's.

Siskin

Carduelis spinus (finches)
L 12 cm   WSp 20–23 cm   Middle distance migrant

rump greenish-yellow

broad yellow wing-bar

Habitat *Breeds in coniferous forests and mixed woodlands; outside of breeding season, also in uncut hedgerows or coppices with deciduous trees.*

> **Breeding season February–August**
> **4–5 bluish, brown mottled eggs**
> **1–2 broods per year**

You usually come across the Siskin in wintertime hanging headfirst from alder cones. It specialises in extracting seeds from the cones using its pointed bill. However it also likes to feed on pine and birch seeds. In flight, swarms of Siskins look especially tightly packed together, as the birds do not maintain much distance from each other.

upperparts greenish-grey, streaked

♀

underparts white, streaked

black forehead and throat

♂

Voice *Inconspicuous song with fine twittering and buzzing flourish; delicate, melancholy call.*

pointed bill

breast yellowish

Redpoll

Carduelis flammea (finches)
L 12–14 cm   WSp 20–25 cm   Short distance migrant

weak whitish wing-bars

Habitat *Birch and coniferous forests, partly also in residential areas with gardens and parks.*

> **Breeding season April–August**
> **4–6 bluish, red mottled eggs**
> **2 broods per year**

Starting from the Alps and Great Britain the redpoll species has gradually populated numerous cities in central Europe. The Lesser Redpoll (*C. caberet*) of central and western Europe is slightly smaller than the Redpoll, with warmer brown plumage. The paler coloured Arctic Redpoll (*C. hornemanni*) also lives in northern Scandinavia.

bill small and yellow

forehead red

♂

♀

smaller red patch on forehead

breast whitish

build more sturdy than Redpoll's

rump white

breast red

Arctic Redpoll

Voice *Calls plaintive 'cherp' (mostly multiple); song consists of similar calls interspersed with hoarse trills.*

Goldfinch

Carduelis carduelis (finches)

L 12 cm   WSp 21–25 cm   Resident bird/Short distance migrant

The Goldfinch prefers to breed in loose association with up to other 10 pairs. They often go foraging for food together and Goldfinches from another group are not tolerated within the flock's territory. While the adults take care of the new brood, the fully-fledged young roam about in groups nearby. Late in autumn the separate flocks unite and form larger ones, thus forming the basis of the following year's breeding pairs. In late winter the males start to look for suitable breeding places.

Habitat *Breeds in open forests and coppices; forages at edges of footpaths and fallow areas.*

> *Breeding season April–September*
> *4–6 bluish eggs with reddish-brown mottles*
> *2–3 broods per year*

99

back light brown

broad yellow wing-bar

juvenile

without colourful marks

Birder's tip

You can often spot Goldfinches flocking around autumn thistles, where they skilfully pull out the seeds from the globular flower heads. For a member of the finch family, the Goldfinch has a relatively long and pointed bill.

head red-white-black

Voice *Characteristic trisyllabic call and quiet twittering song interspersed with liquid 'swit-witt-witt-witt' calls.*

bill long and pointed

Linnet
Carduelis cannabina (finches)
L 13 cm   WSp 21–25 cm   Short/Middle distance migrant

no wing-bars

head grey

upperpart diffusely streaked ♀

Habitat Open country with thick shrubs; also in residential areas.

> *Breeding season April–August*
> *4–6 bluish, dark mottled eggs*
> *1–3 broods per year*

The Linnet is being deprived of many breeding sites due to clearing of hedgerows. However the bird is also flexible enough to breed successfully in some residential areas where it builds its nest in ornamental shrubs. It looks for food outside these areas at the edges of paths and on fallow land.

forehead red

bill grey

breast red

back monochrome brown

♂

Voice Two double or tri-syllabic calls, softer than the Greenfinch's (p. 96) ('teu' and 'chup'); song consists of calls with screeching and trills.

---

rump pink

no distinct wing-bar

Twite
Carduelis flavirostris (finches)
L 14 cm   WSp 22–24 cm   Resident bird/Short distance migrant

Habitat Breeds on moors and in the tundra; in winter on salt marsh on the coast as well as fallow areas.

> *Breeding season March–August*
> *5–6 bluish, reddish-brown mottled eggs*
> *1–2 broods per year*

In winter the Twite is a coastal bird. It searches the coastline in flocks for seeds that have been washed ashore from saline meadows. In its breeding habitat it also feeds almost exclusively on seeds, and softens them in its crop and feeds its young on them. In winter on the continent large flocks of Twites sometimes stay overnight in alcoves on extensive inner-city buildings.

bill yellow

upperparts strongly streaked

bill dark grey

breeding plumage

breast brownish, darkly mottled

winter plumage

Voice Song is a rapid succession of trills; calls screeching and slightly ascending 'chweet', also with soft 'tweit'.

Hawfinch

Coccothraustes coccothraustes (finches)
L 18 cm WSp 29–33 cm Resident bird/Short distance migrant

cigar-shaped body

wings
black-white

The Hawfinch uses its extremely strong bill
to crack open seeds as tough as cherry stones. As it spends most
of its time in treetops, it is rarely seen from early springtime
onwards when the trees come into leaf. However you might spot
the Hawfinch drinking at puddles.

Habitat Breeds in
deciduous forests and
mixed woodlands;
also visits parks and
gardens.

> *Breeding season
> April–August*
> 4–6 grey, dark brown
> spotted eggs
> 1 brood per year

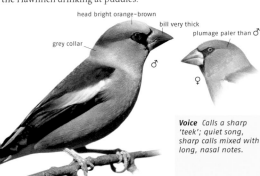

head bright orange-brown

bill very thick

plumage paler than ♂

grey collar

♂

♀

Voice Calls a sharp
'teek'; quiet song,
sharp calls mixed with
long, nasal notes.

Bullfinch

Pyrrhula pyrrhula (finches)
L 15–17 cm WSp 22–29 cm Resident bird/Middle distance migrant

rump white

Bullfinch pairs often get together in early autumn.
In winter they roam different areas together and start their
search for a nesting site from March. As vegetarians they prefer
shoots of plum and maple trees as well as stinging nettle and
maple seeds, although they raise their young on insects.

Habitat Breeds in
mixed woodlands and
parks; in winter also
in gardens.

> *Breeding season
> April–July*
> 4–6 pale blue, black
> spotted eggs
> 2 broods per year

bill thick, very short

black crown

♀

still lacks
black crown

juvenile

underparts
brownish-pink

♂

underparts
bright
pinkish-red

white wing-bar

Voice Soft, slightly
descending, subdued
calls ('djee-ur-ur');
song consists of
quiet whistles and
trills.

Scarlet Rosefinch
Carpodacus erythrinus (finches)
L 15 cm   WSp 24–26 cm   Long distance migrant

head and breast red

Habitat *Breeds in different, mostly damp habitats with shrubberies.*

> **Breeding season May–July**
> 4–6 blue-green, brown mottled eggs
> 1 brood per year

Year in year out, the Scarlet Rosefinch returns to the same nesting site. However once they are fully fledged, the young usually settle far away from their parents' nest. This is probably why the species, which remains in India over the winter, has expanded its habitat considerably further west.

♂ **first year and ♀**

wings brown with faint wing-bars

upperparts greenish-grey

underparts streaked

Voice *Song 4–5 loud, alternately ascending and descending whistling notes; call a low 'weeje-wiiweeja'.*

♂ **at least 2 years old**

Pine Grosbeak

♀

head and breast green, tinged orange

Pinicola enucleator (finches)
L 18 cm WSp 31–35 cm Resident bird/Short distance migrant

Habitat *Open coniferous forests and mixed woodlands.*

> **Breeding season May–August**
> 3–4 pale blue, black mottled eggs
> 1 brood per year

The Pine Grosbeak is very secretive while out foraging for blossoms and seeds and is therefore not easily spotted in its breeding habitat. In autumn and winter it largely feeds on berries and this is the best time to spot the bird. If food is scarce, many Pine Grosbeaks move southwards in Scandinavia, although they rarely cross the borders.

heavy, round hooked bill

head and area around the head more intensely orange coloured than ♀

♂ **juvenile**

narrow white wing-bars

Voice *Rapid, vibrating song consists of clear, thin notes; loud warbling calls.*

♂

head and breast red

Crossbill

Loxia curvirostra (finches)
L 16 cm   WSp 27–30 cm   Short distance migrant

The Crossbill is a true nomad. It settles in any number of different places for breeding, depending on the availability of spruce cones. Spruces do not bear cones every year, so occasionally food becomes scarce for the Crossbill. This results in irruptive migration. If an abundant supply of Spruce cones is available, the Crossbill will also breed in winter. Even the juveniles are able to start breeding at the age of only five months. The Scottish Crossbill (*L. scotica*) is native to Scotland.

sturdy build

Habitat *Coniferous forests and mixed woodlands, preferably with spruces.*

> **Breeding season** *December–September*
> *3–5 bluish, brown mottled eggs*
> *1–2 broods per year*

103

Voice *Calls loudly and clearly 'glipp'; song consists of loud, harsh notes.*

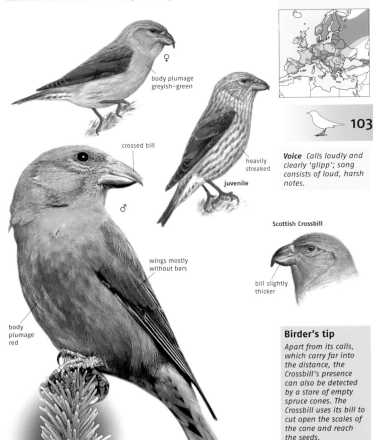

♀

body plumage greyish–green

crossed bill

heavily streaked

juvenile

♂

wings mostly without bars

body plumage red

Scottish Crossbill

bill slightly thicker

Birder's tip

Apart from its calls, which carry far into the distance, the Crossbill's presence can also be detected by a store of empty spruce cones. The Crossbill uses its bill to cut open the scales of the cone and reach the seeds.

Parrot Crossbill
Loxia pytyopsittacus (finches)
L 17 cm   WSp 31–33 cm   Resident bird

♂

very thick
crossed bill

Habitat Coniferous
forests, preferably with
large pine tree reserves.

> Breeding season
December–August
> 3–5 bluish, brown
mottled eggs
> 1–2 broods per year

Thanks to its very strong bill the
Parrot Crossbill is able to open
even the thickest pine cones to
get at the seeds. Pine trees
regularly bear fruit, so food
for the Parrot Crossbill is
rarely scarce. As a result the
Parrot Crossbill is seldom
forced temporarily to leave
its breeding habitat.

body
plumage
red

♀

Voice Calls a little
lower and hollower
than Crossbill's
(p. 103) ('chup'), only
distinguished by
experienced birders.

body plumage
greyish-green

blackish wings,
without bars

body
plumage green

♀

back
mottled
black

Two-barred Crossbill
Loxia leucoptera (finches)
L 15 cm   WSp 26–29 cm   Short distance migrant

cross bill rather flat

body
plumage
red

Habitat Exclusively in
coniferous forests.

> Breeding season
February–September
> 3–5 bluish, brown
mottled eggs.
> 1–2 broods per year

The Two-barred Crossbill has
the smallest bill of all the
crossbills. It therefore specialises
in opening small cones (such as
larch cones). Although it likes to
roam about its breeding habitat,
it rarely migrates to central
Europe. Often several pairs
breed together in groups.

♂

two broad,
plain white
wing-bars

juvenile

plumage
heavily
streaked

Voice Calls reminiscent
of Chaffinch
(p. 94) ('chwink');
characteristic nasal,
trumpet-like call.

Corn Bunting

Emberiza calandra (buntings)

L 18 cm WSp 26–32 cm Resident bird/Short distance migrant

often with legs hanging down in flight

The male Corn Bunting marks the borders of its territory with its penetrating song but is often ignored by females. Therefore it often happens that some males have numerous mates whereas others have none. As a result of intensified farming in many areas of central Europe the Corn Bunting has lost its breeding habitat and has disappeared.

bill thick, yellowish

upperparts grey-brown, darkly streaked

song delivered from elevated perch

breast whitish, darkly streaked

Voice Metallic, tinny sounding song; calls quietly 'tip'.

Habitat Fields and uncultivated open country.

> *Breeding season May–August*
> 4–5 reddish, black marked eggs
> 1–2 broods per year

Rock Bunting

Emberiza cia (buntings)

L 16 cm WSp 22–27 cm Resident bird/Short distance migrant

The Rock Bunting generally behaves inconspicuously. It quietly forages for food well hidden among shrubs or on the ground, where it also prefers to build its nest, such as under shrubs or piles of rocks, in vineyards or also in nooks and crannies of walls. The Rock Bunting sometimes starts a second or even third brood before the previous one has fledged.

head striped black-grey

♂

back striped black-brown

♀

colour of plumage paler than ♂

Voice Clear, rhythmical song, sometimes sounds at high pitch; calls high 'seea'.

long tail

underparts reddish-brown

Habitat Breeds on steep, often rocky slopes with the occasional shrub.

> *Breeding season April–August*
> 2–5 greyish white, brown mottled eggs
> 2–3 broods per year

Cirl Bunting

more striped head than
Yellowhammer

Emberiza cirlus (buntings)
L 16 cm   WSp 22–25 cm   Resident bird/Short distance migrant

Habitat Bushy and rocky hillsides and vineyards.

> **Breeding season April–August**
> **2–5 greyish, dark brown spotted eggs**
> **2–3 broods per year**

The male marks its breeding territory with its song and sometimes never leaves its winter breeding ground. The female and juveniles also stay in this territory after the breeding season and roam about for weeks, but they move to other areas in winter. In some areas, intensified viniculture and an increasingly humid climate have negatively affected the expansion of this handsome species.

♀

head striped
black and yellow

♂

black
throat

breast band
grey

Voice Song more rapid and lower than Yellowhammer's and without final flourish; calls high 'sip'.

Black-headed Bunting ♀

Emberiza melanocephala (buntings)   belly yellowish
L 16–17 cm   WSp 26–30 cm   Long distance migrant

under tail-coverts yellow

Habitat Steppes and dry farmland with bushes, also orchards.

> **Breeding season May–July**
> **4–5 bluish, darkly mottled eggs**
> **1 brood per year**

The Black-headed Bunting stays in India over the winter and only frequents its breeding habitat between April and August. In its breeding territory, the Black-headed Bunting collects insects as large as locusts to feed the young. In autumn it switches to seeds and flocks of Black-headed Buntings sometimes plunder cornfields.

crown subtly striped
upperparts grey-brown, with dark stripes

breast brownish

juvenile

Voice Sings hoarse short, twittering stanzas; different hoarse or harsh calls.

head black

♂

back rufous-brown

underparts golden brown

Yellowhammer

Emberiza citrinella (buntings)
L 16–17 cm   WSp 23–29 cm   Resident bird/Short distance migrant

The males are the first to leave the winter flocks in February and March in order to occupy its future breeding territory. The females follow afterwards. The nest is built in a place sheltered by vegetation, with early broods nests often being situated in the undergrowth. As a result, different predators often plunder the nests, so the later broods are more successful as the foliage becomes thicker on the bushes and provides more shelter. The adults collect insects for the young and switch to grains in autumn. This is also the season for socialising with finches (pp. 94–96) and sparrows (p. 91–91).

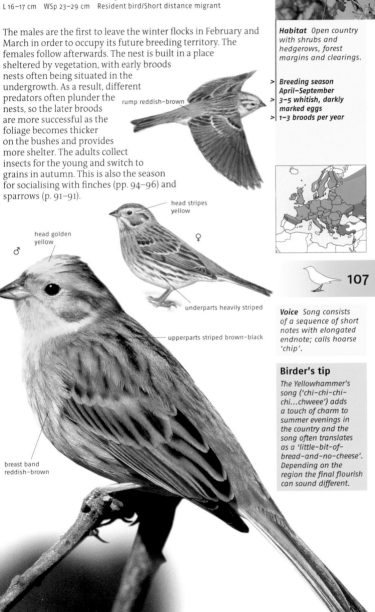

rump reddish-brown

head stripes yellow

♀

head golden yellow

♂

underparts heavily striped

upperparts striped brown-black

breast band reddish-brown

Habitat *Open country with shrubs and hedgerows, forest margins and clearings.*

> *Breeding season April–September*
> *3–5 whitish, darkly marked eggs*
> *1–3 broods per year*

107

Voice *Song consists of a sequence of short notes with elongated endnote; calls hoarse 'chip'.*

Birder's tip

The Yellowhammer's song ('chi-chi-chi-chi...chweee') adds a touch of charm to summer evenings in the country and the song often translates as a 'little-bit-of-bread-and-no-cheese'. Depending on the region the final flourish can sound different.

Ortolan Bunting

Emberiza hortulana (buntings)
L 16–17 cm   WSp 23–29 cm   Long distance migrant

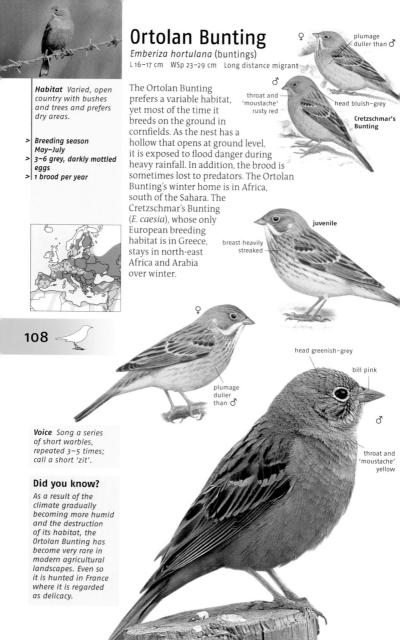

♀ plumage duller than ♂

♂ throat and 'moustache' rusty red

head bluish-grey

Cretzschmar's Bunting

Habitat *Varied, open country with bushes and trees and prefers dry areas.*

> Breeding season May–July
> 3–6 grey, darkly mottled eggs
> 1 brood per year

The Ortolan Bunting prefers a variable habitat, yet most of the time it breeds on the ground in cornfields. As the nest has a hollow that opens at ground level, it is exposed to flood danger during heavy rainfall. In addition, the brood is sometimes lost to predators. The Ortolan Bunting's winter home is in Africa, south of the Sahara. The Cretzschmar's Bunting (*E. caesia*), whose only European breeding habitat is in Greece, stays in north-east Africa and Arabia over winter.

juvenile

breast heavily streaked

♀ plumage duller than ♂

head greenish-grey

bill pink

♂ throat and 'moustache' yellow

Voice *Song a series of short warbles, repeated 3–5 times; call a short 'zit'.*

Did you know?
As a result of the climate gradually becoming more humid and the destruction of its habitat, the Ortolan Bunting has become very rare in modern agricultural landscapes. Even so it is hunted in France where it is regarded as delicacy.

Reed Bunting

Emberiza schoeniclus (buntings)
L 15–16 cm   WSp 21–28 cm   Resident bird/Middle distance migrant

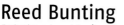

The female builds her nest among old reeds or tall weed clusters, so that it is well hidden by foliage. Nests that are built directly above the water's surface are more likely to stay intact because predators cannot reach them. In autumn most Reed Buntings migrate to the Mediterranean. The Rustic Bunting (*E. rustica*), which only breeds in Europe in Sweden's and Finland's coniferous forests and mixed woodlands, migrates as far as China.

back with light lengthways stripes

Habitat *Breeds in reedbeds, along ditches and on damp fallow areas.*

> **Breeding season April–August**
> **4–5 brownish, black mottled eggs**
> **2 broods per year**

ear-coverts warm brown
light brown supercilium
juvenile

ear-coverts blackish-brown
whitish supercilium
♀

white supercilium
reddish-brown mottled flanks
head and throat black
white collar
♂ **Rustic Bunting**

♂
underparts whitish with streaked flanks

109

Birder's tip

Apart from reed warblers (p. 41–44), the Reed Bunting is the most frequent occupant of reedbeds. The male, with its black head, is easily spotted delivering its song from the top of a reed or on a bush.

Voice *Song consists of single, slowly delivered notes; call a stretched, slightly descending 'tsiu'.*

Little Bunting
Emberiza pusilla (buntings)
L 13–14 cm   WSp 22–23 cm   Long distance migrant

white eye-ring
open behind the eye

reddish–brown crown stripe

bill thinner than Reed Bunting's

ear-coverts chestnut

Habitat *Breeds in open coniferous and Birch forests; outside of breeding season also in open country.*

> **Breeding season June–August**
> 4–6 greenish, darkly mottled eggs
> 1–2 broods per year

The Little Bunting's winter habitat ranges from north India to China. In these areas, it populates fields and meadows in flocks sometimes of several hundred birds. Some Little Buntings take a south-westerly route in autumn and arrive in central and western Europe. They can be distinguished from the Reed Bunting (p. 109) by their head markings.

delicate black streak on breast

Voice *Song starts similar to Yellowhammer's (p. 107) but then ends in a short, variable melody; calls shortly and delicately 'tick'.*

Lapland Bunting
Calcarius lapponicus (buntings)
L 15–16 cm   WSp 26–28 cm   Short distance migrant

♀
face and throat pale

Habitat *Breeds in the Tundra; during winter in steppes and along coasts.*

> **Breeding season May–August**
> 4–7 yellowish-white mottled eggs
> 1 brood per year

The Scandinavian Lapland Buntings take two different migratory routes: most of them migrate in a south-easterly direction and stay in the steppe area between the Ukraine and the Near East. Only a small number take a south-westerly route to reach the North Sea coast. The Lapland Bunting likes to creep stealthily through the grass and stands out mostly because of its flight calls.

yellow bill

chestnut nape

♂

face and throat black

Voice *Hard, trilling call, often followed by soft 'tick'; song consists of short phrases of melodious, ringing notes.*

head reddish-brown

juvenile

chestnut wing patch

Snow Bunting
Plectrophenax nivalis (buntings)
L 16–17 cm   WSp 32–38 cm   Short/Long distance migrant

The Snow Bunting's magnificent white breeding plumage is not the result of any moulting but simply emerges after the wing-tips of the brownish winter plumage are worn out. The white plumage is an ideal camouflage in a snowy environment. In the breeding season, the Snow Bunting benefits from large quantities of insects found in the tundra. In winter it specialises on collecting seeds from the tide line around the coast. The birds native to Greenland have an unusual migratory route across the North Sea to Norway and on to the Russian steppe for winter.

♀ juvenile
almost no white on wings

lots of white on wings

♂ adult winter plumage

bill yellow

white wing patch

breast orangey-brown

♂ winter plumage

♀ winter plumage

white belly

white head and belly

♂ breeding plumage

black back

wing-tip black

Habitat *Breeds in sparse environment of the rocky tundra; in winter along the coast and in steppe regions.*

> *Breeding season May–August*
> *5–6 greenish-white, reddish-brown mottled eggs*
> *1–2 broods per year*

111

Birder's tip
You can identify flocks of Snow Buntings from afar because of their flashy white wing patches. If you take a closer look, you will notice the difference between the distributions of white on the wings – older males tend to have a lot of white, whereas young females have almost none.

Voice *Softly trilling calls, often followed by plaintive 'teup'. Song is a bright, scratching chatter.*

Pin-tailed Sandgrouse

Pterocles alchata (sandgrouse)
L 31–39 cm   WSp 54–65 cm   Resident bird

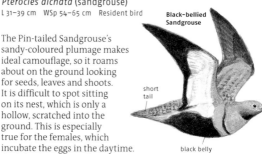

Black-bellied Sandgrouse

short tail

black belly

long forked tail

belly white

Habitat *Deserts and semi-deserts, also arid cultivated land.*

> **Breeding season April–August**
> **3 brownish-yellow, lightly mottled eggs**
> **1 brood per year**

The Pin-tailed Sandgrouse's sandy-coloured plumage makes ideal camouflage, so it roams about on the ground looking for seeds, leaves and shoots. It is difficult to spot sitting on its nest, which is only a hollow, scratched into the ground. This is especially true for the females, which incubate the eggs in the daytime. At night-time, the males take over. The less common Black-Bellied Sandgrouse (*P. orientalis*) lives in Spain's semi-deserts and arid habitats.

112

♀ upperparts grey-brown patterned

head orange-brown

♂

upperparts greenish-grey, mottled yellow

Birder's tip

Sandgrouse prefer arid regions. To obtain their required water intake they make long flights to watering places during the mornings and evenings. They also take up water with their belly plumage and transport it back to their chicks.

Voice *Calls nasal or 'catarr' in repetitive series.*

Wood Pigeon

Columba palumbus (pigeons and doves)
L 41–45 cm   WSp 75–80 cm   Resident bird/Short distance migrant

The Wood Pigeon is among the most successful species to inhabit cultivated landscapes. Trees in residential areas also offer a variety of nesting opportunities. The Wood Pigeon finds numerous leftover grains on open fields, especially maize cobs. These areas have plenty of food supplies to offer and the Wood Pigeon is therefore a resident bird in many parts of central Europe. In winter and during migration, you will often see them in small parties, and also in flocks of a few thousand birds.

Habitat Forests, parks, gardens, other densely wooded areas; also forages on open fields.

> *Breeding season April–October*
> *2 white eggs*
> *1–3 broods per year*

no black wing-bars

white wing-bar

Birder's tip
The male marks its territory and performs its courtship display with its song and mating flight. It ascends up to 20–30 m and, at the peak of this display flight, clatters its wings and then slowly glides downwards.

Voice Muffled song, often translated as 'Take-two-coos, taffy. Take-two-coos, taffy, take'.

113

juvenile

without white patch on neck

eye yellowish

nape glossy green

white patch on neck

Rock Dove, Feral Pigeon

Columba livia (pigeons and doves)
L 31–34 cm   WSp 63–70 cm   Resident bird

back and scapulars pale grey

Habitat *Rocky areas, cities and villages; also forages on fields.*

> **Breeding season March–September**
> 1–2 white eggs
> 2–6 broods per year

nape glossy green

Because of its skill at finding its way back home over long distances, the Rock Dove was traditionally used as a carrier pigeon, and was also kept as a source of meat. Today its feral descendents populate European city streets. Genuine wild birds are only spotted in mountainous regions.

feral pigeons

black bill

two broad wing-bars

feral pigeons with variable plumage colours

Voice *Deep, sometimes hoarse croon in different variations.*

Stock Dove

Columba oenas (pigeons and doves)
L 32–34 cm   WSp 63–69 cm   Short distance migrant

back and scapulars dark grey

Habitat *Breeds in forests and field copses, along the coast, also in sand dunes. Often forages on open landscape.*

> **Breeding season March–October**
> 2 white eggs
> 3 broods per year

The Stock Dove builds its nest in tree holes, often in a Black Woodpecker's (p. 124) old nest. Because of the relatively sparse supply of tall trees on coastlines, the Stock Dove uses rabbit warrens and other holes in the ground when breeding in these areas. Stock Doves are easiest to spot when they forage on fields or during migration.

bill yellow

juvenile

without glossy neck patch

nape glossy green

breeds in tree holes

Voice *Song consists of a series of short, muffled crooning 'druoo' sounds.*

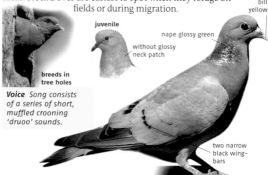

two narrow black wing-bars

Collared Dove

Streptopelia decaocto (pigeons and doves)
L 30–32 cm   WSp 47–55 cm   Resident bird

upper-parts have monochrome appearance

white terminal tail band

The Collared Dove has spread from the Balkans throughout Europe since 1920 and has established itself as a breeding bird. It feeds on grass seeds and leftover corn grains and also takes advantage of food scattered out on chicken runs. The Collared Dove builds its nest from a few twigs, usually on trees but sometimes also on buildings.

black half-collar

plumage beige-grey

often forages in flocks

Habitat Villages and cities with coppices.

> *Breeding season March–October*
> *2 white eggs*
> *2–6 broods per year*

Voice Sings strongly and clearly 'ooo-roo-oo'; hoarse call at take-off and landing.

Turtle Dove

Streptopelia turtur (pigeons and doves)
L 26–28 cm   WSp 47–53 cm   Long distance migrant

upperpart appears colourful
white terminal tail band

The Turtle Dove is not only Europe's smallest but also its most secretive dove species. It keeps itself well hidden in foliage at its breeding site and is also rarely spotted while foraging for seeds on the ground. It is the only dove species that migrates south of the Sahara over winter.

black and white patch on neck

rust brown wings

juvenile

without patch on neck

breast tinged pink

Habitat Breeds at forest margins and field copses; forages out on open country of all kinds.

> *Breeding season May–September*
> *2 white eggs*
> *1–2 broods per year*

Voice Song an elongated crooning, repeated 'roor-r-r'.

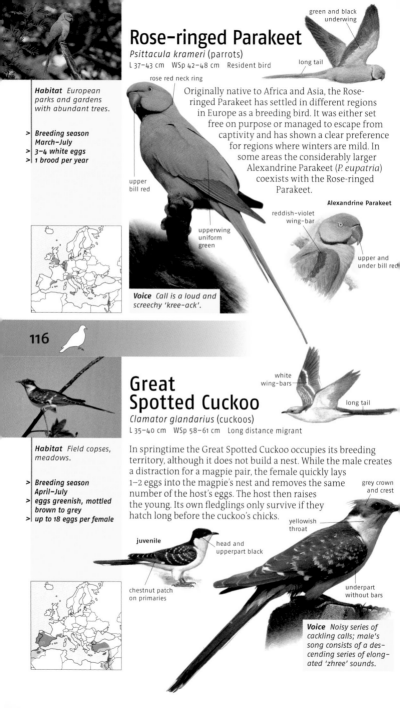

Rose-ringed Parakeet

Psittacula krameri (parrots)
L 37–43 cm   WSp 42–48 cm   Resident bird

green and black underwing

long tail

rose red neck ring

Habitat *European parks and gardens with abundant trees.*

> **Breeding season March–July**
> **3–4 white eggs**
> **1 brood per year**

upper bill red

Originally native to Africa and Asia, the Rose-ringed Parakeet has settled in different regions in Europe as a breeding bird. It was either set free on purpose or managed to escape from captivity and has shown a clear preference for regions where winters are mild. In some areas the considerably larger Alexandrine Parakeet (*P. eupatria*) coexists with the Rose-ringed Parakeet.

upperwing uniform green

Alexandrine Parakeet

reddish–violet wing-bar

upper and under bill red

Voice *Call is a loud and screechy 'kree-ack'.*

Great Spotted Cuckoo

white wing-bars

long tail

Clamator glandarius (cuckoos)
L 35–40 cm   WSp 58–61 cm   Long distance migrant

Habitat *Field copses, meadows.*

> **Breeding season April–July**
> **eggs greenish, mottled brown to grey**
> **up to 18 eggs per female**

In springtime the Great Spotted Cuckoo occupies its breeding territory, although it does not build a nest. While the male creates a distraction for a magpie pair, the female quickly lays 1–2 eggs into the magpie's nest and removes the same number of the host's eggs. The host then raises the young. Its own fledglings only survive if they hatch long before the cuckoo's chicks.

grey crown and crest

yellowish throat

juvenile

head and upperpart black

chestnut patch on primaries

underpart without bars

Voice *Noisy series of cackling calls; male's song consists of a descending series of elongated 'zhree' sounds.*

Cuckoo
Cuculus canorus (cuckoos)
L 32–34 cm   WSp 55–60 cm   Long distance migrant

The Cuckoo is famous for its characteristic call and unusual breeding behaviour. The female lays each egg in a different bird's nest and the host then hatches it. 50–100 host species are known – often they are the Pied Wagtail (p. 29), Dunnock (p. 34), Meadow Pipit (p. 27) or Reed Warbler (p. 43). Shortly after hatching, the young Cuckoo pushes the other eggs out of the nest. Adult and juvenile Cuckoos start migrating to their African winter home from the beginning of August.

young cuckoos much bigger than their hosts (here: Reed Warbler)

Habitat Varied landscape; forests, open country and reedbeds near water.

> *Breeding season April–September*
> *Eggs adapted to host's eggs in colour*
> *9–25 eggs per female*

117

long tail

narrow, pointed wing

small, black bill

some females with plumage brown

chest grey

belly barred

Did you know?

The Cuckoo is among the few bird species that eat large, hairy caterpillars. It generally feeds on many other insects too. The female also eats eggs from the nests where she deposits her own eggs.

Voice Male calls distinctively 'cuck-coo'; also chuckling and hoarse sounds.

Hoopoe

Upupa epops (hoopoes)
L 26–28 cm   WSp 42–46 cm   Short/Long distance migrant

wings striped black and white

Habitat *Open forests, orchards, vineyards and agricultural areas with trees in dry regions.*

> **Breeding season April–August**
> 5–8 bluish-grey eggs
> 1–2 broods per year

The Hoopoe has fairly specific tastes, preferring to eat large insects such as crickets and larger beetles. To find them it needs habitats with sparse vegetation. At the same time the Hoopoe requires suitable breeding holes, which it usually finds in old trees, rock crannies, alcoves of buildings or in piles of rocks.

large, expandable crest

bill long and thin

head and neck orange-brown

breeds mostly in tree holes

Voice *Calls low and mostly trisyllabic 'poo-poo-poo'.*

Roller

Coracias garrulus (rollers)
L 29–34 cm   WSp 66–73 cm   Long distance migrant

wing blue/black

Habitat *Forests with old tree stocks, field coppices, other tree groups; also breeds in rock faces and ruins.*

> **Breeding season May–August**
> 3–5 white eggs
> 1 brood per year

The colourful Roller likes to display itself perched upright on posts or wires. From here it pounces on passing bugs, worms or lizards. The Roller breeds in tree holes, partly also in rock crannies or earth holes. The male marks its breeding territory with spectacular flight displays: a steep ascent is usually followed by a vertical dive.

pale plumage

juvenile

back chestnut

head and belly azure blue

Voice *Thin, cawing calls, displayed in rapid series during nuptial flight.*

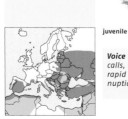

Nightjar
Caprimulgus europaeus (nightjars)
L 25–28 cm   WSp 57–64 cm   Long distance migrant

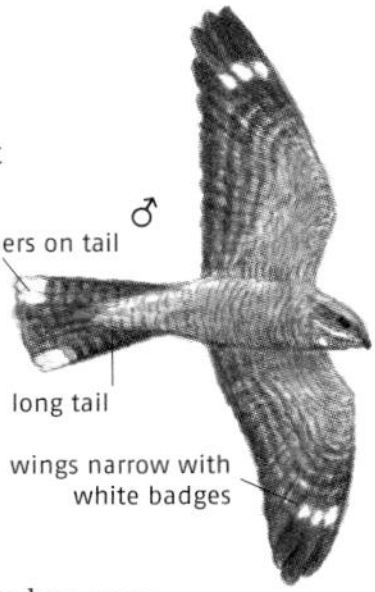

During the day the Nightjar sits motionless on branches or on the ground and depends on its plumage for camouflage. At dusk, it becomes active and flies around with its bill wide open to catch moths and other insects. The female lays the eggs straight on the ground, without building a nest, and the male occasionally takes over from the female to incubate for a short while. The Red-Necked Nightjar (*C. ruficollis*), which also stays south of the Sahara over winter, breeds in Spain in sandy regions.

♂
white corners on tail
long tail
wings narrow with white badges

Habitat Open forests and heaths, dry ground and moors.

> *Breeding season June–August*
> *2 white, brown mottled eggs*
> *1–2 broods per year*

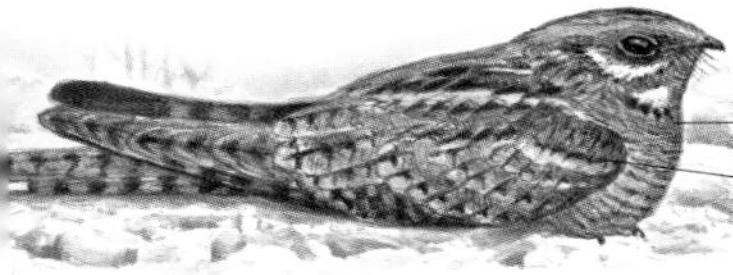

Red-Necked Nightjar
chestnut collar
bend of wing grey

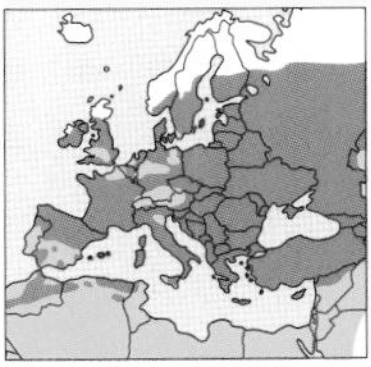

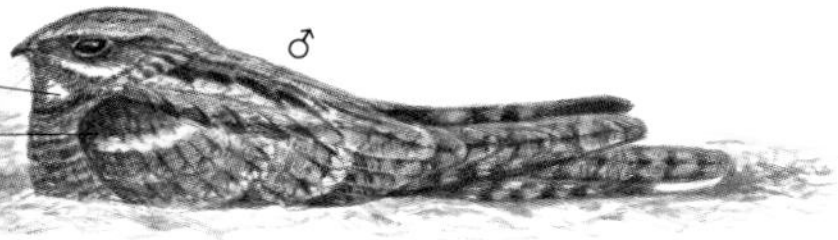

♂
white patch on throat
bend of wing blackish

119

tiny bill (but very large gape)

Did you know?
Apart from the remarkable purring song, you can occasionally hear a loud clapping at night. This is caused by the male clapping its wings above its back as a courtship display and is also designed to drive away rivals.

♀
plumage looks like bark

Voice Song consists of a minute-long, hoarse purr that is only heard at night.

Alpine Swift
Apus melba (swifts)
L 20–22 cm   WSp 54–60 cm   Long distance migrant

wings long and narrow
forked tail
belly white

Habitat *Rocky areas (especially in mountains) and cities; hunting flights in diverse landscapes.*

> **Breeding season** *May–August*
> *1–3 white eggs*
> *1 brood per year*

During daytime, the Alpine Swift is often in the air where it catches insects. It achieves a flight speed lies of 60–100 km/h. The Alpine Swift breeds in colonies. Its nest is built in alcoves of buildings or in rock crannies using straws and feathers, which are glued together with saliva. In contrast to the Swift (p. 121), the Alpine Swift does not sleep on the wing during the breeding season but remains at the nest.

Voice *High, trilling calls, sometimes reminiscent of falcons.*

upperpart brown
white throat

Pallid Swift
Apus pallidus (swifts)
L 16–17 cm WSp 42–46 cm Long distance migrant

Habitat *Cities, preferably in lowlands.*

> **Breeding season** *April–October*
> *2–3 white eggs*
> *1–2 broods per year*

The Pallid Swift often appears together with the Swift (p. 121) and can be regarded as its southern equivalent because of its similar way of life. It also breeds in building alcoves, is always in the air and hunts for insects. Pallid Swift parents manage to provide their young with up to 20,000 insects per day.

belly palely scaled

whi patch c thro

Voice *Gives shrill flight calls, but slightly lower and softer than Swift's.*

greater wing-coverts brighter coloured than back

underwing coverts riche in contrast than Swift's

wing-tip slightly rounder than Swift's

Swift

Apus apus (swifts)
L 16–17 cm   WSp 42–48 cm   Long distance migrant

The Swift is always in the air, apart from when it spends time at the nest. It even sleeps during flight, mates in the air and hovers above the water's surface when it drinks. If there are no insects in the air during bad weather spells the Swift takes a detour, sometimes of more than 100 km, to find food and only returns to its breeding territory after a few days. The fledglings reduce their body temperature in the meantime and can survive without food in this energy-saving mode for one to two weeks.

whitish throat

plumage uniform black-brown

narrow, crescent-shaped wings

forked tail

Habitat Breeds in cities and villages, rarely also in forests; forages over all types of land.

> **Breeding season May–September**
> **2–3 white eggs**
> **1 brood per year**

121

Voice The characteristic elongated flight-calls are shrill and hoarse chirp.

Birder's tip
The Swift's flying height is adjusted to its prey's flying height and therefore indirectly to weather conditions. During warm periods insects and swifts fly high, during rainy and cold periods the Swift will be spotted flying close above ground and water surfaces.

nest

Kingfisher
Alcedo atthis (kingfishers)
L 16–17 cm   WSp 24–26 cm   Resident bird/Short distance migrant

Habitat *Breeds near water and needs steep banks or cliffs to dig nesting tunnels into the soil.*

> **Breeding season March–September**
> 6–7 white eggs
> 2–4 broods per year

This 'flying gem' dives into the water after little fish from branches that overhang the water's surface. Many Kingfishers starve if the winter is very cold and the waters freeze. Surviving birds compensate for the loss by producing a larger number of broods the following breeding season.

azure blue upperpart

long bill

underpart orange

short tail

Voice *Call is a high and penetrating 'chee'.*

underwing coverts brightly coloured

tail fork

Bee-eater
Merops apiaster (bee-eater)
L 27–29 cm   WSp 44–49 cm   Long distance migrant

Habitat *Diverse landscapes, with steep faces and trees.*

> **Breeding season May–August**
> 5–7 white eggs
> 1 brood per year

The Bee-eater is a skilled hunter that catches airborne insects. Before eating them it kills the insects by smashing them against its perch. The Bee-eater mostly breeds in colonies where every pair bores a tunnel, up to 2m long, into a mud wall. Out on the hunt and during migration the Bee-eater prefers to live in flocks.

juvenile

upperpart greenish

adult at nesting tunnel

Voice *Characteristically hoarse call ('prruip'), almost constantly uttered by bee-eaters in flight.*

yellow throat

back yellowish-chestnut

long bill, slightly curved

underparts azure blue

Wryneck
Jynx torquilla (woodpeckers)
L 16–17 cm   WSp 25–27 cm   Long distance migrant

The Wryneck perching at a tree trunk is perfectly camouflaged by its bark-patterned plumage. However, it mostly searches for food on the ground. It pecks open anthills with its bill, pushes its sticky tongue inside and thus takes larvae and pupae. It uses tree holes to breed and sometimes destroys existing songbird broods. With the gradual disappearance of old fruit trees, and since ants have become rarer, the Wryneck population is in serious decline.

long tail

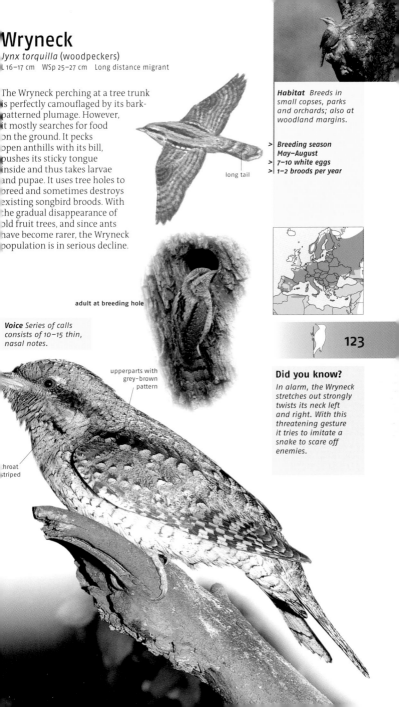

Habitat Breeds in small copses, parks and orchards; also at woodland margins.

> **Breeding season May–August**
> **7–10 white eggs**
> **1–2 broods per year**

adult at breeding hole

Voice Series of calls consists of 10–15 thin, nasal notes.

upperparts with grey-brown pattern

throat striped

123

Did you know?
In alarm, the Wryneck stretches out strongly twists its neck left and right. With this threatening gesture it tries to imitate a snake to scare off enemies.

Black Woodpecker

Dryocopus martius (woodpeckers)
L 45–57 cm   WSp 64–68 cm   Resident bird

Habitat Coniferous and deciduous forests as well as mixed woodland, breeds here in old wood reserves.

> **Breeding season March–August**
> **3–5 white eggs**
> **1 brood per year**

The Black Woodpecker starts breeding by constructing a nesting hole that is up to 50 cm deep. It pads out the floor with wood chip. Occasionally it also uses nesting holes from the previous year. The Black Woodpecker provides nesting sites for other hole-breeders like the Stock Dove (p. 114) and Jackdaw (p. 86), as it constantly produces new holes and also reuses old ones. Without the Black Woodpecker, there would otherwise be a shortage of larger holes suitable for nesting purposes in forests. This bird also does a great service to forestry, as it feeds on insect larvae that bore into the wood as well as ants.

slightly crested red crown

brightly coloured eye

♂

feeds fledglings in breeding hole

broader wing and narrower tail in comparison to crows

♀

red restricted to rear crown

Birder's tip

The Black Woodpecker performs the longest drum-roll of European woodpeckers. It lasts for 2–3 seconds and is quite loud. The drumming serves as an acoustic territorial demarcation fence. Each spell of drumming consists of about 50 pecks.

Voice Calls a series of 'kwick-kwick-kwick-...', hoarsely 'krri-krri-krri-...' or plaintive 'kleeaa'; with long drum-roll of pecks.

Green Woodpecker

Picus viridis (woodpeckers)

L 31–33 cm, WSp 40–42 cm, Resident bird

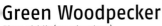

The Green Woodpecker pecks its breeding hole in rotten wood. While out foraging, it drums less on wood than other woodpeckers, mainly because it spends most of the time on the ground where it uses its bill in various ways to catch ants. It can dig holes in the ground with its bill, shovel snow and remove moss from cracks in cobblestone surfaces.

rump yellowish-green

plenty of red on head

red crown

black around the eye

♀

green nape

♂ red 'moustache'

♀ black 'moustache'

Voice *Laughing, gurgling series of calls that maintain their high pitch ('keoo-keoo-keoo-keoo-...').*

Habitat *Field coppices, forests clearings as well as parks and gardens with plenty of trees (also residential areas).*

> *Breeding season April–August*
> *5–8 white eggs*
> *1 brood per year*

125

Grey-headed Woodpecker

Picus canus (woodpeckers)

L 25–27 cm WSp 38–40 cm Resident bird

rump yellowish–green

♂ narrow black 'moustache'

grey head

As soon as the climate becomes milder in February or March the male Grey-headed Woodpecker's subdued calls can be heard throughout its breeding habitat. This is how it marks its territory and attracts a mate. Together they build a breeding hole that takes up to three weeks. Like the Green Woodpecker, the Grey-headed Woodpecker mainly feeds on ants.

Habitat *Prefers deciduous forests and mixed woodland, but also in parks, gardens and alleys.*

> *Breeding season April–July*
> *7–9 white eggs*
> *1 brood per year*

♀ grey forehead

♂ red forehead

Voice *Descending series of calls that gradually slows down (e.g. 'ku-ku-ku-kuuh'); drums in long bursts.*

Middle Spotted Woodpecker

Dendrocopos medius (woodpeckers)
L 20–22 cm   WSp 33–34 cm   Resident bird

Habitat Deciduous forests and mixed woodlands, preferably with oaks; also parks and gardens.

> *Breeding season April–August*
> *5–6 white eggs*
> *1 brood per year*

red crown

belly streaked

black half-collar

The Middle Spotted Woodpecker stays in its breeding territory for the whole year but stays well hidden all the time, even during the mating season. It uses the breeding holes that it has hammered into the wood for a few years at a time. When looking for insects, the Middle Spotted Woodpecker searches by picking at rotten wood. In autumn and winter, however, its food mainly consists of nuts and other tree fruits.

white round scapular patch

Voice Calls hoarse, screeching with shorter calls, partly in series; drums rarely.

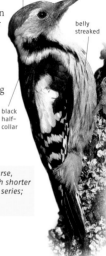

Lesser Spotted Woodpecker

Dryobates minor (woodpeckers)
L 14–16 cm   WSp 25–27 cm   Resident bird

wings heavily barred
middle-back whitish

Habitat Inhabits sparse deciduous forests, coppices on fields, alleys, parks and gardens.

> *Breeding season March–August*
> *5–7 white eggs*
> *1 brood per year*

♂
belly streaked

The smallest European Woodpecker is light-weight and can even sit on herbaceous shrubs while foraging for food, although it is mostly found roaming in treetops. It chisels its breeding holes in tree trunks or in strong branches. Some females have two mates with whom they produce one brood each.

upperpart with white bars

black crown
♀

red crown
♂

Voice Falcon-like call series; rapid, deliberate drumming most of the time.

Great Spotted Woodpecker

Dendrocopos major (woodpeckers)
L 20–24 cm   WSp 34–39 cm   Resident bird

The Great Spotted Woodpecker is resourceful when it comes to choosing its habitat and diet. In summer it mostly prefers insects but also opens up the nest-holes of tits to devour their eggs and chicks. In winter the Great Spotted Woodpecker primarily feeds on conifer seeds, nuts and beechmast. It also likes to lick up the juicy sap of trees.
The Syrian Woodpecker (*D. syriacus*), which is very similar, can also be seen in south-eastern Europe.

white longish scapular patch

Habitat *Forests, field coppices, parks and gardens.*

> *Breeding season April–August*
> *4–7 white eggs*
> *1 brood per year*

127

Voice *Calls sharply 'kik' or 'krrk-krrk-krrk-...' in series; drums more rapidly and in shorter bursts than Black Woodpecker.*

Birder's tip

An ideal time to watch the Great Spotted Woodpecker is when it is out foraging. Its drumming drives out insect larvae from tree trunks in gardens and parks. It wedges pine-cones in branch forks for easier processing ('woodpecker forges').

♂

closed black collar

open black collar

Syrian Woodpecker

black back

black rear head and nape   ♀

red under-tail coverts

red patch on nape   ♂

juvenile
red crown

White-backed Woodpecker

Dendrocopos leucotos (woodpeckers)
L 24–26 cm   WSp 38–40 cm   Resident bird

white lower back and rump

wings heavily barred

black band under cheeks, not reaching nape

Habitat *Deciduous forests and mixed woodlands with a high percentage of dead wood.*

> **Breeding season April–July**
> **3–5 white eggs**
> **1 brood per year**

The White-backed Woodpecker destroys rotten tree trunks by drumming on them to drive out insect larvae. In its northern- and eastern European habitats and in mountainous regions it often has to work on tree trunks. The White-backed Woodpecker stays in its habitat throughout the year, as long as the availability of food is guaranteed. If this is not the case it moves onto another habitat.

♂ belly streaked

red crown ♂   black crown ♀   upperparts heavily barred

Voice *Calls shortly 'kuck'; long bursts of drumming, accelerating towards the end.*

128

Three-toed Woodpecker

Picoides tridactylus (woodpeckers)
L 20–24 cm   WSp 32–35 cm   Resident bird

back barred black and white

Habitat *Coniferous forests with many dead and rotten trees.*

> **Breeding season May–September**
> **3–4 white eggs**
> **1 brood per year**

head striped black and white

underparts strongly mottled

♀

This woodpecker species is specialised at extracting larvae and pupae from beneath the bark of dead trees. It therefore depends on the stock of dead wood in its habitat and is absent from forests that are subject to intensive forestry. On the other hand the Three-toed Woodpecker finds excellent living conditions in forests with storm damage.

yellow crown ♂

whitish crown ♀

Voice *Calls briefly 'kuck', also in series; drum longer and slower than the Great Spotted Woodpecker's.*

Barn Owl

Tyto alba (barn owls)

L 33–35 cm   WSp 85–93 cm   Resident bird

Barn Owl populations can strongly fluctuate within a period of a few years. Their numbers depend on the supply of rodents and the harshness of the winters. If the Barn Owl finds them in sufficient quantities, it will breed up to three times a year. However if rodents are not in constant supply in its habitat, the broods will be small or not produced at all. If the ground is completely covered in snow for a long period, the Barn Owl will not be able to catch its prey and many birds starve. Cars also kill many Barn Owls during their nocturnal hunting flights.

underparts orange-brown in central and eastern Europe

Habitat Mostly breeds in buildings adjacent to suitable hunting grounds, open country with hedgerows or ditches.

> *Breeding season March–December*
> *4–12 white eggs*
> *1–2 broods per year*

129

Voice Shrieking and hissing sounds are heard at night in breeding habitats.

face white, heart-shaped

underwing coverts very brightly coloured

underparts white in western and southern Europe

family in nesting box

Birder's tip

The Barn Owl breeds in holes in attics, barns or church towers, if it finds an entrance. Special nesting boxes make it easier for it to find a suitable nesting site and provide protection from predators.

Tawny Owl

Strix aluco (owls)
L 37–42 cm   WSp 90–104 cm   Resident bird

broad and rounded wings

Habitat Breeds in old trees in forests, parks and other woodland; nocturnal hunting also in open country.

> **Breeding season February–August**
> **3–5 white eggs**
> **1 brood per year**

The Tawny Owl's hoot, well known from horror movies, can be heard in autumn and early springtime. The Tawny Owl breeds in large tree holes, at the age of only four weeks, the owlets can be found perching on branches or on the ground. The bigger Ural Owl (*S. uralensis*) inhabits the mountainous forests of south-eastern Europe.

dark eye

head big with white streaks

Voice Male calls with long, quavering hoots; female calls short and sharp 'quitt'.

owlet

plumage fluffy and barred

mono-chrome face

Ural Owl   long tail

short tail

Great Grey Owl

Strix nebulosa (owls)
L 62–70 cm   WSp 134–158 cm   Resident bird

face grey with white centre

big head

yellow eye

Habitat Dense coniferous forests with clearings.

> **Breeding season April–September**
> **3–6 white eggs**
> **1 brood per year**

This large owl breeds in old nests of birds of prey. Juveniles leave the nest after three to four weeks but will remain under their parents' care for another five months. Because of this long period of parental care some pairs do not produce a brood every year. Also, the lack of vole numbers can result in a brood deficit.

pale brown wing patch

thick neck

owlet

dark face

Voice Male calls in a series of muffled, short 'ho'-notes; female's calls like a cat's miaow

Little Owl
Athene noctua (owls)
L 21–23 cm   WSp 54–58 cm   Resident bird

The Little Owl generally stays in its breeding territory for its entire life. Its offspring usually also settle only a few kilometres from the parents' nest, once they leave the nest at the age of two to three months. The Little Owl's preferred nesting sites in central Europe are tree holes, especially in old willows and fruit trees. In southern Europe it frequently breeds in rock caves or buildings. If there is a lack of these natural nesting sites, artificial nesting boxes can replace them.

Habitat *Open country with shrubs and also in villages and small towns, depending on the region.*

> *Breeding season March–August*
> *3–5 white eggs*
> *1 brood per year*

131

juvenile

longish neck

short tail

crown speckled white

yellow eye

broad face

juvenile in front of nesting hole

Voice *Call is a strong 'hoooh', mostly given in a loose series.*

Birder's tip
The Little Owl hunts at dawn and dusk. Perched on a fencing post or wall it looks out for its prey and plummets to catch mice, little birds or earthworms in a rapid dive.

Tengmalm's Owl

Aegolius funereus (owls)
L 24–26 cm   WSp 53–62 cm   Resident bird

stocky head

head seems square

open facial expression

yellow eye

Habitat *Deciduous forests, mostly in mountains.*

> **Breeding season March–September**
> 3–6 white eggs
> 1–2 broods per year

Tengmalm's Owl is a nocturnal hunter and locates its prey simply by listening to the sounds in the vicinity of its perch. If it hears a mouse or a little bird rustling in the leaves, it will quietly but rapidly seize it in a steep dive. The Tengmalm's Owl almost always moves into a Black Woodpecker's old tree hole to breed. In summer and winter it also uses the tree hole to store extra prey.

adult in breeding hole

Voice *Male's song is a slightly screechy ascending series of sounds ('hoo-hoo-hoo-hoo'); the female gives short, sharp calls.*

plumage dark brown

juvenile

Pygmy Owl

Glaucidium passerinum (owls)
L 16–19 cm   WSp 34–38 cm   Resident bird

short tail

elongated head

Habitat *Inhabits coniferous forests and mixed woodlands, mostly in mountainous regions.*

> **Breeding season April–August**
> 4–7 white eggs
> 1 brood per year

The smallest European Owl is often active long before dusk. Its preferred prey are songbirds and, especially during breeding season, mice. From February onwards the male shows the female several prospective nest holes (made by Great Spotted or Three-toed Woodpeckers) and the female chooses one.

roundish head

view from breeding hole

narrow streaked patch on breast

back faintly mottled

juvenile

flank dark brown

Voice *Song consists of loud initial note followed by lower hoots ('huhuhu'); also stretched calls.*

Hawk Owl
Surnia ulula (owls)
L 36–41 cm WSp 74–81 cm Resident bird

wings rather pointed

tail long

face bordered black

This owl resembles a hawk (p. 148) in flight outline. It is mainly active during the day and can be seen sitting on treetops. It locates mice and little birds with its acute sense of hearing and sharp eyes. For breeding it adapts natural tree holes or tree holes built by woodpeckers and breeds twice a year if there is enough food.

Habitat *Open coniferous forests, forest margins and coppices, also in the vicinity of houses.*

> *Breeding season March–August*
> *5–10 white eggs*
> *1–2 broods per year*

underparts barred crosswise

owlet

underparts faintly barred

Voice *Song (of male and female) consists of rolling trills.*

Scops Owl
Otus scops (owls)
L 18–20 cm WSp 49–54 cm Short/Middle distance migrant

'ear-tufts'

underparts streaked vertically

white bar on scapulars

The Scops Owl is perfectly camouflaged for a secretive existence in trees, thanks to its bark-coloured plumage. Therefore it is rarely spotted and only becomes noticeable in the dark when its monotonous song is heard and it hunts small mammals and insects. The Scops Owl breeds in tree holes or holes in walls and spends the winter in Africa, south of the Sahara.

Habitat *Trees of all kinds in dry areas, but absent from closed forests.*

> *Breeding season April–August*
> *3–5 white eggs*
> *1 brood per year*

Voice *Song a monotonous series of sad sounding notes ('duh...duh...duh...').*

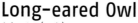
upper- and underwing coverts with faint contrast

Long-eared Owl

Asio otus (owls)

L 35–40 cm WSp 90–100 cm Resident bird/Short distance migrant

large, mostly erected 'ear-tufts'

eye orange

Habitat Breeds at edges of forests, in shrubs on fields and in coppices; nocturnal hunt in open country.

> **Breeding season March–August**
> **3–8 white eggs**
> **1 brood per year**

The Long-eared Owl uses the nests of crows and birds of prey. It marks its breeding territory with calls and its mating flight display when it bats its wings above its head. In winter Long-eared Owls often congregate at communal daylight roosts in coniferous trees. Later on, the regurgitated remains of prey in the form of pellets can be found scattered on the forest floor.

owlet — already with little 'ear-tufts'

Voice Male sings muffled series of 'oo'-sounds; juveniles produce feebly cheeping calls.

greater wing coverts rich in contrast

tip of primaries black-barred

Short-eared Owl

Asio flammeus (owls)

L 34–42 cm WSp 95–110 cm Resident bird/Short distance migrant

Habitat Wetland and open country (marshes, dunes, wet meadows).

> **Breeding season March–August**
> **7–10 white eggs**
> **1 brood per year**

The Short-eared Owl is not only active at twilight, but also during the daytime. Similar to the harriers (p. 146–147), the Short-eared Owl patrols while hovering close to the ground in a wavering search-flight and, with a rapid about-turn, it dives to carry off rodents it has spotted. The female bird scrabbles together a nest on the ground that is well concealed in among clusters of tall grass.

yellow eye

small, almost invisible 'ear-tufts'

juvenile, 3 weeks old

Voice Song of male is a slightly ascending row of muffled, repeated sounds ('boo-boo').

Eagle Owl
Bubo bubo (owls)
L 60–75 cm   WSp 160–188 cm   Resident bird

power bird of prey stature

As the largest owl, the Eagle Owl can carry off prey the size of hares and herons. This owl almost became extinct in many parts of Europe. However, protective precautions, such as watching the eyries, have ensured that stocks are once again increasing. Breeding takes place in eyries, with the adults feeding juveniles for periods of up to five months.

narrow 'ear-tufts'

eye orange

breast heavily mottled

pale face

juvenile, 2 months old

***Voice** Male calls low and muffled 'ooo–hu' (emphasis on first syllable).*

Habitat *Varied landscape, with rock faces or large trees as nesting sites.*

> ***Breeding season February–July***
> ***2–4 white eggs***
> ***1 brood per year***

135

Snowy Owl
Bubo scandiaca (owls)
L 53–66 cm   WSp 142–166 cm   Short distance migrant

more or less distinctive terminal tail bar

large head

The Snowy Owl often breeds on the ground and defends its nest so frequently against Arctic Foxes that Brent Geese prefer to breed close by, thus profiting from the Snowy Owl's protection. However, the Snowy Owl will not breed if lemmings, which are its staple food source, are not readily available.

♂ plumage almost pure white

juvenile, 7 weeks old

almost all feathers with dark tip

♀

yellow eye

intermediate plumage dark grey

***Voice** The male's song consists of a monotonous series of hoarse notes, reminiscent of a dog barking.*

Habitat *On the tundra, often along coastal areas.*

> ***Breeding season May–September***
> ***4–9 white eggs***
> ***1 brood per year***

Griffon Vulture

Gyps fulvus (hawks and relatives)
L 95–105 cm   WSp 240–280 cm   Resident bird

contrasting underwing

Tail round

Habitat *Mountainous, rocky regions.*

> **Breeding season January–August**
> 1 white egg, sometimes lightly mottled
> 1 brood per year

The Griffon Vulture flies almost without wingbeats and only sets out on flights after sunrise. It uses thermal uplifts to rise into the sky. At altitudes of up to 3,000 m, the Griffon Vulture surveys vast areas of land in search of animal carcasses and carefully scans the horizon for other vultures that may already be in descent. Breeding colonies are located on cliff and rock faces.

head and neck naked and pale grey

brown ruff (with adults white)

back pale brown

juvenile

Voice *Shrieking and cackling calls, especially when fighting for carcasses.*

Black Vulture

Aegypius monachus (hawks and relatives)
L 98–107 cm   WSp 250–295 cm   Resident bird

Habitat *Mountainous regions with forests.*

> **Breeding season March–September**
> 1 white, brown mottled egg
> 1 brood per year

In contrast to the Griffon Vulture, the Black Vulture searches for its food, which mainly consists of carrion, in low, swooping flight. The Black Vulture is not so gregarious and mostly breeds alone, building its massive nest out of thick twigs high up in a tree. It takes 7–8 weeks for the egg to hatch. The juvenile bird spends up to four months in the nest and is still supplied with food afterwards.

crown bright-coloured
naked black neck
grey-brown ruff

body and wings with dark brown feathers

Voice *Mostly silent but produces grunting sounds at carcasses.*

Bearded Vulture

Gypaetus barbatus (hawks and relatives)
L 100–115 cm   WSp 250–282 cm   Resident bird

adult   **juvenile**
head
black–
brown

diamond–
shaped
tail

The Bearded Vulture hunts down its
prey both in a high, soaring flight
as well as hovering low in a search
flight. It not only con-
sumes the meat from
carcasses, but also the
bones. It smashes
larger pieces of bone
or tortoise shells by dropping them
from a height. Bearded Vulture pairs
remain faithful throughout their
lifetime and build several
nests on cliff or
rock faces.

head bright-
coloured with
black 'moustache'

blackish
upperside

belly
orange-
brown

belly
brown

Habitat Rocky regions,
mostly in remote
mountain ranges.

> *Breeding season*
> *December–August*
> *1–2 brownish eggs*
> *1 brood per year*

Voice Few whistling
and trilling notes,
rarely heard.

Egyptian Vulture

Neophron percnopterus (hawks and relatives)
L 58–70 cm   WSp 155–180 cm   Long distance migrant

The Egyptian Vulture eats carrion and all kinds of
refuse. It has to wait until other, bigger vultures
have dissected larger carcasses until it can feed.
Only when the other vultures have their fill is it
the turn of the Egyptian Vulture.

thin,
hooked bill

forehead naked
and yellow

Habitat Open country
with rock faces as
nesting sites.

> *Breeding season*
> *March–July*
> *2 pale, mottled brown*
> *eggs*
> *1 brood per year*

adult

diamond–
shaped
tail

juvenile

underparts
dark brown

underparts
black and
white

Voice Calls infrequent,
hissing, grunting or
trilling notes in
alarm.

Osprey

Pandion haliaetus (ospreys)
L 55–58 cm   WSp 145–170 cm   Long distance migrant

Habitat *Near water with plentiful supply of fish, in tall trees; also on seashores.*

> **Breeding season March–August**
> **3 white, brown mottled eggs**
> **1 brood per year**

If you are lucky enough to see an Osprey plunge into the water with outstretched feet, you will enjoy this spectacular sight. Shortly afterwards, it emerges again with a large fish. The Osprey only needs two fish for its daily food intake. However its needs grow as the youngsters require feeding for a period of three months. It begins its migration to Africa in August.

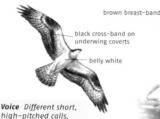

black cross-band on underwing coverts

belly white

Voice *Different short, high-pitched calls, mostly in series.*

head white with dark stripe reaching nape

upperparts blackish-brown

brown breast-band

138

Black-shouldered Kite

Elanus caeruleus (hawks and relatives)
L 31–35 cm   WSp 75–87 cm   Resident bird

extended wing-tip black

hovering

Habitat *Dry, open country with loose tree population; also meadows and fields.*

> **Breeding season March–August**
> **3–5 brightly coloured eggs, distinctly mottled brown**
> **1 brood per year**

Only 2,000 pairs of Black-shouldered Kites breed in Europe, making it one of Europe's rarest birds. It breeds in eyries up in the trees. It feeds on mice, lizards and small birds that it catches either from its perch or in harrier-like search light or by hovering.

black eye-pit

head white

black shoulders and under-surface to primaries

grey back

brown chest

juvenile

upperparts scaled white

adult

Voice *Hoarse and miaowing calls.*

White-tailed Eagle

Haliaeetus albicilla (hawks and relatives)
L 69–92 cm   WSp 200–245 cm   Resident bird

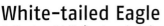

The White-tailed Eagle only begins breeding from the age of four years. Pairs stay together for life and mostly stay in their breeding territory throughout the year. The White-tailed Eagle constructs its nest, up to 1 m in diameter, high up in a tree and uses this nest for many years. It is a versatile hunter and snatches large fish from the water, fighting with waders on the water's surface or pursuing them in flight. It also takes carrion and in winter catches starving swans.

dark bill tip

head and neck dark brown

dark tail

juvenile

white tail, slightly diamond-shaped

adult

strong, yellow bill

head and neck warm light brown

Did you know?
The White-tailed Eagle was in steep decline due to hunting, disturbances and poisoning. However, through increased protection and banning dangerous environmental pollutants, this development could be averted. Today the species has returned to habitats that it previously vacated.

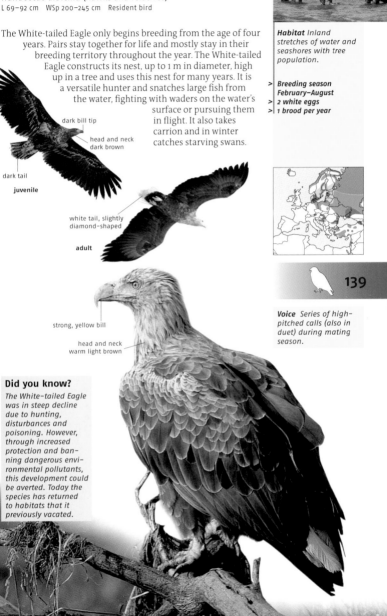

Habitat Inland stretches of water and seashores with tree population.

> Breeding season February–August
> 2 white eggs
> 1 brood per year

139

Voice Series of high-pitched calls (also in duet) during mating season.

Golden Eagle

Aquila chrysaetos (hawks and relatives)
L 77–90 cm   WSp 190–210 cm   Resident bird

golden brown wing patch

Habitat *Breeds in mountains, in winter also in lowland regions.*

> Breeding season March–August
> 2 whitish, brown mottled eggs
> 1 brood per year

The Golden Eagle is a typical sight in European mountainous regions and mainly hunts small animals such as hares, young goats and also grouse and other birds. The Golden Eagle only breeds from the age of five years and builds a nest on a rocky ledge or in a tree.

head orange-brown

golden brown middle coverts on upperwing

large white wing patch

black terminal tail bar

tail faintly barred

juvenile

adult

Voice *Rarely heard cackling and miaowing calls.*

underwing coverts very dark

juvenile

adult

Imperial Eagle

Aquila heliaca (hawks and relatives)
L 72–84 cm   WSp 185–220 cm   Short/Middle distance migrant

yellowish-grey brown

centre of tail light-coloured

Habitat *Woodland steppes, also on open cultivated land.*

> Breeding season March–August
> 2–3 whitish, brown mottled eggs
> 1 brood per year

The Imperial Eagle builds its nest in isolated trees and its surrounding breeding and feeding area covers about 50 km². The Imperial Eagle feeds on small mammals about the size of a hare and hamsters or ground squirrels form its most important prey. The similar Spanish Imperial Eagle (*A. adalberti*) replaces this species in southern and central Spain.

head light yellowish-brown

whiter 'braces' on scapulars

Voice *Barking series of calls in nuptial flight, also trilling calls.*

juvenile

adult

outer wing edge whitish

body plumage red-brown

Spanish Imperial Eagle

Greater Spotted Eagle

faint light wing patch

tail light at base

juvenile

Aquila clanga (hawks and relatives)

L 62–75 cm   WSp 155–182 cm   Medium/Long distance migrant

strong bill

body plumage dark brown

It is notoriously difficult to distinguish the Greater and Lesser Spotted Eagles. The Greater Spotted Eagle is slightly more powerful in stature and darker in colour. It is more inconspicuous in its search flight for mice and frogs and also often sets out 'on foot' to hunt its prey. It migrates to its winter habitat at the end of September.

Habitat Forests, also hunts on open countryside.

> *Breeding season April–September*
> 2 white eggs, occasionally mottled brown
> 1 brood per year

smaller, light wing patch

underpart very dark

juvenile

adult

light brown tail parts

wing broader than Lesser Spotted Eagle

Voice Barking and hoarse series of calls.

Lesser Spotted Eagle

marking more noticeably white than Greater Spotted Eagle

juvenile

fore-wing coverts lighter brown

Aquila pomarina (hawks and relatives)

L 57–66 cm   WSp 134–170 cm   Long distance migrant

The Lesser Spotted Eagle can easily strut across meadows with its very long legs. It catches mice, frogs and large insects. This bird usually only moves 1–2 km from its nest when out hunting for prey. However, in its winter habitat, in the southern half of Africa it is nomadic, ranging over hundreds of kilometres.

juvenile

warm brown plumage contrasted with black wing coverts

Habitat Breeds in forests and hunts in clearings as well as nearby meadows and fields.

> *Breeding season April–August*
> 1–2 white, brown or violet mottled eggs
> 1 brood per year

bill thinner than Greater Spotted

light tail base

plumage warmer brown than Greater Spotted

adult

Voice Loud, light calls, often delivered in a series.

Booted Eagle

Aquila pennata (hawks and relatives)
L 45–53 cm   WSp 100–121 cm   Long distance migrant

light variant
underwing coverts black and white

dark variant

underwi cov

bre

belly dark brown

The Booted Eagle has a distinctive almost 'hanging' flight when out hunting. It virtually 'stands' motionless in mid-air, turning its head from side to side. Any rabbits, lizards and birds that it spots are captured in diving flight. The Booted Eagle has light and dark colouring. The similar, much rarer Bonelli's Eagle (*A. fasciata*) inhabits the Mediterranean.

light variant

small, white shoulder patch

underparts whitish with streaked breast

only toes unfeathered

Bonelli's Eagle
underparts reddish-brown

broad black wing-bar

adult

juvenile

black termina tail bar

Voice Long call series, often audible at breeding site.

Habitat Disturbed forests in lowlands and mountainous regions.

> **Breeding season**
> April–August
> 2 white, light brown mottled eggs
> 1 brood per year

Short-toed Eagle

Circaetus gallicus (hawks and relatives)
L 62–67 cm   WSp 170–185 cm   Long distance migrant

long and broad wing

tail barred

underwing coverts strongly barred

big head

breast dark, belly mottled

The Short-toed Eagle preferably feeds on snakes, although it also catches lizards and frogs. It always carries its prey in its bill to its nest that is usually in a tree. It needs over 200 snakes to rear its youngsters. Its habitat tends to be restricted to areas where there are a large number of snakes.

Habitat Breeds in forests, hunts in semi-open and open country, also in mountains.

> **Breeding season**
> April–August
> 1 white egg
> 1 brood per year

Voice Male call consists of one high and one low note ('hee-jaw'), usually in a series.

Red Kite

Milvus milvus (hawks and relatives)
L 60–66 cm WSp 175–195 cm Short distance migrant

whitish bases to underwing primaries with black tip

chestnut tail, deeply forked

wings invariably slightly bent

The Red Kite prefers carrion and often feeds on remains of animal carcasses left after traffic accidents. The Red Kite scans the ground in a fairly low, swooping flight. Each pair has its own territory during the breeding season. Otherwise, the Red Kite is very gregarious. You can watch larger groups at refuse sites. In the evening, they flock to spend the night in a group of trees.

light grey head

light band on upper wing-coverts

Voice *Ascending and descending warble ('pee-oo-ee-oooo-ee-oo').*

Habitat Breeds in forests and shrubs on fields; forages and hunts in open country.

> **Breeding season April–August**
> 2–3 white, brown mottled eggs
> 1 brood per year

143

Black Kite

Milvus migrans (hawks and relatives)
L 55–60 cm WSp 160–180 cm Long distance migrant

underwing primaries slightly lightened

dark brown tail only slightly forked

The Black Kite has the widest distribution of any bird of prey, colonising Africa, Asia and Australia as well as Europe. It predominantly feeds on carrion, like the Red Kite, but also searches stretches of water for dead fish. European Black Kites spend winter south of the Sahara in Africa.

crown slightly lightened

body plumage dark brown

slightly lightened panel on otherwise dark upperwing

Voice *Long whistles ending with a trill, at the nest also duets by male and female.*

Habitat Breeds in forests, field copses; forages and hunts in open country and near water.

> **Breeding season April–August**
> 2–3 whitish, brown mottled eggs
> 1 brood per year

Rough-legged Buzzard

Buteo lagopus (hawks and relatives)
L 50–61 cm   WSp 120–150 cm   Short distance migrant

often wind-hovering
when hunting

Habitat *Breeds in tundra and mountainous regions, in winter on meadows and in similar open country.*

> **Breeding season May–August**
> **2–7 white, brown mottled eggs**
> **1 brood per year**

Mice and lemmings are this species' main food source, but the numbers of these animals fluctuate from year to year. The Rough-legged Buzzard adapts to this situation by reducing the size of its clutch to match the available food, by not breeding at all or by switching breeding sites. If possible, the Buzzard nests on cliffs or in trees and on the ground in tundra regions.

black carpal patch

head light-coloured

white tail with black terminal band

belly black-brown

foot feathered except for toes

Voice *Calls longer and lower than Buzzard's ('kee-aah').*

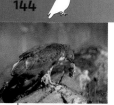

Honey Buzzard

Pernis apivorus (hawks and relatives)
L 52–60 cm   WSp 130–150 cm   Long distance migrant

adults (plumage colour variable)

black carpal patch

underwing coverts strongly barred

small head

Habitat *Breeds in forests but also hunts in open country.*

> **Breeding season May–August**
> **2 whitish, brown mottled eggs**
> **1 brood per year**

From its perch, the Honey Buzzard watches wasps fly into their nest that it then nudges to the ground with its foot and bill. It eats the wasp larvae immediately or carries the comb back to its nest as food for its youngsters. It often migrates to its African winter quarters in large groups.

juvenile
tail longer than Buzzard's

grey head

yellow eye

breast mottled

Voice *Juvenile's calls trisyllabic 'pee-lee-u', many other calls also familiar.*

Buzzard

Buteo buteo (hawks and relatives)
50–57 cm   WSp 113–128 cm   Resident bird/Short distance migrant

Hardly any other bird species has such a wide variety of plumage colours as the Buzzard – from monochrome black brown to almost white, with various different patterns also possible. It feeds on mice and other small animals, building its nest in trees. This is the most common bird of prey in Europe: there are about one million breeding pairs. The red-brown plumage of the Long-legged Buzzard (*B. rufinus*) is a common sight in the Balkans and it looks very similar to the north-eastern European subspecies of Buzzard.

Habitat Breeds in forests and coppices; hunts in open country.

> **Breeding season March–August**
> **2–3 white, brown mottled eggs**
> **1 brood per year**

tail short and round, subtly barred, dark terminal band

in north-eastern Europe plumage chestnut coloured

145

Voice High, plaintive call ('peeoo').

Birder's tip

The Buzzard is easy to observe on the hunt for food. It often perches on fencing posts and scans the surrounding fields and meadows. Sometimes it uses thermal currents to spiral itself upward and search the area from the air.

compact build

black carpal patch

Long-legged Buzzard

tail monochrome chestnut

foot yellow and unfeathered

plumage very variable

Hen Harrier

Circus cyaneus (hawks and relatives)
L 43–52 cm   WSp 99–121 cm   Resident bird/Short distance migrant

Habitat Breeds in
marshes, swamps,
dunes and forest
clearings; hunting
habitat also includes
meadows and fields.

> **Breeding season
> April–August**
> 3–7 whitish, occasionally
> mottled eggs
> 1 brood per year

The Hen Harrier only spends winter where rodents are in sufficient supply. During the daytime, it takes off alone to hunt in open
meadows and fields. At night-time, the birds congregate to sleep,
mostly in reedbeds. The Hen Harrier builds its nest
out of grasses and twigs directly on the ground.

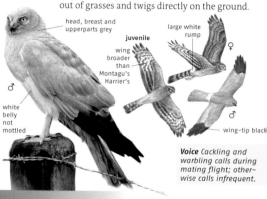

head, breast and
upperparts grey

juvenile

wing
broader
than
Montagu's
Harrier's

large white
rump

♂

white
belly
not
mottled

♂

wing-tip black

*Voice Cackling and
warbling calls during
mating flight; other-
wise calls infrequent.*

Montagu's Harrier

Circus pygargus (hawks and relatives)
L 43–47 cm WSp 105–120 cm Long distance migrant

whitish collar
underwing
coverts dark

diamond-
shaped

lighter collar

juvenile

♂

Pallied Harrier

Habitat Breeds and
hunts in marshes,
meadows and
cornfields.

> **Breeding season
> May–August**
> 3–5 bluish-white, rust
> red mottled eggs
> 1 brood per year

The Montagu's Harrier breeds on
the ground or occasionally in loose
colonies. It spends the winter in Africa.
In addition to rodents, it eats
large insects, lizards
and small birds.
The Pallid Harrier
(*C. macrourus*), which
is also slender in
build and very
similar in colour,
breeds from the
Black Sea eastwards.

hint of
light collar

narrow
white rump

black
wing-bar

wings very
narrow

♀

juvenile

head, breast and
upperparts grey

♂

*Voice Cackling call
series during male's
mating flight.*

belly mottled chestnut

Marsh Harrier

Circus aeruginosus (hawks and relatives)
48–56 cm   WSp 110–130 cm   Middle/Long distance migrant

The male begins its mating flight shortly after arrival in the breeding territory. It performs its aerial display high in the sky and utters chattering, shrill calls. The female is mainly in charge of building the nest while the male supplies the nesting material.
The Marsh Harrier eats mice and small birds and in the breeding season also feeds on eggs and fledglings of other bird species. If enough food is available, a male can keep two females, although he then has two nests, which need supplying with food for hungry chicks.

fledglings in nest

Habitat Breeds in areas with reeds and cornfields; hunts in open country, preferably by water.

> *Breeding season April–August*
> *4–5 bluish-white eggs, occasionally mottled*
> *1 brood per year*

outer edge of dark brown lesser wing-coverts yellowish

♀

juvenile

head light brown

uniform blackish except for head

♂

wings brown–grey-black

147

Voice Nasal screeching calls during male's mating flight; cackling calls in alarm.

back brown

Birder's tip

A fluttering search flight is typical of all harriers. The bird flies close to the ground, holding its wings upward in a shallow V-shape when gliding and 'rocks' around its own axis. If the harrier spots its prey it stops and turns around in mid-flight, diving on it immediately.

♂

long legs

Goshawk

Accipiter gentilis (hawks and relatives)
L 48–62 cm   WSp 135–165 cm   Resident bird

upperparts brown
underparts reddish, mottled brown

juvenile

Habitat Breeds in forests; usually hunts at forest edges, also in open country.

> **Breeding season March–July**
> **2–5 whitish eggs**
> **1 brood per year**

The male bird is considerably smaller than the female. The size of prey taken also varies between the sexes. While the male mostly catches birds the size of pigeons, the female can overpower large gamebirds. The Goshawk also feeds on rodents, especially squirrels, and rabbits.

upperparts dark grey

underparts white with black bars

♀ adult

underparts barred crosswise
strong build

♂ juvenile

long tail
underparts mottled vertically

Voice Buzzard-like calls at nest; long series of short sounds in alarm ('kye-kye-kye').

Sparrowhawk

Accipiter nisus (hawks and relatives)
L 28–38 cm WSp 55–70 cm Resident bird/Short distance migrant

Levant Sparrowhawk
♂   ♀

wing-tip black

slim build

wing broad and round

♂

♀

Habitat Breeds in coniferous forests and in shrubs on fields, likes to hunt in open country but also in areas with many opportunities for cover.

> **Breeding season April–August**
> **4–6 bluish-white, dark mottled eggs**
> **1 brood per year**

As with the Goshawk, male and female Sparrowhawks differ considerably in size. The Sparrowhawk can only chase its prey for short distances, so it has to launch surprise attacks and use the cover of bushes and trees. The similar, though dark-eyed Levant Sparrowhawk (*A. brevipes*) breeds from the Balkans eastwards.

upperparts grey-brown

eye yellow

underpart white with black bars

♀

Voice Long call series, also in duets ('kek-kek-kek...'), more rapid in alarm.

upperparts bluish-grey ♂

underpart barred chestnut

Kestrel

Falco tinnunculus (falcons)
32–39 cm   WSp 65–82 cm   Resident bird/Long distance migrant

The Kestrel uses many different nesting sites
 often old nests left by crows and magpies
in trees or electricity pylons.
However it also breeds in
rock crevices and building
alcoves. In cities it occupies
church towers and other buildings,
though it flies to hunt on open
fields. Sometimes several pairs form a breeding
colony, yet with separate feeding territories. The
similar Lesser Kestrel (*F. naumanni*) breeds in colonies in the
Mediterranean.

hovering

head
brownish

♀

♂

black terminal
tail band

♂

tail grey

upperparts
chestnut, not
mottled

♂

Lesser Kestrel

grey wing-bar

♂

head grey

♂

upperparts
chestnut, dark
mottled

breast densely
mottled

Habitat *Breeds in rocky
areas, in towns and
field coppices as well
as forest edges; hunts
in open country.*

> **Breeding season**
  March–July
> **4–6 yellowish, brown
  mottled eggs**
> **1 brood per year**

149

Voice *Calls penetrating
'kee-kee-kee...'.*

Birder's tip
*Hovering flight is
characteristic for the
Kestrel. It hovers in the
air with fanned tail
and rapid wingbeats
while scanning the
ground. If it discovers
a mouse or vole it
immediately drops
down on it.*

Merlin

Falco columbarius (falcons)
L 25–30 cm WSp 50–67 cm Short/Middle distance migrant

wings more pointed than Sparrowhawk's

tail barre

Habitat Breeds in moorland, swamps and sparse coppices; in winter on meadows and fields.

> **Breeding season** May–August
> 3–5 yellowish, chestnut mottled eggs
> 1 brood per year

The Merlin flies in rapid flight over the ground in order to surprise and catch small songbirds. Even when migrating over the sea it captures other migrating birds by this method. In the breeding season, the smaller male bird, which is grey on the upperparts, mainly takes charge of hunting. However, the female feeds the prey to the chicks.

head marks with faint con

upperpart
brow

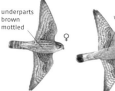

underparts brown mottled

underparts with reddish tinge

Voice Calls 'ki-ki-ki-ki' in series.

Red-footed Falcon

Falco vespertinus (falcons)
L 28–31 cm WSp 65–78 cm Long distance migrant

belly and underwing coverts orange-brown

underwing coverts black

Habitat Marshes and meadows with small coppices, preferably near water.

> **Breeding season** May–August
> 3–4 yellowish, chestnut mottled eggs
> 1 brood per year

The Red-footed Falcon is a gregarious bird of prey, often hunting in groups and generally breeding in colonies. From its perch it follows airborne insects, whereas it captures locusts and mice on the ground. In autumn, its migratory route leads to southern Africa. On the return journey some birds fly too far and arrive in central Europe.

first year
rufous breast band

crown orange-brown

underparts mottled brown

upperparts dark brown
juvenile

plumage mostly dark grey ♂

older than 1 year   underpart orange-brown

Voice Call series reminiscent of Kestrel (p. 149), partly more nasal ('kikikiki').

lower belly rufous

Hobby

Falco subbuteo (falcons)

28–36 cm WSp 74–84 cm Long distance migrant

wings narrow, pointed

lower belly chestnut

underwing coverts light

The Hobby rears its young in an old crow's nest. It prefers to hunt while airborne, following swallows (p. 18–21), swifts (p. 120–121) and other birds in rapid flight. However, large flying insects are also part of its diet. After sustained periods of bad weather, broods can be lost due to a shortage of nourishment.

Habitat Breeds in forests and field copses; hunts near water and in open, humid countryside.

> **Breeding season** May–August
> 2–4 whitish, chestnut mottled eggs
> 1 brood per year

head marks rich in contrast

upperparts black-grey

underparts densely mottled black

juvenile

upperparts brown

underparts faintly mottled brown

Voice Call similar to Kestrel, also performs duets with mate.

151

Eleonora's Falcon

Falco eleonorae (falcons)

L 36–42 cm WSp 110–130 cm Long distance migrant

underwing coverts dark

breast densely streaked

head marks black and white

lower belly chestnut

light colouring

dark colouring

Eleonora's Falcon is a pathfinder among the birds of prey. It breeds on Mediterranean islands and lurks here for migratory birds that fly over the Mediterranean en route for Africa. It only breeds in autumn so it can feed its young on the plentiful supply of migrating birds. Later it sets off on its own migration flight.

Habitat Breeds on cliffs, preferably on small rocky islands.

> **Breeding season** July–October
> 2–3 light, chestnut mottled eggs
> 1 brood per year

upperparts black-brown

upperparts brown slightly scaled

faint head marks

juvenile

Voice Call series ('kje–kje–kje–kjah') lower than Kestrel's (p. 149).

Gyrfalcon
Falco rusticolus (falcons)
L 48–60 cm   WSp 130–160 cm   Resident bird/Short distance migrant

Habitat Tundra and steep cliffs; in winter also on coasts and open country.

> **Breeding season April–August**
> 3–4 yellowish, chestnut mottled eggs
> 1 brood per year

The Gyrfalcon builds its nests on cliff faces. It also uses nests constructed in trees by buzzards and Ravens. While the adult birds usually spend the winter in the breeding territory, a few juveniles move to northern central Europe. The Saker (*F. cherrug*), with slightly warmer colouring, is also a little smaller than the Gyrfalcon. It lives in the steppes and semi-deserts of south-eastern Europe, catches mammals the size of hares and can even take small deer.

strong, Buzzard-like build (broad, thick belly)

152

upperparts variable
Greenland

underparts dark brown streaked
Scandinavia

adult

juvenile

head marks poor in contrast

light head with narrow moustachial stripe

Saker

upperparts warm brown

underparts spotted blackish

brown 'trousers'

Voice Call series lower than Peregrine's ('aaahi').

Did you know?
The Gyrfalcon is Europe's largest falcon species. Thanks to its power and beauty is is very popular with falconers. High prices are earned in illegal trade and make this bird an endangered species, even though its nests are not easily accessible.

Peregrine
Falco peregrinus (falcons)
L 36–48 cm   WSp 80–120 cm   Resident bird/Short distance migrant

underwing coverts light

relatively short tail for a falcon

The Peregrine Falcon's diet consists of birds up to its own size and occasionally larger. Illegal hunting and environmental pollution almost caused this bird's extinction in Europe. Protective measures and banning certain chemicals mean that the breeding population has significantly recovered, so that the species is now native to many cities where it occupies church towers. The Lanner (*F. biarmicus*) is another large falcon species that is found from Italy to Greece.

Habitat Breeds on rock faces and tall buildings, also in forests; hunts in open country and near water.

> **Breeding season March–June**
> **3–4 yellowish, brown mottled eggs**
> **1 brood per year**

153

juvenile

upperparts brown

underpart vertically mottled

rufous nape

narrow moustachial stripe

adult

underpart mottled crosswise

Lanner

Voice Call series ('kek–kek–kek') more penetrating than Kestrel's (p.149).

Did you know?
The Peregrine is among the fastest birds on earth. When it spots its prey during its circling search flights, it dives down with closed wings reaching a speed of more than 300 km/h.

head with black 'cap'

juvenile

upperparts dark brown

upperparts slate grey

underparts dark barred

underparts brownish, dark brown mottled

Black Grouse

Tetrao tetrix (gamebirds)
L 32–39 cm   WSp 65–80 cm   Resident bird

small bill

Habitat *Heaths and moorland by forests.*

> **Breeding season April–September**
> 6–10 yellowish-brown mottled eggs
> 1 brood per year

In springtime during the early morning and evening, several males meet up in a mating arena to perform a mating display or 'lek'. They perform various poses and leaps to win favour with watching females. The most successful males mate with several females, although they do not join in with rearing the young.

neck and belly barred brown

Voice *Mating males produce bubbling and hissing notes; females cackling calls.*

scarlet wattle

glossy blue-black plumage

Hazel Grouse

Bonasa bonasia (gamebirds)
L 35–40 cm   WSp 48–54 cm   Resident bird

Habitat *Varied forests with lots of undergrowth and berries.*

> **Breeding season April–July**
> 7–11 yellowish-brown mottled eggs
> 1 brood per year

white bands on forehead reaching down along scapulars

upperparts barred crosswise

The Hazel Grouse lives concealed in undergrowth and you would be fortunate to see one. It searches for berries, shoots and leaves on the ground and on trees if there is a snow covering. The female hatches and rears the youngsters alone. However they can already fly at the age of two weeks and soon feed themselves.

♀

barred throat

♂ black throat

Voice *The male marks his territory with polysyllabic warbles, whistling and gurgling notes.*

Capercaillie

Tetrao urogallus (gamebirds)

L 54–95 cm   WSp 87–125 cm   Resident bird

Intensive forestry, hunting and predators have wiped out the Capercaillie in many locations. Also the bird does not tolerate damp climates and the chicks are sensitive to wet and cold. The mother has to take them under her wing up to the age of 2–3 weeks to protect them. In addition to shoots and berries, the Capercaillie also eats needles from coniferous trees that it cuts with its sharp bill and breaks up with the help of tiny stones it has swallowed.

strong bill

♀

rufous patch on breast

heavy build

♀

scarlet skin above eyes

brown back

♂

long tail

Habitat Remote coniferous forests and mixed woodland with open areas.

> *Breeding season April–August*
> *5–11 yellowish dark mottled eggs*
> *1 brood per year*

155

Voice The male's mating call consists of gurgling, popping and trilling notes; females cackle.

Birder's tip

If you are lucky you will get the chance to observe the Capercaillie's famous mating behaviour in springtime. A certain number of males pose with upright neck and fanned tail to perform their mating display.

Willow Grouse
Lagopus lagopus (gamebirds)
L 37–42 cm   WSp 55–66 cm   Resident bird

Habitat Moors and
heaths in the tundra
and similar habitats;
also in forests.

> *Breeding season
April–July*
> *5–12 yellowish mottled
brown eggs*
> *1 brood per year*

Willow Grouse spend the winter in groups. In springtime
they leave in pairs to settle in their breeding territories.
The female takes over the task of hatching the brood
and the male acts as guardian to the young family.
The Willow Grouse feeds on shoots and twigs of
willow shrubs.

scarlet skin, swollen
during breeding season

Scotland

back, neck and breast
reddish-brown

northern
Europe

brown belly

white belly and legs

*Voice Many calls
familiar, along with
barking song-flight
and trilling song from
perch.*

156

wings plain white

Ptarmigan
Lagopus muta (gamebirds)
L 33–38 cm   WSp 54–60 cm   Resident bird

Habitat Tundra and in
mountainous regions
above tree line.

> *Breeding season
May–September*
> *5–8 brownish mottled
eggs*
> *1 brood per year*

The Ptarmigan's plumage fades into the undergrowth. In summer
it is grey brown like its rocky habitat and in winter it is pure white
like snow. To reach shoots and leaves in winter, the Ptarmigan
burrows tunnels in the snow. It spends the night in snow holes
and is well protected from the icy
polar winds and exposed mountain
climate.

back, neck and breast grey-brown

♀ camouflaged plumage when breeding

summer

belly white

*Voice Croaking and
barking song phrases;
also different grating
and sharp calls.*

Grey Partridge
Perdix perdix (gamebirds)
L 29–31 cm   WSp 45–48 cm   Resident bird

chestnut tail

Young partridges quickly learn to be
independent, although they prefer to
stay with the family until the end of winter. Intensive farming
has made it difficult for the Grey Partridge to survive.
In many places hedgerows are no longer available
as breeding sites or shelter. Pesticides and early
ploughing of stubble fields reduce the
supply of insects and
plant seeds.

chestnut
face

wing mottled brown

grey
breast

chicks search
for food on
their own
very early

Voice Male's call a
grating 'kree-arit'.

Habitat Dry
landscapes,
agricultural land,
fallow land and
marshes, preferably
with bushes or hedges.

> *Breeding season
> April–October*
> *10–20 brownish eggs*
> *1 brood per year*

157

Quail
Coturnix coturnix (gamebirds)
L 16–18 cm   WSp 32–35 cm   Long distance migrant

upperparts streaked

long wings

When Europe's smallest game bird creeps through
fields and meadows, it is almost impossible to see.
However, you can hear its song from a long distance.
Juveniles develop extremely quickly and can breed at the age of
four months. Juveniles from the Mediterranean region possibly
fly to central Europe for this reason during the summer months.

upperparts with yellowish vertical streaks

♀

black throat
patch

♂

light
throat

Voice Male sings
rhythmically 'whic-
whic-ic', mostly repeat-
edly, also at night
during migration.

Habitat Cornfields,
meadows and fallow
areas with not too dry
ground.

> *Breeding season
> March–October*
> *7–13 yellowish dark
> mottled eggs*
> *1–2 broods per year*

Red-legged Partridge

Alectoris rufa (gamebirds)

L 32–34 cm   WSp 47–50 cm   Resident bird

Habitat *Varied open country, also in agricultural areas.*

> **Breeding season April–September**
> 10–16 yellow, chestnut speckled eggs
> 1–2 broods per year

broad white supercilium

brown back

black mottled collar

The Red-legged Partridge has been resident in northern Europe for several centuries. In England, the species is successfully reared for shooting and there are 200,000 breeding pairs. Unlike the Red-legged Partridge, the north African Barbary Partridge (*A. barbara*) is found on Sardinia.

light grey throat

brownish-grey back

brown collar with white spots

Barbary Partridge

Voice *Song consists of hard 'chuck'-sounds; harsh, grating calls on take off.*

Rock Partridge

Alectoris graeca (gamebirds)

L 32–35 cm   WSp 46–53 cm   Resident bird

Habitat *Dry, rocky slopes in mountainous regions; sometimes in open woods.*

> **Breeding season May–September**
> 8–14 yellowish-brown, red speckled eggs
> 1 brood per year

flanks strongly streaked

rufous tail

In the breeding season, the male Rock Partridge marks his territory with a series of calls. The female constructs a nesting hollow in the ground. The parents share rearing the young that pick at food from their very first day. The similar Chukar (*A. chukar*) is resident on Crete and from Turkey, further east.

black frontal band

white throat

back grey-brown

yellowish throat

Chukar

Voice *Harsh, grating song.*

Pheasant

Phasianus colchicus (gamebirds)

L 53–89 cm   WSp 70–90 cm   Resident bird

The Pheasant forages on the ground for its food that includes plant seeds, young shoots, earthworms and insects. At night-time, it roosts in shrubs and trees. During the breeding season the male bird keeps a harem of several females that he attracts into his territory with calls. The female is in charge of hatching the eggs under the protection of dense vegetation in a ground hole. The chicks can already fly a little after only two weeks, although they are still supervised for at least three months.

chick

Habitat *Agricultural land and meadows with shrubs that provide cover, reeds or shrubs on fields.*

> *Breeding season April–September*
> *8–12 grey-brown eggs*
> *1 brood per year*

159

very long tail

♀

scarlet wattles around eyes

plumage light brown, dark mottled

♂

blue and green glossy head plumage

body plumage reddish-brown with black bars

Did you know?

The Pheasant is a traditional game bird reared for shooting. Presumably the Romans introduced the bird to Europe. Pheasants are still released from breeding in large numbers because without husbandry the population would decline.

Voice *Male calls with loud 'korrk-kok' followed by burst of loud wing flapping.*

Bittern

Botaurus stellaris (herons, bitterns)
L 64–80 cm   WSp 125–135 cm   Resident bird/Short distance migrant

upwards
elongated
pose

Habitat *Extensive stretches of reedbeds; in winter on edges of ditches.*

> **Breeding season March–September**
> 5–6 olive-brown eggs
> 1 brood per year

In the presence of danger, the Bittern momentarily adopts its striking, upwards-elongated pose. With its neck stretched upright, you can scarcely distinguish its plumage from the surrounding reeds and grass blades. It is usually difficult to spot the Bittern, as its nest is well concealed in reedbeds. Under cover of dusk and by night, it searches for fish and frogs.

dark crown

hunched
posture

thick neck
between hunched
shoulders

short legs

Voice *Penetrating, low, muffled calls ('woommp') during breeding season.*

Little Bittern

Ixobrychus minutus (herons, bitterns)
L 33–38 cm   WSp 52–58 cm   Long distance migrant

light brown
wing patch

Habitat *Reedbeds on lake shores, backwaters and rivers.*

> **Breeding season May–October**
> 5–6 white eggs
> 1–2 broods per year

Although the Little Bittern is more active during the daytime than its larger relative, you will rarely glimpse this bird. It spends its life mostly hidden in the reeds where it builds its nest and forages for food. In September, it leaves its breeding ground to spend winter in Africa south of the Sahara.

black crown

black brown back

black back

♂

♀

striped neck

Voice *The male's short, hoarse calls ('rrroo') can be heard day and night during the breeding season.*

juvenile

Grey Heron

Ardea cinerea (herons, bitterns)
L 90–98 cm   WSp 175–195 cm   Short distance migrant

The Grey Heron breeds in colonies and
leaves them to fly in search of food, covering
distances of up to 40 km. On land, it mainly feeds on rodents.
On water, it takes frogs and fish. Its hunting tactics are similar.
It stalks its prey almost silently
then quick as lightning
it seizes its catch with its
dagger-like bill.

thick neck between
hunched shoulders

Habitat *Mainly breeds
in shrubs and coppices
near water; forages on
fields, meadows and in
shallow waters.*

> *Breeding season
> February–August*
> *3–5 light blue eggs*
> *1 brood per year*

ead black and white

bill strong
and yellow

grey crown

**part of a
breeding colony**

juvenile

Voice *Hoarse,
elongated calls
('rrrreck').*

Purple Heron

Ardea purpurea (herons, bitterns)
L 78–90 cm WSp 120–150 cm Long distance migrant

long toes   thick neck, striped

Unlike the Grey Heron, the Purple
Heron prefers to remain hidden in reeds. Thanks to its long toes,
it can cling onto several reed stems and is an excellent climber.
Its behaviour is similar to the Bittern (p. 160). If exposed to
danger it occasionally also adopts an upright position. Purple
Herons spend the winter in Africa's
steppe regions.

Habitat *Large reedbeds
and adjacent waters.*

> *Breeding season
> April–August*
> *4–5 blue-green eggs*
> *1 brood per year*

narrow head

red-buff neck

juvenile

upperparts
brown

belly chestnut

Voice *Hoarse calls,
little higher than
Grey Heron's.*

Night Heron

Nycticorax nycticorax (herons, bitterns)
L 56–65 cm   WSp 105–112 cm   Long distance migrant

grey wings

short, thick neck

True to its name, this bird is usually
only active at night-time or dusk. During the daytime, the
Night Heron stays motionless under cover of bushes and trees.
You are most likely to spot this bird in flight, when it is searching
for food away from the breeding colony and covers distances of
up to 20 km.

Habitat *Breeds in
bushy coppices at
lake shores and along
banks of large rivers,
sometimes also in
reeds.*

> *Breeding season
April–September*
> *3–5 bluish-green eggs*
> *1–2 broods per year*

brown plumage,
light mottled

juvenile

black crown

black back

adult

underparts light gre

Voice *Characteristic
nasal 'kwack' calls
at breeding site and
during flight.*

Cattle Egret

Bubulcus ibis (herons, bitterns)
L 46–56 cm   WSp 88–96 cm   Resident bird/Short distance migrant

winter
plumage

yellow
bill

The Cattle Egret's name derives from the fact that it prefers to
look out for insects swarming around grazing cattle. It even sits
on the back of the animals to do so.
The similar Squacco Heron
(*Ardeola ralloides*) is native
to southern Europe.

orange tufts on crown

**breeding
plumage**

bill orange

breast
orange

Habitat *Breeds in
coppices, forages on
pastures, fields and
marshes.*

> *Breeding season
April–August*
> *4–5 white or bluish eggs*
> *1–2 broods per year*

back beige
brown

wing white

plumage
plain
white

legs grey

**Squacco
Heron**

Voice *Various mono-
or disyllabic muffled
calls.*

winter plumage

Great White Egret

Casmerodius albus (herons, bitterns)
L 80–104 cm   WSp 140–170 cm   Resident bird/Short distance migrant

legs protruding
under tail by far

The Great White Egret only has long white
ornamental quills on neck and back during the
breeding season. For the mating display, the
feathers are outspread in wheel-like formation.
The male constructs a platform of twigs and
reeds for the display and these are later used
for the nest. Although the Great White Egret is
common throughout the world, the species
is a relative newcomer to northern parts
of Europe.

long,
yellow bill

plumage
plain white

winter
plumage

dark legs

mating display

Voice Low, hoarse
calls.

Habitat Breeds in
reedbeds or on trees
by water; forages on
meadows, fields and in
shallow water.

> *Breeding season
> April–August*
> *3–5 pale blue eggs*
> *1 brood per year*

Little Egret

Egretta garzetta (herons, bitterns)
L 55–65 cm   WSp 86–95 cm   Resident bird/Short distance migrant

plumage plain white

The Little Egret looks like a smaller version of the Great White
Egret and its ornamental quills are also an important part of
the mating ritual. Indeed these feathers once endangered the
Little Egret as they were sought after and
the bird was hunted down. The breeding
population in Europe has recovered
and increased to about 100,000
pairs.

black bill

adult with ornamental
quills at nest

yellow toes

black leg

Voice Various hoarse
calls.

Habitat Forages in
open, shallow water;
breeds close to water in
shrubs or trees.

> *Breeding season
> April–September*
> *3–5 greenish-blue eggs*
> *1 brood per year*

Spoonbill

Platalea leucorodia (ibises)
L 70–95 cm WSp 115–135 cm Middle/Long distance migrant

bill bent

brown glossy plumage

Glossy Ibis

Habitat *Different types of water, also on mudflats.*

> Breeding season April–September
> 3–5 white-brown mottled eggs
> 1 brood per year

The bill shape of this bird is unmistakable and the Spoonbill moves it from side to side in calm water to scoop up small fish and other water animals. It often joins colonies of other birds to breed, mostly herons (pp. 161–163). The related Glossy Ibis (*Plegadis falcinellus*) is resident in the south of France as far as the Caspian Sea.

neck extended

juvenile

black wing-

white crown

spoon-like bill

yellow breast

pink bill

juvenile

Voice *Relatively mute, grunting or howling sounds only at breeding site.*

164

neck very long

wing black and red

Greater Flamingo

Phoenicopterus roseus (flamingos)
L 120–145 cm WSp 140–165 cm Resident bird/Short distance migrant

Habitat *Flat, mostly salty lakes and coastal lagoons.*

> Breeding season April–September
> 1 white egg
> 1 brood per year

The Greater Flamingo lives in scattered colonies on lakes and lagoons. The nests are tightly packed together by the water's edge and built out of mud. The flamingo's bill has special lamellas inside that are used to sift shellfish and insects from the water. Escaped Chilean flamingos (*P. chilensis*) also live in parts of Europe.

grey bill

juvenile

plumage grey-brown

adult

bill pink and bent

legs long, reddish

half of bill black

only 'knee' red

Chilean Flamingo

Voice *Low, hoarse calls reminiscent of geese.*

White Stork

Ciconia ciconia (storks)
L 100–102 cm WSp 155–165 cm Long distance migrant

wing black and white — neck extended

The White Stork's nests can be spotted in the middle of villages and this bird is a popular symbol of nature adapting to a manmade environment. However, especially in the western part of Europe, intensive farming has seriously jeopardised the bird's survival and populations have been in decline for several decades.

bill red, strong

nest on chimney

head to back white

legs red

Habitat *Forages on water meadows and fields; breeds in trees as well as on rooftops.*

> **Breeding season March–September**
> **3–5 white eggs**
> **1 brood per year**

Voice *Loud bill clappering on nest; otherwise quiet hissing sounds.*

Black Stork

Ciconia nigra (storks)
L 95–100 cm WSp 144–155 cm Long distance migrant

neck extended

belly white

The Black Stork is a shy bird that you will spot, if you are lucky, in flight between its nest and feeding ground. Unlike its slightly larger relative, it prefers to search for fish and frogs when it is well hidden. Undisturbed woodland areas are especially important as cover.

head to back black

bill red, strong

legs red

head to back blackish–brown

brownish bill

juvenile

brownish legs

Habitat *Deciduous forests and mixed woodland; forages at ponds, creeks, streams and marshy tracts.*

> **Breeding season April–September**
> **3–5 white eggs**
> **1 brood per year**

Voice *Call Buzzard-like 'feeo' during flight; various sounds at nest.*

Great Bustard

♂ mating display

Otis tarda (bustards)
L 75–105 cm   WSp 190–260 cm   Resident bird/Short distance migrant

Habitat Dry areas as well as varied agricultural and meadowland areas.

> **Breeding season April–August**
> **2–3 green to olive-brown eggs**
> **1 brood per year**

The male presents a strange figure during the mating display. It swells its neck, spreads its wings and cocks its tail upright. Successful 'players' manage to attract several of the much smaller females that take care of rearing the young alone. The males do not join in the mating display until they are five years old.

white 'whiskers'
♂
grey head
thick neck
lower neck chestnut

♀
breast grey-brown
lesser and median wing-coverts black and white-brown
belly white
goose-like build

Voice Muffled sounds during mating display; otherwise groaning and barking calls.

wing with plenty of white

Little Bustard

sturdy neck

Tetrax tetrax (bustards)
L 40–45 cm   WSp 105–115 cm   Resident bird/Short distance migrant

Habitat Dry, steppe-like terrain.

> **Breeding season May–September**
> **3–4 olive-brown eggs**
> **1 brood per year**

During the mating display the male jumps up into the air with one or two flaps of his wings and with his neck plumage ruffled up. The female lays her eggs in a hollow in the ground and is not only camouflaged on the nest due to her sand-coloured plumage, but also covers herself with plants. Outside the breeding season, the Little Bustard lives in large groups.

grey head
♂
brown plumage with dark marks
♀
neck striped black and white
♂ mating display
belly white

Voice Male song consists of 'ptrrr'-notes that is repeated in regular but long intervals; short calls during flight.

Crane

Grus grus (cranes)

110–120 cm WSp 200–220 cm Middle distance migrant

In the breeding season, Cranes are shy and often only revealed by their mating calls. However, during migration and in its winter quarters, it congregates conspicuously in flocks. You can watch this majestic, sizeable bird in many rest areas as it forages for seeds, earthworms and potatoes. At night, massive assemblies form at sleeping places. For a long time this species was regarded as endangered. However, protective measures have ensured that the bird population has reached 200,000 birds in Europe.

Habitat Breeds in marshes and wet bogs; forages on fields and meadows.

> *Breeding season March–September*
> 2 olive- to rufous, brown mottled eggs
> 1 brood per year

167

long black neck

legs protruding far beyond tail

neck long and extended

adult

head black and white with crimson central crown

brownish head

juvenile

long drooping inner flight feathers

Voice Loud trumpet-like sounds at breeding site; penetrating 'kr-rooh' during flight.

Birder's tip

It is worth paying attention to the crane's flight calls when the first days of milder spring weather begin or in autumn with the first crisp frost. Then, long chains of cranes will start their journey to their breeding habitat or winter home, sometimes also at night.

very long legs

group mating display

Water Rail

Rallus aquaticus (rails)
L 23–28 cm WSp 38–45 cm Resident bird/Short distance migrant

light supercilium

head and breast brownish

juvenile

Habitat Along shores of ponds or lakes with dense reedbeds or shrubs.

> **Breeding season April–September**
> 6–11 whitish, brown or grey spotted eggs
> 1–2 broods per year

The Water Rail has long toes and a very slender build that enables it to climb through reedbeds. In marshy and muddy areas, it can search for worms with its long bill. It also feeds on insects, frogs and fish. Water Rails are difficult to spot as their nests are covered and well concealed in the reeds.

long, red bill, slightly bent downwards

head and breast bluish-grey

flanks barred

Voice Piglet-like squealing and many more short calls, sometimes in series.

males rarely out in the op

Corncrake

Crex crex (rails)
L 27–30 cm WSp 42–53 cm Long distance migrant

grey head

strong b

Habitat Preferably in water meadows, lush vegetation; also in cornfields and marshes.

> **Breeding season May–August**
> 7–12 brownish, dark red mottled eggs
> 1–2 broods per year

You would not notice the presence of the Corncrake, if it were not for its constant scratchy calling all through the night and sometimes also during the day. It loves damp grassland and is therefore endangered by floods. Many broods are also lost due to early and repeated mowing of meadowland.

long neck

wings chestnut

female feeds chicks during their first days

Voice The male's monotonous scratching, disyllabic song ('krrrt-krrrt') can be mainly heard at night.

Spotted Crake
Porzana porzana (rails)
22–24 cm WSp 37–42 cm Middle-/Long distance migrant

The Spotted Crake has to be flexible in its choice of breeding and nesting sites. It reacts sensitively to changes in water levels. It can occupy flooded areas in April, but if high tides do not arrive until summer, it only appears in June. In very wet areas, the nest is constructed on a platform. Baillon's Crake (*P. pusilla*) breeds on wetland meadows of eastern Europe and also in parts in west and south Europe and the Little Crake (*P. parva*) breeds in reedbeds.

Habitat Water meadows, marshes, swamps with reeds.

> **Breeding season** April–August
> 8–12 cream coloured, reddish mottled eggs
> 1–2 broods per year

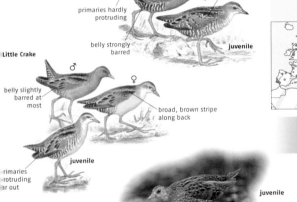

adult

Baillon's Crake

white 'scribbles' on upperparts

primaries hardly protruding

belly strongly barred

juvenile

Little Crake

♂

belly slightly barred at most

♀

broad, brown stripe along back

juvenile

primaries protruding far out

169

juvenile

Voice Hard, warbling 'whitt', mostly delivered in monotonous series at night.

neck and flank slightly spotted

area around eyes dark

yellow bill with red base

Did you know?
The chicks leave the nest after only a few hours and are only fed during the first few days. After that they venture forward on the mud to search for insects, snails and worms on their own.

Coot

Fulica atra (rails)
L 36–39 cm   WSp 70–80 cm   Resident bird/Short distance migrant

juvenile

grey plumage
whit breas shiel

Habitat Shores of gently flowing and still waters of all types, in winter also along coastal shores.

> **Breeding season March–August**
> 5–10 grey, dark speckled eggs
> 1–2 broods per year

Instead of webbed feet, the Coot only has slightly lobed, extended toes. It swims with jerky movements and uses its neck to propel itself forwards. The Coot feeds both on plant fragments and small water animals. You often spot the Coot diving or picking titbits from the water's surface, but it also forages on land.

young chicks have bare, red heads

white frontal shield

plumage greyish-black

white bill

Voice Calls loudly 'twek' or 'twrek'.

Purple Gallinule

Porphyrio porphyrio (rails)
L 45–50 cm   WSp 90–100 cm   Resident bird

red frontal shield
thick red bill

Habitat Lake shores and lagoons with dense vegetation.

> **Breeding season March–September**
> 3–5 brownish, dark mottled eggs
> 1–2 broods per year

The largest European species of rail is generally a resident bird. However dried out rivers or lakes can cause minor excursions that evidently take place 'on foot'. The Purple Gallinule usually feeds on shoots of water and riverside plants that it bites or snaps off with its powerful bill. Outside of the breeding season, it prefers to live in groups.

juvenile
plumage bluish-grey

plumage iridescent dark blue

Voice Very vocal, varied call repertoire of trumpeting, nasal and shrieking sounds.

long red legs

Moorhen

Gallinula chloropus (rails)

32–35 cm   WSp 50–55 cm   Resident bird/Short distance migrant

Moorhens hide their nests away in dense undergrowth or reeds
along riverbanks and lake shores. The chicks are fed here for a
few days, before the parents take them to tour their breeding
territory. The youngsters then catch their own food and rest
on rafts that the male bird builds alone. Northern and eastern
European Moorhens are migratory birds, but central European
birds remain in the breeding territory,
unless heavy frosts force
them to leave.

Habitat Shores with
dense reeds or shrubs;
also forages in open
country.

> **Breeding season
> April–September**
> 5–11 yellowish, brown
> mottled eggs
> 1–3 broods per year

young chicks have bare, bluish heads

tail often cocked upwards

plumage brownish

juvenile

171

Voice Calls bubbling
'purrck'; also varied
short, sharp calls.

white line along
top of flanks

bill red with
yellow tip

under-tail white

Birder's tip

*The Moorhen's very
long toes enable it
to climb reeds and
branches and walk on
floating pondweed.
However, its feet are
not ideal for swim-
ming, so the Moorhen
appears much clumsier
than the Coot when it
swims along with its
head nodding in jerky
movements.*

wing-tip black, mottled white

two white wing-bars

Stone Curlew

Burhinus oedicnemus (stone curlew)
L 40–44 cm WSp 77–85 cm Middle/Long distance migrant

Habitat *Dry, rocky regions on open country; also barren fields and fallow areas.*

> *Breeding season March–July*
> *2 light brown, darkly mottled eggs*
> *1 brood per year*

During the day the Stone Curlew stays motionless among sparse vegetation or cowers on the ground. It only becomes active at dusk, utters its mating calls and forages for all types of small animals as large as mice. Its large, owl-like eyes help it to spot its prey.

eye large, yellow

strong, yellow and black bill

legs long and yellow

Voice *Curlew-like, wailing calls at night ('coo-ree') , also short and trilling calls.*

172

Collared Pratincole

Glareola pratincola (pratincoles)
L 22–25 cm WSp 60–65 cm Long distance migrant

Habitat *Barren, steppe-like country; often breeds near water.*

> *Breeding season April–August*
> *3 brownish, darkly marked eggs*
> *1 brood per year*

This species chases after insects in flight, similar to the Swallow, although it also picks its prey off the ground. It breeds in colonies, mostly near the water's edge. During migration and in its African winter quarters, it is very gregarious. The similar Black-winged Pratincole (*G. nordmanni*) breeds from the Black Sea further east.

underwing completely blackish-brown

Black-Winged Pratincole

slight red patch on bill

forked tail distinctly shorter than wing

lots of red on bill

cream-coloured throat with black edge

chestnut under-wing coverts

white trailing edge of wing

Voice *Sharp, tern-like calls ('kitti-kirrik-kitik-tik').*

Oystercatcher

Haematopus ostralegus (oystercatcher)
40–47 cm   WSp 80–86 cm   Resident bird/Short distance migrant

The Oystercatcher is one of the easiest birds to spot along
Europe's coastlines due to its penetrating calls. It is also common
in many places: during summer months, one breeding territory
borders another; and in winter this species can gather in large
flocks. The Oystercatcher escorts
its chicks to feeding areas on
the day they hatch. Feeding
sites may be located a
considerable distance from
the nesting place. Initially,
adults help the chicks
forage for food by alerting
them to prey with
their bill.

broad white
wing-bar

adult shows prey
to chick

long, orange red bill

plumage black and white

pink legs

winter plumage

white collar

Habitat Breeds
on beaches, saline
meadows and
grassland; forages on
mudflats.

> **Breeding season**
> April–August
> 3 brownish, darkly
> mottled eggs
> 1 brood per year

173

Birder's tip

*The Oystercatcher can
use its very strong
bill in various ways
to search for food. It
pokes the soft ground
on mudflats looking
for worms and opens
shells by hammering
on them or using its
bill as a lever.*

Voice *Calls often;
mating call 'keewick-
keewick-keewick'
(ending in trill); during
flight 'keeweep'.*

Avocet

Recurvirostra avosetta (avocets)
L 42–45 cm WSp 77–80 cm Resident bird/Middle distance migrant

wing black and wh

Habitat Shallow water at sea shores and inland waters, often in lagoons and on mudflats.

> **Breeding season April–August**
> **4 brownish, darkly mottled eggs**
> **1 brood per year**

The Avocet moves its distinctive bill from side to side as it searches for food in shallow water. With its specially shaped bill it catches worms, crabs and other small water animals. It often places its nesting hollow very close to lake shores or riverbanks, so high water levels may quickly wash away its brood.

long neck

slender upcurved bill

chick's bill already upcurved

long, bluish legs

Voice Calls 'kloo-it' loudly and mostly in series.

Black-winged Stilt

Himantopus himantopus (avocets)
L 35–40 cm WSp 67–83 cm Middle distance migrant

Habitat Shallow salt water on open country.

> **Breeding season April–August**
> **4 light brown, black mottled eggs**
> **1 brood per year**

In relation to its body size, the Black-winged Stilt has incredibly long legs. This is how it wades in deeper water than related species while searching for insects and other small animals. It breeds in loose colonies, mostly protected on tiny islands. Its legs are tucked beneath its body while incubating, though they still extend over the edge of the nest.

bill slender and straight

body plumage white

wing black

legs protruding beneath tail by far

extremely long, red legs

Voice Calls 'kyik' and 'kweeit' hoarsely and in series.

Lapwing

Vanellus vanellus (plovers)

28–31 cm   WSp 82–87 cm   Short distance migrant

The Lapwing has adapted to man's presence in most of its breeding territory, as it breeds on agricultural land. However, since this bird breeds on the ground, intensive use of farm machinery and early mowing of meadows have nowadays severely depleted the population. Additionally, suitable habitats are destroyed as land dries out. In many places the Lapwing only appears to rest during its migratory flight and you can sometimes see large flocks. It searches the ground for worms and other animals during the day and also on moonlit nights.

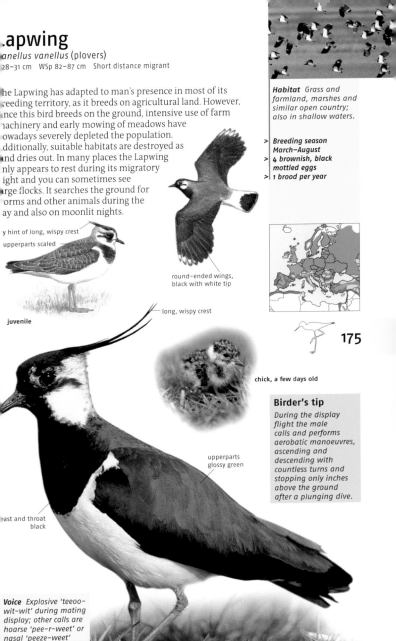

Habitat Grass and farmland, marshes and similar open country; also in shallow waters.

> *Breeding season March–August*
> *4 brownish, black mottled eggs*
> *1 brood per year*

only hint of long, wispy crest

upperparts scaled

juvenile

round-ended wings, black with white tip

long, wispy crest

chick, a few days old

175

upperparts glossy green

breast and throat black

Birder's tip

During the display flight the male calls and performs aerobatic manoeuvres, ascending and descending with countless turns and stopping only inches above the ground after a plunging dive.

Voice Explosive 'teeoo-wit-wit' during mating display; other calls are hoarse 'pee-r-weet' or nasal 'peeze-weet'

Golden Plover
Pluvialis apricaria (plovers)
L 26–29 cm   WSp 67–76 cm   Short distance migrant

underwing white

Habitat Marshes, moors and tundra; outside breeding season mostly fields, meadows and mudflats.

> **Breeding season April–August**
> **4 light brown, black mottled eggs**
> **1 brood per year**

The disappearance of peat and marshy moorlands almost caused the Golden Plover's extinction in central Europe. In Scandinavia, the bird's melancholy calls are a typical part of the acoustic backdrop. Outside the breeding season, the Golden Plover is often seen in flocks of several thousand birds as they rest during day and search for food at night.

face and neck black

upperparts spotted golden brown

breeding plumage

belly black

ey larg da

upperparts warm brown

breast mottle warm brow

**juveni
(winter plumage simila**

Voice *Calls melancholy 'tlui'; song sounds similar and consists of several syllables.*

176

Grey Plover
Pluvialis squatarola (plovers)
L 27–31 cm   WSp 71–83 cm   Long distance migrant

black axillaries

Habitat Tundra; outside breeding season mainly on mudflats and similar coastal areas.

> **Breeding season June–August**
> **4 eggs**
> **1 brood per year**

The Grey Plover is a true cosmopolitan breeding in the Arctic and spending winters along coastlines of all five continents. While searching for food it stays motionless and looks for worms and other animals out on the mudflats. It then catches them in a few quick strides. Its powerful eyes enable it to forage for food at night.

upperparts sombre greyish-brown

pale looking plumage

juvenile

bill stronger than Golden Plover's

whitish crown

upperparts marked black/white

winter plumage

Voice *Calls thin 'tlee-u-ee'; call sounds less melancholy than Golden Plover's.*

breeding plumage

face an underpart blac

Little Ringed Plover

Charadrius dubius (plovers)

14–17 cm   WSp 42–48 cm   Long distance migrant

no wing-bar

This bird's eggs are well hidden in a hollow among gravel stones. Adults feign illness in the event of danger and attract potential predators with their legs dangling from the nest or by sending out a chick. Alarmed by warning calls, the chicks cower on the ground and are almost impossible to spot due to their camouflaged colouring.

crown
brown

dark brown collar,
open at front

juvenile

black bands over forehead through eye

yellow eye-ring

breeding plumage

black bill

black collar, closed

pale brownish-pink legs

Voice Calls descending 'tee-u', often call series like 'tree-a, tree-a' or hoarse 'tree-tree' during display flight.

Habitat Sandy areas and gravel pits at freshwater sites, e.g. river shores, artificial lakes at gravel pits or clear ponds.

> **Breeding season April–September**
> **4 brownish, black speckled eggs**
> **1–2 broods per year**

Ringed Plover

Charadrius hiaticula (plovers)

18–20 cm   WSp 48–57 cm   Short/Long distance migrant

distinctive white wing-bar

With a few strides, the Ringed Plover catches small animals living in the mud. If it is not satisfied after its catch, it tramples the ground and unearths organisms from the mud. Although it spends the winter many thousands of kilometres away, it always returns to the same breeding site every year.

black collar, closed

distinctive white spot behind eye

dark brown collar open at front

juvenile

orange bill with black tip

breeding plumage

orange legs

legs greenish-yellow

Voice Calls 'too-li'; during mating display flight calls 'too-eh'.

Habitat Sandy areas and gravel pits, mostly on coast; winters on coasts and mudflats.

> **Breeding season March–August**
> **4 sandy coloured, black spotted eggs**
> **1–2 broods per year**

Kentish Plover

Charadrius alexandrinus (plovers)
L 15–17 cm WSp 42–45 cm Resident bird/Middle distance migrant

distinctive white wing-bar

Habitat Sandy areas and gravel pits at coastal shores (lagoons, mudflats) and saltwater inland lakes.

> **Breeding season April–September**
> **3 brownish, dark mottled eggs**
> **1 brood per year**

The Kentish Plover prefers sparsely vegetated ground for breeding, althought it makes its nesting hollow near the protection of a small cluster of grass. The males and females share incubation of the eggs and, a few hours after the chicks hatch, they escort them to feeding areas.

dull brown crown

orange-brown crown

black bill

lightly edged feathers on upperparts

collar black, open at front

collar on fai

♀

blackish legs

breeding plumage

juvenile

Voice Calls short 'wit-tit-tit'; during display purring notes.

Dotterel

Charadrius morinellus (plovers)
L 20–22 cm WSp 57–64 cm Long distance migrant

no wing-bar

juvenile

white tail

Habitat Breeds in tundra and mountainous regions; during migration and in winter on fields, meadows and on (semi-) deserts.

> **Breeding season May–August**
> **3 grey brown, dark mottled eggs**
> **1 brood per year**

Depending on the distribution of birds in a breeding site, one male can keep up to three females or one female up to three males. The Dotterel is polygamous, although an adult only starts another brood once the chicks hatch, while others take care of the youngsters.

cream-coloured supercilium

feathers of upperparts strongly marked

light breast band only faint

white rear supercilium joining in 'V'

breeding plumage

whit breas banc

chestnut breast

juvenile

Voice Various short calls, during mating display also in series; also hoarse 'churr'.

Red-necked Phalarope

Phalaropus lobatus (sandpipers and relatives)
18–19 cm   WSp 31–41 cm   Long distance migrant

narrow, white
wing-bar

The Red-necked Phalarope swims about in circular movements. It picks up insects and at sea, in winter, it also feeds on shellfish. The male looks after the brood and rears the youngsters alone, so some females begin a second brood with a different partner.

Habitat Breeds at ponds and coves in tundra and on meadows; in winter at sea, during migration also on inland waters.

> **Breeding season
> May–August**
> 4 light brown, dark mottled eggs
> 1 brood per year

head marked black and white

upperparts with golden brown vertical stripes

juvenile

upperparts grey with light white marks

winter plumage

breeding plumage

blackish head

very thin bill

chestnut neck

Voice Calls quietly 'eeee' (also in series); song more hoarse 'too-li, too-li, too-li'.

179

Grey Phalarope

Phalaropus fulicarius (sandpipers and relatives)
20–22 cm   WSp 37–44 cm   Long distance migrant

upperparts unmarked grey

winter plumage

sturdier build than Red-necked Phalarope

Most of the year, the Grey Phalarope is a shore bird. You rarely see it from the beach as it breeds in loose colonies and prefers to settle near terns (pp. 203–207) so that it is protected by their fierce mobbing of predators. The female performs mating flight displays and, after laying her clutch, she no longer participates in incubating or rearing the young.

Habitat Breeds on ponds and other small lakes in tundra; in winter at sea, rarely on inland waters.

> **Breeding season
> June–August**
> 4 olive-green, dark mottled eggs
> 1 brood per year

bill strong with yellow base

head white

breeding plumage

dark feathers on upperside edged yellowish

juvenile

nape warm brownish

underparts chestnut

Voice Calls mono or disyllabic 'whit' or 'prip-prip'.

Black-tailed Godwit

Limosa limosa (sandpipers and relatives)
L 36–44 cm WSp 70–82 cm Middle-/Long distance migrant

broad white wing-bar
white tail with black terminal band

long orange bill with black tip

neck and breast orange red

belly barred

juvenile

legs protruding tail by far

brea[st]
yellowish-brow[n]

The Black-tailed Godwit prods meadow ground looking for earthworms with its long bill, and pulls bristle worms out of mudflats. Not all Black-tailed Godwits spend winters along the coast. Outside of the breeding season, many birds populate wetlands in the interior of western Africa, where they feed on plant seeds.

upperparts greyish-brown

underpar[ts] light

breeding plumage

winter plumage

Habitat Breeds on wetland meadows; stays in shallow waters and on mudflats over winter.

> **Breeding season April–July**
> **4 greenish, dark mottled eggs**
> **1 brood per year**

Voice During mating display flight loud and clear 'wheddy-whit-o'; in breeding area also nasal 'quee-yit'.

Bar-tailed Godwit

Limosa lapponica (sandpipers and relatives)
L 37–41 cm WSp 70–80 cm Long distance migrant

no wing-bar
tail barred

European breeding birds winter at the North Sea and Atlantic coasts. Siberian birds travel considerably further, starting in March in western Africa and making a transitory stop here on the mudflats. The plentiful food supply means they can then fly non-stop to their Arctic breeding ground.

Habitat Breeds in tundra and swamps near or beyond tree line; outside breeding season on mudflats.

> **Breeding season May–August**
> **3–4 olive-green, slightly mottled eggs**
> **1 brood per year**

upperparts greyish-brown

winter plumage

neck to belly rufous

bill pink and black, slightly upturned

chestnut from head and mantle to vent

white rump extending up back

legs protruding back a little

juvenile

black bill, a little shorter than Black-tailed Godwit's

breeding plumage

Voice Flight call screeching 'kirrik'; during mating display flight reminiscent of Black-Tailed Godwit's.

Curlew

Numenius arquata (sandpipers and relatives)

L 50–60 cm   WSp 80–100 cm   Short distance migrant

You can enjoy the Curlew's mating flight display out on moors and wetland meadows and listen to the trilling song – surely one of nature's most pleasant sounds. Unfortunately, however, in many places the Curlew is quite rare. Its habitat is largely destroyed due to land drying out and the use of meadows for arable land. Many broods are also lost due to mowing of meadows. Outside the breeding season, most Curlews live on mudflats where they search the muddy ground for mussels and earthworms and assemble in hundreds in resting sites at high tide.

Habitat Breeds in marshes and damp meadows; in winter on mudflats, meadows and fields.

> **Breeding season March–August**
> 4 greenish or brownish, mottled eggs
> 1 brood per year

outside breeding season mostly in groups

181

no wing-bar

whitish rump extends to lower back

tail barred

legs protruding tail

plumage brown with black streaks

bill long, decurved

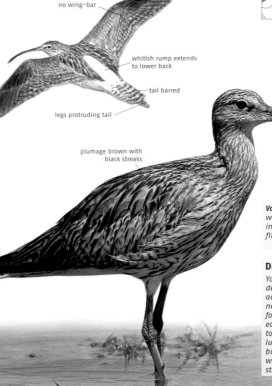

Voice Melancholy, warbling song, ending in trills; ascending flight call 'cour-li'.

Did you know?

You can consider the decurved bill as an adaptation to the needs of searching for food on mudflats. It is easier for the Curlew to gain access to the lugworm's curved burrows than it would be with a straight bill.

Whimbrel
Numenius phaeopus (sandpipers and relatives)
L 40–46 cm   WSp 76–89 cm   Long distance migrant

Habitat *Breeds in tundra, marshes and swamps; during migration and in winter on coastal cliffs and on mudflats.*

> **Breeding season May–August**
> **4 olive green, dark mottled eggs**
> **1 brood per year**

The Whimbrel has a similar bill to its larger relative, the Curlew, although it has a different diet. It prefers berries and, especially in its African winter quarters, has specialised in catching crabs. It removes the legs and claws by shaking the crabs in its bill and finally swallows the fleshy meat.

legs not protruding beneath tail

head streaked light brown dark brown

bill shorter and more sharply decurved than Curlew's

Voice *Flight call laughing, slowly trilling ('tee-tee-tee-tee'); song recalling Curlew.*

182

Woodcock
Scolopax rusticola (sandpipers and relatives)
L 33–35 cm   WSp 56–60 cm   Short distance migrant

plump shape

Habitat *Forests with clearings and aisles; during migration and in winter sometimes in open country.*

> **Breeding season March–September**
> **4 yellowish, brown mottled eggs**
> **1–2 broods per year**

Unlike the snipes, the Woodcock does not live on countryside, but prefers woodland. You hear them at dawn and dusk as they take off from their breeding ground with their curious calls. The population is mainly under threat due to hunting, as every year three to four million Woodcocks are shot around Europe.

broad wings

steep forehead

eyes large and dark

Voice *During mating display flight at dusk muffled croaking notes, followed by whistle ('orrrrt-orrrrt-tsiwick').*

plumage strongly barred

Snipe

Gallinago gallinago (sandpipers and relatives)
L 25–27 cm   WSp 44–47 cm   Short distance migrant

trailing white
wing edge

During the mating flight, the Snipe produces a
'moaning' humming noise due to the vibration of its
tail feathers. It probes muddy ground with its with its long
bill when searching for earthworms. The very similar Great Snipe
(*G. media*) breeds on wetland meadows and moors of northern
and eastern Europe.

bill long, straight

several white
wing-bars

plump shape

Great Snipe

bill shorter
than Snipe's

belly also
barred

belly white, only
flanks barred

Voice *Flight call a
nasal 'gwat', often in
series; song in long
series, sharp 'chic-ka-
chic-ka'.*

Habitat *Breeds on
marshes and damp
meadows; also on
muddy shores and
other wetlands.*

> *Breeding season
March–July*
> *4 greenish, dark
mottled eggs*
> *1 brood per year*

183

Jack Snipe

Lymnocryptes minimus (sandpipers and relatives)
L 17–19 cm   WSp 38–42 cm   Short/Middle distance migrant

small,
stout
shape

wingbeat
flapping,
bat-like

In times of danger, the Jack Snipe relies on
its camouflage colouring. When it cowers
motionless on the ground it is virtually
invisible due to the streaks on its back that
are reminiscent of reed blades. It only flushes
at the last minute. It is also very
particular in its choice of nesting
ground, preferring inaccessible
muddy areas with protective
plant growth.

bill much
shorter
than Snipe's

back with yellow-
brown vertical stripes

Voice *Rhythmic flight
song ('kollorap-kollo-
rap'); otherwise mostly
mute.*

Habitat *Breeds in
marshes and wetland
meadows; during
migration and in winter
on riverbanks, lake
shores and bogs with
plenty of cover.*

> *Breeding season
April–August*
> *4 olive brown, dark
brown mottled eggs*
> *1 brood per year*

Green Sandpiper
Tringa ochropus (sandpipers and relatives)
L 21–24 cm   WSp 57–61 cm   Short/Long distance migrant

underwing black

white tail with broad black bars

legs hardly protruding beyond tail

upperwing uniform black–brown

Habitat *Breeds on ponds with trees on shore and marshes; outside breeding season on shores and riverbanks with dense vegetation.*

> **Breeding season April–July**
> **4 greenish to yellow, mottled eggs**
> **1 brood per year**

In contrast to most other waders, the Green Sandpiper does not breed on the ground but in thickets of young conifers. It does not build its own nest, but looks for abandoned thrushes nests. At the end of May some females begin their migration to winter quarters. For some birds these are in central Europe, for others in tropical Africa.

bill longer than Common Sandpiper's   belly white   legs pale green

Voice Calls bright and yodelling 'tlui-tit-tit'.

Wood Sandpiper
Tringa glareola (sandpipers and relatives)
L 19–23 cm   WSp 56–57 cm   Long distance migrant

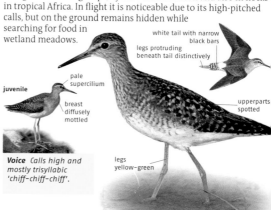

underwing pale

Habitat *Breeds on marshes and swamps in tundra and taiga; outside breeding season on various types of shallow water.*

> **Breeding season May–August**
> **4 brownish, dark mottled eggs**
> **1 brood per year**

The Wood Sandpiper only remains for a few weeks on its breeding ground and spends the remainder of the year on its travels. In doing so it lives in groups, by the Mediterranean and also in flocks in tropical Africa. In flight it is noticeable due to its high-pitched calls, but on the ground remains hidden while searching for food in wetland meadows.

white tail with narrow black bars

legs protruding beneath tail distinctively

upperparts spotted

juvenile

pale supercilium

breast diffusely mottled

legs yellow-green

Voice Calls high and mostly trisyllabic 'chiff-chiff-chiff'.

Common Sandpiper

Actitis hypoleucos (sandpipers and relatives)
L 19–21 cm WSp 38–41 cm Middle-/Long distance migrant

broad, white wingbar

white, widely barred sides to long tail

The Common Sandpiper bobs its tail almost incessantly as it forages for insects. Its flight is also unmistakeable as it beats its wings with short fluttering actions alternating with gliding phases. It usually flies low over water. The Terek Sandpiper (*Xenus cinereus*), which breeds in north-eastern Europe, is similar but feeds on small crabs.

Terek Sandpiper

black bar on back

bill upcurved

legs short, orange

Habitat Breeds on shingle areas on riverbanks and gravel pits; during migration and in winter also on other types of shores and banks.

> **Breeding season April–July**
> **4 light brown, dark brown speckled eggs**
> **1 brood per year**

breast brown mottled

belly white

legs short, greyish-brown

Voice Call high-pitched and sharp 'hee-dee-dee', often in long series; in alarm elongated 'eeht'.

Greenshank

Tringa nebularia (sandpipers and relatives)
L 30–35 cm WSp 68–70 cm Middle/Long distance migrant

no wing-bar

white wedge on back

You often see the Greenshank wading through shallow water and plunging its bill repeatedly into the water. This is how it catches worms, crabs and insects and also tadpoles and small fish. The slightly smaller Marsh Sandpiper (*T. stagnatilis*), with similar plumage colouring, is the Greenshank's equivalent in the steppe regions of eastern Europe.

Habitat Breeds on waters in marshes, tundra and open woods; also in shallow water and on mudflats.

> **Breeding season April–August**
> **4 light brown, dark mottled eggs**
> **1 brood per year**

head and neck streaked grey

upperparts brownish-grey

bill very slender

greyish-green legs longer than Greenshank's

bill slightly upcurved

Marsh Sandpiper

legs greyish-green

Voice Flight calls harsher than Redshank's, trisyllabic 'tiu-tu-tu', sometimes more penetrating.

Spotted Redshank
Tringa erythropus (sandpipers and relatives)
L 29–32 cm WSp 61–67 cm Middle/Long distance migrant

juvenile

tail barred

no wing-bar

narrow white wedge in centre of back

Habitat *Breeds in marshes in taiga and tundra; during migration and in winter in shallow waters and on mudflats.*

> **Breeding season May–August**
> **4 olive green, dark mottled eggs**
> **1 brood per year**

The female only remains in the breeding territory for a short time. Soon after laying her clutch, she leaves and the male is in charge of rearing the young. Adults assemble together from June to August and moult into their grey winter plumage. They then migrate to their winter quarters, which, for many, is in Africa. The juveniles follow the adults separately during autumn.

winter plumage

back grey

white supercilium

bill tip slightly decurved

upperparts speckled white

body plumage black

breeding plumage

juvenile
legs orange-red

legs dark red

Voice *Calls 'tchuit' with emphasis on higher 2nd syllable.*

Redshank
Tringa totanus (sandpipers and relatives)
L 27–29 cm WSp 59–66 cm Short/Long distance migrant

narrow white wedge in centre of back

tail barred

broad white inner primary tips

Habitat *Breeds on coastal saline meadows, water meadows and marshes; also in shallow waters and on mudflats.*

> **Breeding season March–August**
> **4 light brown, dark mottled eggs**
> **1 brood per year**

The Redshank often perches on fence posts at its breeding site. It keeps watch from here for predators, whose approach it signals with loud calls. The chicks then immediately hide beneath clusters of grass. Many Redshanks migrate to western Africa during autumn, some spend winter at the North Sea, where they feed on shellfish and worms.

wings mottled

bill red with black tip

breast and belly strongly mottled

legs orange
juvenile

breeding plumage

legs red

Voice *Calls melancholy trisyllabic 'tiu-du-du', also long 'teuk'; yodelling song.*

Ruff

Philomachus pugnax (sandpipers and relatives)
20–32 cm   WSp 48–58 cm   Long distance migrant

Male Ruffs dance around their mating arena with their feathery
crests and neck ruffs puffed out. After mating, the female rears
the young alone, as while it supervises the chicks, the male
already disappears to its moulting ground
and sheds its magnificent plumage.
Outside the breeding season, you
usually always spot the Ruff in
groups searching for small
water animals or seeds in
shallow waters.

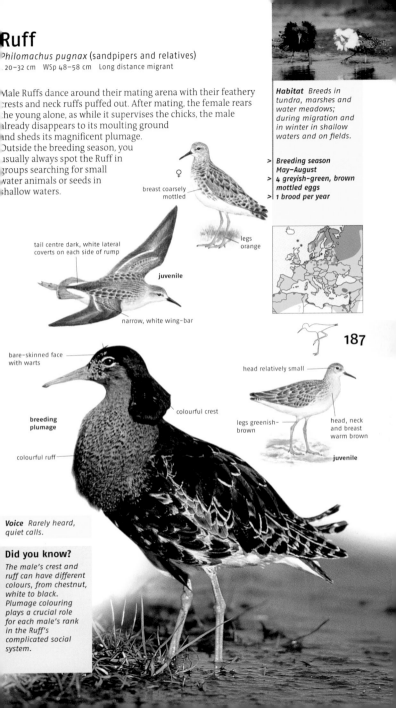

Habitat Breeds in
tundra, marshes and
water meadows;
during migration and
in winter in shallow
waters and on fields.

> • Breeding season
>   May–August
> • 4 greyish-green, brown
>   mottled eggs
> • 1 brood per year

♀

breast coarsely
mottled

legs
orange

tail centre dark, white lateral
coverts on each side of rump

juvenile

narrow, white wing-bar

187

bare-skinned face
with warts

colourful crest

**breeding
plumage**

colourful ruff

head relatively small

legs greenish-
brown

head, neck
and breast
warm brown

juvenile

Voice Rarely heard,
quiet calls.

Did you know?
The male's crest and
ruff can have different
colours, from chestnut,
white to black.
Plumage colouring
plays a crucial role
for each male's rank
in the Ruff's
complicated social
system.

Turnstone

Arenaria interpres (sandpipers and relatives)

L 21–26 cm   WSp 50–57 cm   Long distance migrant

white wing-bar

white stripes on central back and along flanks

This bird's name derives from the
fact that it turns stones or seaweed with its bill looking
for hidden small animals. It hammers barnacles to open them
or chisels at snails clinging fast to stones. Northern European
breeding birds spend winter in Africa, while Canadian and
Greenland birds stay in Europe during the winter.

**winter
plumage**

upperparts
blackish-brown

head black and white

upperparts
orange brown-
black marked

dark
breast
band

belly white

Voice Calls hard 'tuk',
mostly in series, also
elongated 'tlioo';
rhythmical song with
similar elements.

short
strong bil

short legs,
bright orange

**breeding
plumage**

---

upperwing fairly dark,
with narrow white
wing-bar

Broad-billed Sandpiper

Limicola falcinellus (sandpipers and relatives)

L 16–18 cm   WSp 34–39 cm   Long distance migrant

light supercilium
forking before eye

Unlike most other
species, the Broad-
billed Sandpiper does not migrate along the
Atlantic coastline. It winters in eastern Africa
and Arabia. Many of the approximately
20,000 pairs rest at the Black Sea en route
to the Crimea. The female builds her nest on
inaccessible muddy areas, while the male
marks the breeding territory with
song flight.

creamy streaks on back

**breeding
plumage**

bill with heavy
base and slightly
decurved tip

Knot

Calidris canutus (sandpipers and relatives)
23–25 cm   WSp 45–54 cm   Long distance migrant

narrow white wing-bar
whitish tail, weakly barred
juvenile

In the breeding season, the Knot takes advantage of the rich supply of insects in the tundra. During migration and in its winter quarters, it specialises in catching mussels, which it finds with its sensitive bill and stabs in the mud. It swallows them whole as it crushes the shells in its gizzards.

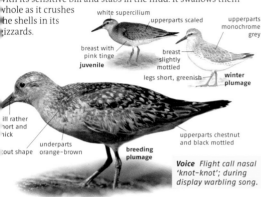

white supercilium
upperparts scaled
upperparts monochrome grey
breast with pink tinge
juvenile
breast slightly mottled
legs short, greenish
winter plumage

bill rather short and thick
out shape
underparts orange-brown
breeding plumage
upperparts chestnut and black mottled

Habitat Breeds in tundra; during migration and in winter on mudflats, less often on inland waters.

> *Breeding season June–August*
> *4 greenish, brown mottled eggs*
> *1 brood per year*

Voice Flight call nasal 'knot-knot'; during display warbling song.

189

Curlew Sandpiper

Calidris ferruginea (sandpipers and relatives)
18–23 cm   WSp 42–46 cm   Long distance migrant

white rump
juvenile
narrow white wing-bar

The Curlew Sandpiper travels from its Siberian breeding ground to Africa and Australia. The number of juveniles shows how breeding conditions were at the other side of the world. If no lemmings are around, Arctic foxes eat the birds eggs and chicks so that the Curlew Sandpiper is left with virtually no youngsters.

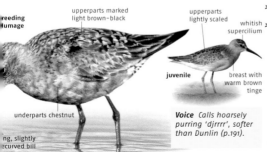

breeding plumage
upperparts marked light brown–black
upperparts lightly scaled
whitish supercilium
juvenile
breast with warm brown tinge
underparts chestnut
ng, slightly ecurved bill

Habitat Breeds in tundra; outside breeding season on mudflats and shallow inland waters.

> *Breeding season June–August*
> *4 olive green, light and dark eggs*
> *1 brood per year*

Voice Calls hoarsely purring 'djrrrr', softer than Dunlin (p.191).

Sanderling

Calidris alba (sandpipers and relatives)
L 20–21 cm   WSp 40–45 cm   Long distance migrant

broad white wing-bar
tail centre black

juvenile

Habitat Breeds in tundra; in winter mainly on sandy beaches, also sandy mudflats; less often on inland waters.

> **Breeding season June–August**
> **4 greenish, brown mottled eggs**
> **1 brood per year**

The Sanderling is a long-distance runner among waders. It appears to run non-stop at the edge of waves along the beach in order to pick up small animals in the sand or washed ashore. When breeding among the red-brown coloured plants in the tundra, it is well camouflaged with its breeding plumage.

upperparts black
white-edged feathers

juvenile

upperparts grey

faint collar on yellow base

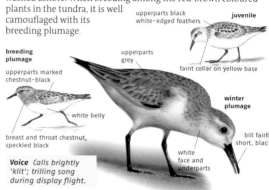

breeding plumage

upperparts marked chestnut-black

white belly

breast and throat chestnut, speckled black

upperparts grey

winter plumage

bill fairl short, blac

white face and underparts

Voice *Calls brightly 'klit'; trilling song during display flight.*

Purple Sandpiper

white wing-bar

upperpart dar

Calidris maritima (sandpipers and relatives)
L 20–22 cm   WSp 42–46 cm   Short/Long distance migrant

Habitat Breeds in sparse tundra; in winter on cliffs and rocky beaches; less often inland.

> **Breeding season May–August**
> **4 greenish, dark brown mottled eggs**
> **1 brood per year**

The Purple Sandpiper has adapted to life on coastal cliffs. It is the only beach wader to do so. In winter it skilfully picks small snails and blue mussels from rock crevices. It can also feed at night, so that it can even winter in Norway in permanent dark conditions. It returns to the same winter quarters every year.

bill black, yellowish at base

head and breast brownish, mottled

breeding plumage

upperparts blackish with weak violet glimmer

winter plumage

breast dark mottled

feathers on upperparts black edged brown and white

legs greenish-yellow (sometimes also orange)

Voice *Calls similar to Swallow 'wit' or 'wit–wit'.*

Dunlin

Calidris alpina (sandpipers and relatives)
16–20 cm   WSp 38–43 cm   Middle/Long distance migrant

The Dunlin spears the muddy ground with its bill and searches for worms, small mussels and snails. It catches its prey with its flexible bill tip as if it is a pincer and it can also open its bill when immersed in the mud. The Dunlin is one of the most common bird species out on mudflats and in many other coastal areas. At low tide, the birds scatter across the mudflats in flocks looking for food and as the tide comes in, they assemble in large flocks at their resting sites.

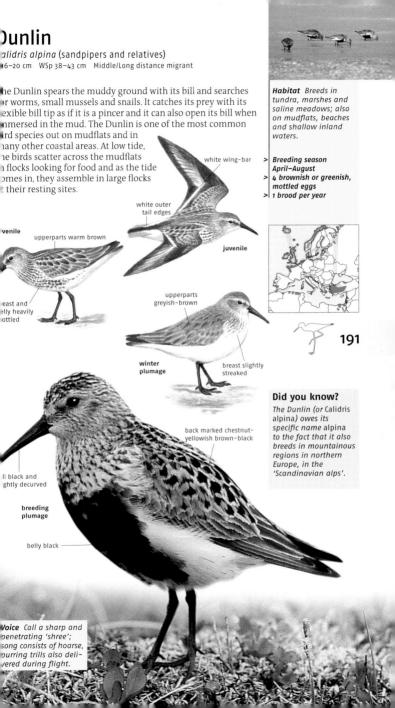

Habitat Breeds in tundra, marshes and saline meadows; also on mudflats, beaches and shallow inland waters.

> Breeding season April–August
> 4 brownish or greenish, mottled eggs
> 1 brood per year

191

white wing-bar

white outer tail edges

juvenile

juvenile

upperparts warm brown

breast and belly heavily mottled

upperparts greyish-brown

winter plumage

breast slightly streaked

Did you know?

The Dunlin (or Calidris alpina*) owes its specific name* alpina *to the fact that it also breeds in mountainous regions in northern Europe, in the 'Scandinavian alps'.*

back marked chestnut-yellowish brown-black

bill black and slightly decurved

breeding plumage

belly black

Voice Call a sharp and penetrating 'shree'; song consists of hoarse, purring trills also delivered during flight.

Little Stint

white wing-bar
pale 'V' on back

Calidris minuta (sandpipers and relatives)
L 12–14 cm   WSp 34–37 cm   Long distance migrant

juvenile

Habitat *Breeds in tundra; outside breeding season on mudflats, on beaches and shallow inland waters.*

> *Breeding season June–August*
> *4 greenish, brown mottled eggs*
> *1–2 broods per year*

In one breeding season, the female Little Stint has two partners. The first male has to incubate and rear the first clutch alone, whereas the female rears the second brood alone. In both cases the adult leaves the breeding territory even before the youngsters can fly, although they are able to make their own way to the winter quarters.

feathers on upperparts edged brown

looks short-tailed

juvenile

upperparts greyish-brown

upperparts reddish-brown

bill relatively sho
and bla

winter plumage

breeding plumage

legs black

head and breast to flanks reddish-brown

Voice Call a short 'dzee'; during mating display flight trilling song.

192

white wing-bar

Temminck's Stint

juvenile

Calidris temminckii (sandpipers and relatives)
L 13–15 cm   WSp 34–37 cm   Long distance migrant

outer tail edges light

Habitat *Breeds in tundra; during migration and in winter on shallow inland waters and coastal lagoons.*

> *Breeding season May–August*
> *4 yellowish-brown, dark brown mottled eggs*
> *1–2 broods per year*

This species was named after a Dutch scientist. You can spot it during migration along coasts and in wetland inland areas. In muddy areas, Temminck's Stint mainly feeds on insects. Both males and females can mate with two partners each in a single summer.

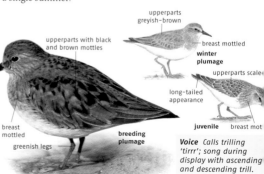

upperparts greyish-brown

upperparts with black and brown mottles

breast mottled

winter plumage

upperparts scale

long-tailed appearance

juvenile   breast mot

breast mottled

greenish legs

breeding plumage

Voice Calls trilling 'tirrr'; song during display with ascending and descending trill.

Arctic Skua

tercorarius parasiticus (skuas)
41–46 cm WSp 110–125 cm Middle/Long distance migrant

underwing dark

long tail feathers

adult

light patch on underwing

tail fork only short   **juvenile**

he Arctic Skua steals the prey of auks,
mall seagulls and terns. In the breeding
eason it chases seabirds in flight and
arrasses them until they drop the fish
hey have caught. In winter it searches
ea areas ahead of the African coast
where the food supply is plentiful. It
ccurs in light and dark forms.

Habitat Breeds in
open country near
coast; outside breeding
season mostly on open
sea.

> Breeding season
> May–September
> 2 olive brown, dark
> mottled eggs
> 1 brood per year

feathers on
upperparts edged
warm brown

light patch on
base of bill

bill thinner than
Pomarine Skua's

underparts barred

veniles (variation)

Voice Miaowing
calls, often in
series, only heard in
breeding habitat.

193

Long-tailed Skua

tercorarius longicaudus (skuas)
48–53 cm WSp 105–117 cm Long distance migrant

grey brown tertials and
secondaries contrasting
dark primaries

adult

he Long-tailed Skua's flight is full of
wists and this is how it chases down
erns (pp. 203–207) to steal their prey.
t spends winter in the South Atlantic
where it catches fish. In its Arctic
reeding ground it catches lemmings
nd other small rodents from hovering
light.

wings narrower than
Arctic Skua's

underwing
strongly
barred

lean body
juvenile

juvenile

feathers on
upperparts edged
greyish-brown

under-tail coverts strongly barred

very long tail

Habitat Breeds in
tundra, also away from
coast; in winter almost
exclusively at sea.

> Breeding season
> June–August
> 1–2 olive green, dark
> mottled eggs
> 1 brood per year

ill thinner than
rctic Skua's

Voice Miaowing calls
at breeding site,
slightly higher than
Arctic Skua's.

Pomarine Skua

Stercorarius pomarinus (skuas)
L 46–51 cm   WSp 125–138 cm   Long distance migrant

two light patches on underwing coverts

adult

juvenile

body more robust than Arctic Skua

Habitat *Breeds in tundra, outside breeding season exclusively at sea.*

> *Breeding season June–August*
> *2 brown, dark mottled eggs*
> *1 brood per year*

With its stately, gull-like flight, the Pomarine Skua cannot really outfly terns (pp. 203–207). However, it can compete with gulls (pp. 195–202) for their prey. In its breeding territory it mainly feeds on lemmings. It migrates from Siberia to Africa via Europe's seas and passes Europe's coasts in smaller numbers than the Arctic Skua (p. 193).

dark crown extending into face

upperparts blackish-brown

brownish breast band

thick bill

juvenile (a few months old)

plumage blackish-brown

legs grey

ample with br twis streame 'spo

adult (da variant)

adult (light variant)

Voice *Chuckling, barking and laugh-like calls, only heard in breeding habitat.*

Great Skua

Stercorarius skua (skuas)
L 51–56 cm   WSp 145–155 cm   Short/Long distance migrant

large white wing patch

tail short

belly thick

Habitat *Breeds on sea shores close to seabird colonies; outside breeding season always on open sea.*

> *Breeding season April–August*
> *2 brown, dark mottled eggs*
> *1 brood per year*

When attacking other seabirds, the Great Skua does not restrict itself to the prey in their bills but occasionally also kills Puffins (p. 208) or other birds. It defends its nest with wild, diving flights and can also injure people. It remains in the North Atlantic in winter and can reach the American coast.

dark brown crown

head dark brown

juvenile

plumage mottled

underparts orange-brown

strong bill

Voice *At breeding site chuckling calls in series; shrieking calls during attacks on enemies.*

Lesser Black-backed Gull

Larus fuscus (gulls)

51–64 cm WSp 135–150 cm Resident bird/Long distance migrant

adult

some white on wing-tip

The Lesser Black-backed Gull migrates the farthest of large seagulls and spends winter in Spain as far as western Africa. Finnish birds migrate to eastern Africa. From its breeding colonies it flies out to sea for up to 100 km to catch fish and crabs or pick up discarded fish from trawlers.

Habitat Breeds on sea shores and large lakes; searches for food mainly on open sea but also on fields.

> **Breeding season April–August**
> 2–3 olive green eggs, mottled black
> 1 brood per year

bill black

mantle blackish-brown, lightly edged

juvenile

upperparts fairly dark brown

upperparts blackish-grey

tail almost white with black terminal band

juvenile

appears lean because of long wings

legs yellow

Voice Reminiscent of Herring Gull but often lower and more nasal.

Great Black-backed Gull

Larus marinus (gulls)

64–79 cm WSp 150–167 cm Short distance migrant

adult

plenty of white on wing-tips

tail barred

juvenile

Europe's largest gull only starts breeding at the age of four to five years and assembles in large colonies. Its diet is varied and it often scavenges around in rubbish tips. It primarily feeds, however, on fish. The Great Black-backed Gull can fish itself, but it relies on discarded fish from trawlers.

Habitat Preferably breeds on rocky coasts; searches for food and winters on coasts and open sea.

> **Breeding season April–August**
> 2–3 greenish, dark mottled eggs
> 1 brood per year

juvenile (few weeks old)

black bill

upperparts marks rich in contrast

upperparts black

white head

thick bill, yellow with red spot

pink legs

Voice Calls distinctly deeper than Herring Gull's, a guttural 'kao' most frequently audible.

Yellow-legged Gull

Larus michahellis (gulls)
L 58–68 cm   WSp 140–158 cm   Resident bird

primaries very dark brown

juvenile

underwing da

black terminal tail band

Habitat *Sea shores and inland waters; searches for food on fields and refuse sites.*

> **Breeding season March–August**
> 1–3 olive brown, dark mottled eggs
> 1 brood per year

In many places the Yellow-legged Gull gorges on tit-bits from household refuse and discarded fish from trawlers. This is how its population swelled in the 20th century and the species spread further north and now occasionally colonises inland waters in central Europe.

upperparts a little darker than Herring Gull's

adult

lots of black on wing-tip

juvenile

head light

legs strongly yellow

black wing-tip with a few white spots

Voice *Call repertoire similar to Herring Gull's, generally a little lower pitched.*

underwing coverts light

dark brown terminal tail band

juvenile

Caspian Gull

Larus cachinnans (gulls)
L 58–67 cm   WSp 140–158 cm   Resident bird/Short distance migrant

Habitat *Sea shores and inland waters; search for food often also on fields and refuse sites.*

> **Breeding season April–August**
> 2–3 olive green to grey, mottled eggs
> 1 brood per year

The Caspian Gull does feed on fish but mostly seeks its food on land. From the Black Sea, the Caspian Gull now occurs in central Europe, where in some places it gathers in hundreds and even breeds in many places. It has hybridised with the Herring Gull (p. 197) and Yellow-legged Gull.

black patch on wing-tip

flat forehead

adult

eye dark

head profile longish

juvenile

long bill

yellowish legs

Voice *Reminiscent of Herring Gull but lower.*

Herring Gull

rus argentatus (gulls)

5–67 cm   WSp 138–150 cm   Resident bird/Short distance migrant

e Herring Gull breeds in large colonies on shores and coastal oftops. Its population has increased in places due to its efficient y of feeding initially on discarded fish and later on household fuse. It now colonises inland coastal areas. Its varied diet also includes fish and crabs caught at sea as well as worms caught on mudflats and on fields. In autumn, northern European birds migrate to the south, others merely roam around the breeding site.

Habitat *Sea shores and inland waters; searches for food also on fields, meadows and refuse sites.*

> **Breeding season** *April–August*
> *2–3 olive green to grey, mottled eggs*
> *1 brood per year*

upperparts partially grey

k bill, ning black ard tip

juvenile (one year old)

barred, terminal tail nd dark brown

wings and back partly grey

tail plain white

enile few months old)

juvenile (one year old)

adult

197

upperparts medium brown with dark brown marks

bill mostly black

alular quills strongly marked

juvenile (a few months old)

yellow h red spot

eye yellowish

Birder's tip

Along seaside promenades you can observe how the Herring Gull opens its larger-sized prey: mussels and other hard-shelled animals. It repeatedly drops them from a considerable height until the shell breaks.

legs pink

Voice *Varied repertoire of barking, miaowing and chuckling calls, also in series.*

Glaucous Gull

Larus hyperboreus (gulls)
L 62–68 cm WSp 150–165 cm Resident bird/Short distance migrant

Habitat *Along coasts and on open sea; mostly breeds in rocky areas.*

> *Breeding season May–August*
> *2–3 greenish, dark mottled eggs*
> *1 brood per year*

For most of the year the Glaucous Gull remains in the far north. Its diet is varied. It also behaves as a 'thieving gull' and robs other seabirds of their prey. However it eats Little Auks (p. 208) whole. Iceland Gulls (*L. glaucoides*) also reach northern European seas.

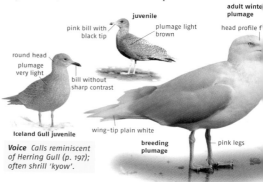

juvenile
wing-tip very light
head streak

adult winter plumage
head profile f

juvenile
pink bill with black tip
plumage light brown

round head
plumage very light
bill without sharp contrast

Iceland Gull juvenile
wing-tip plain white

breeding plumage
pink legs

Voice *Calls reminiscent of Herring Gull (p. 197); often shrill 'kyow'.*

198

Audouin's Gull

Larus audouinii (gulls)
L 48–52 cm WSp 115–148 cm Resident bird/Short distance migrant

juvenile
white tail with broad black terminal band

Habitat *Along coasts; breeds on rocky or sandy islands.*

> *Breeding season March–August*
> *2–3 olive brown, dark mottled eggs*
> *1 brood per year*

A few decades ago this species was almost extinct with only 1,000 surviving breeding pairs. Conservation measures and the use of discarded fish meant that the population rose to almost 20,000 pairs, almost half of this number breeding in the Spanish Ebro Delta. Audouin's Gull roams about the Mediterranean in winter as far as the north-western African coast.

adult
pler of bla on win ti

red bill with yellowish–black tip
eye dark

juvenile (one year old)
grey bill wi black t
legs dark grey

long wing

legs dark grey

Voice *Calls hoarsely 'gi-errk'; also chuckling and barking calls.*

Common Gull

Larus canus (gulls)
40–46 cm WSp 110–130 cm Resident bird/Short distance migrant

adult

Habitat Breeds along coasts and on inland waters; searches for food at sea and on meadows and fields.

The Common Gull often breeds in large colonies and travels in flocks to search for food for the chicks. It mainly finds earthworms on meadows and fields. At sea, it feeds on fish. In winter you mostly see the Common Gull in flocks and assemblies of several thousand birds at roosts.

plenty of white on wing-tips

> **Breeding season April–July**
> 2–3 olive green, black mottled eggs
> 1 brood per year

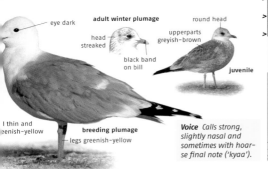

eye dark

adult winter plumage

head streaked

black band on bill

round head

upperparts greyish-brown

juvenile

bill thin and greenish-yellow

breeding plumage
legs greenish-yellow

Voice Calls strong, slightly nasal and sometimes with hoarse final note ('kyaa').

199

Kittiwake

Rissa tridactyla (gulls)
38–40 cm WSp 91–120 cm Resident bird

juvenile

black terminal tail band

adult

white wing lining

black wing-tip without white spots

black wing-bar

Habitat Breeds on steep cliffs, otherwise exclusively on open sea.

The Kittiwake's rear toe is ideally adapted to clinging onto narrow rock faces and ledges. The Kittiwake usually stays far out at sea and can be blown inland in storms. It feeds on small fish that it catches, or chases terns (p. 203–207) or guillemots (p. 209) for their food or collects tit-bits from trawlers.

> **Breeding season May–August**
> 1–3 grey or brown, dark mottled eggs
> 1 brood per year

faint patch on back of head

greyish blurred head marks

eye dark

thin yellow bill

adult winter plumage

black bill
juvenile

legs black
breeding plumage

Voice Calls nasal, screeching 'kiti-wa-ak'.

Mediterranean Gull
Larus melanocephalus (gulls)
L 36–38 cm   WSp 92–105 cm   Short distance migrant

juvenile
grey wing-bar
wing-tips
plain white
adult

Habitat Breeds on coasts and inland waters; searches for food mostly on meadows and fields, in winter at sea.

> **Breeding season** May–July
> **2–3 brownish, black mottled eggs**
> **1 brood per year**

Over the last 50 years, the Mediterranean Gull spread from south-eastern Europe further north and west and now several thousand breeding pairs are in central Europe. They mostly live in colonies with Common or Black-headed Gulls. The largest dark-headed gull in Europe, the Great Black-headed Gull (*L. ichtyaetus*), breeds from the Black Sea further east.

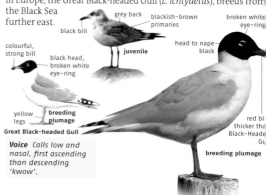

grey back
black bill
blackish-brown primaries
juvenile
broken white eye-ring
head to nape black
colourful, strong bill
black head, broken white eye-ring
yellow legs
breeding plumage
Great Black-headed Gull
red bil thicker tha Black-Heade Gu
breeding plumage

Voice Calls low and nasal, first ascending than descending 'kwow'.

blackish wing-bar
juvenile
straight tail end with black band

Little Gull
Hydrocoloeus minutus (gulls)
L 25–30 cm   WSp 70–80 cm   Short/Middle distance migrant

adult breeding plumage

Habitat Breeds on inland waters and fish ponds; winters on open sea.

> **Breeding season** May–August
> **2–3 brown, dark mottled eggs**
> **1 brood per year**

Europe's smallest gull primarily breeds inland, although in winter it is a true seabird and stays away from the coast. Its hunting technique is very reminiscent of terns (pp. 203–207). It repeatedly dives to the water's surface to catch insects or small fish in flight.

underwing coverts black
wing-t plain whi

adult winter plumage
dark patch behind eye
dark patch behind eye
head to nape black
bill black
dark patch behind eye
blackish wing band
eye dark, without surrounding light area

juvenile

Voice Calls high and nasally, rhythmical 'ek-kek-kek-kek', also single, sharp alarm call 'kay-ee'.

breeding plumage

Black-headed Gull

Larus ridibundus (gulls)

L 34–43 cm   WSp 94–110 cm   Resident bird/Short distance migrant

The Black-headed Gull is by far the most common species inland. Its breeding colony is often near water and it also constructs a nesting platform on the water. After a few days the chicks leave the nest, although they remain nearby hidden from danger beneath leaves. At sea the Black-headed Gull feeds on various small animals and fish and especially earthworms and insect larvae inland. It often follows ploughs to pick up insects that they unearth.

juvenile

outer wings show broad white leading panel

trailing edge of wing black

outer wings show broad white leading panel

underwing coverts light

adult

Habitat Sea shores and inland waters; also searches for food on adjacent meadows and fields.

> *Breeding season April–July*
> 3 brown to green, dark mottled eggs
> 1 brood per year

201

orange bill with black tip

upperwing coverts brown

juvenile

orange legs

upperparts grey

slight black patch behind eye

adult winter plumage

eye dark, partly ringed white

head chocolate brown, nape white

dark red bill

Voice Calls hoarsely crowing 'kraaka'; also short 'kek-kek'.

Birder's tip

Black-headed Gulls like to hunt swarming insects. You can observe how gracefully they fly and how skilfully they catch their prey, when you feed them with bread on park lakes.

breeding plumage

legs bright red

Slender-billed Gull

Larus genei (gulls)

L 42–44 cm WSp 100–110 cm Short distance migrant

upperwing coverts with paler markings than Black-headed Gull — juvenile

upperwing coverts similar to Black-headed Gull — adult

flatter crown than Black-headed

bill long, black

Habitat *Breeds along coastlines, inland lakes and hunts for food on meadows; also winters along coastal waters.*

> **Breeding season April–August**
> **2–3 yellowish or bluish mottled eggs**
> **1 brood per year**

The Slender-billed Gull mostly hunts for food at sea. With its neck outstretched it scans the waters for insects, small crabs or fish. In Europe, its breeding colonies are very sparsely distributed across the Mediterranean. Most of the approximately 50,000 breeding pairs nest in the Ukraine on the Black Sea coast.

eye bright

small patch behind eye

underparts tinged pink

bill long, orange with dark tip

juvenile

breeding plumage

Voice *Hoarse calls 'yep, yep' (lower than Black-headed Gull.*

Sabine's Gull

Larus sabini (gulls)

L 27–33 cm WSp 90–100 cm Long distance migrant

characteristic three-tone wing pattern: grey-white-black

tail forked, white — **adult**

juvenile

tail with black end bar

back and inner upperwing coverts with even colouring

upper crown brownish-grey

upperparts brownish grey, scaled

bill blackish

juvenile

Habitat *Breeds on tundra near coastlines; outside breeding season only on open seas.*

> **Breeding season June–August**
> **2 olive brown, dark mottled eggs**
> **1 brood per year**

Sabine's Gull breeds in the Arctic and then travels across the Atlantic to waters where the food supply is plentiful, along the south-west African coastline. Some birds arrive on European shores on autumn storms and reach as far as the North Sea. If you are lucky, you can marvel at this bird's tern-like, floating flight.

head blackish-grey

bill black with yellow tip

breeding plumage

Voice *Calls harsh 'kee-jah', also laughing and cackling sounds.*

Sandwich Tern

Sterna sandvicensis (terns)

L 36–41 cm WSp 95–105 cm Medium/Long distance migrant

upperwing coverts relatively dark

juvenile

upperwing coverts pale grey

adult

tail forked, without tip

The Sandwich Tern dives almost vertically into the water from a height of about 10 m to catch small fish. It uses fish in its mating display as well as for food. The younger generation grows up in four to five weeks in tightly packed, large colonies that are often right next to Black-headed Gulls (p. 201).

Habitat Near sea coasts, breeds on sandy or gravel islands and saline meadows.

> **Breeding season April–August**
> **1–2 whitish, black mottled eggs**
> **1 brood per year**

black crown with crest

forehead white

upperparts brownish-grey, scaled

adult winter plumage

juvenile

bill long, black with yellow tip

breeding plumage

legs black

Voice High-pitched, shrill call 'keer-reck'.

Little Tern

Sternula albifrons (terns)

L 22–28 cm WSp 47–55 cm Long distance migrant

juvenile

lots of black on tail tip

adult

forked tail

rapid, fluttering wingbeat

The Little Tern lays its eggs in hollows on sandy or gravel banks without plants and where they are well camouflaged. However, foxes often find the eggs and Kestrels take the chicks. In many places conservationists maintain protective fencing so these terns breed successfully. Broods are also lost to high tides.

Habitat Breeds on sandy beaches and gravel banks along coastlines and inland waters; forages in shallow water.

> **Breeding season May–August**
> **2–3 whitish, dark mottled eggs**
> **1 brood per year**

crown white

crown streaked

upperparts brownish, scaled

juvenile

bill yellow

legs orange

Voice Long rasping calls ('kree-ik'), also interspersed with series of rattling calls.

Gull-billed Tern

Gelochelidon nilotica (terns)
L 33–38 cm   WSp 100–115 cm   Long distance migrant

upperwing coverts with faint pattern

juvenile

adult

black trailing edge of wing

Habitat *Breeds along shallow coastal areas and inland lakes. Hunts for food on fields, meadows and open countryside.*

> **Breeding season May–August**
> **2–3 brownish eggs, darkly mottled**
> **1 brood per year**

Unlike other tern species, the Gull-billed Tern does not hunt over water, but on land. It catches insects and small animals including mice in flight. It mostly breeds in smaller colonies where, after only a few days, the young hide beneath plants. Its winter quarters are south of the Sahara in Africa.

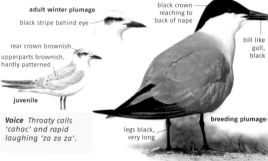

adult winter plumage
black stripe behind eye

black crown reaching to back of nape

bill like gull, black

rear crown brownish
upperparts brownish, hardly patterned

juvenile

Voice *Throaty calls 'cahac' and rapid laughing 'za za za'.*

legs black, very long

breeding plumage

Caspian Tern

Hydroprogne caspia (terns)
L 47–56 cm   WSp 127–145 cm   Medium/Long distance migrant

upperwing coverts faintly patterned

juvenile

lots of black on wing-t

tail forked, without tip

adult

Habitat *Calm sea coasts and wider stretches of inland water.*

> **Breeding season May–August**
> **2–3 light brown, dark speckled eggs**
> **1 brood per year**

The largest tern catches fish up to 20 cm in size by diving into the water. The Caspian Tern population is in severe decline, as its winter quarters in Africa have dried out and because of hunting on migration routes.

black crown with white streaks
upperparts brownish-grey, scaled

juvenile

bill thick, bright red

legs black

Voice *Call hoarse and urgent 'kraa-uh', reminiscent of Grey Heron.*

Common Tern

Terna hirundo (terns)
31–39 cm   WSp 72–98 cm   Long distance migrant

In springtime Common Terns return from their winter quarters. In the breeding colony, the oldest birds are first to occupy the best nesting sites as younger birds often have to make do with less favourable nesting places. Male and female birds breeding when rearing their young. After the chicks have hatched, the female keeps them warm and supervises them while initially only the male supplies small fish and worms. The rare Roseate Tern (*T. dougallii*) primarily breeds on the Azores and in Ireland.

black-edged wing-tip very broad

adult

tail forked, marked tail tip

juvenile

black bar on trailing edge of wing

Habitat Breeds along coasts and inland waters with gravel banks; winters mainly on coastal sea areas.

> *Breeding season April–August*
> 2–3 brown to green eggs with dark speckles
> 1 brood per year

205

Voice Call shrill, grating 'kee-yah', often with cackling sounds.

Birder's tip
You can watch the mating ritual near breeding colonies: display flights are performed in pairs. The mating feed is common, with the male offering the female a small fish.

crown white

juvenile
back brownish, scaled

bill black

chest tinged pink

Roseate Tern

all orange red with black tip

underparts white

legs red, longer than Arctic Tern

Arctic Tern

Sterna paradisaea (terns)
L 33–36 cm   WSp 75–85 cm   Long distance migrant

white trailing edge of primaries

juvenile

adult

narrow black margin at wing-tip

very long tail

Habitat Breeds along coasts and inland waters on tundra; spends winter at sea within reach of coastline.

> **Breeding season May–August**
> 1–3 green, brown or blue mottled eggs
> 1 brood per year

The Arctic Tern surely holds the world record as a migratory bird. From Arctic breeding grounds near the North Pole, it travels to the Antarctic to spend winter and virtually reaches the South Pole. It dives into the water to catch fish and uses the same technique to defend its breeding colony against predators. Any intruders must expect sharp treatment.

eye area white

back grey, scaled

juvenile

bill dark red

underpa often greyer th Common Tern

legs red, notably sh

Voice Similar to Common Tern, but slightly higher-pitched and clearer.

Whiskered Tern

Chlidonias hybridus (terns)
L 23–29 cm   WSp 74–78 cm   Long distance migrant

back yellow brown-black streaked

juvenile

upperwing coverts pale

underwing coverts white

breeding plumage

Habitat Breeds on lakes with floating plant material. Outside breeding season also along coastal waters.

> **Breeding season April–September**
> 2–3 grey or greenish, brown mottled eggs
> 1 brood per year

This tern's habitat is very changeable. It depends on the water level in its breeding territory and colonies can disappear again as quickly as they appeared. As the birds usually depart their breeding territories in different directions, new areas are constantly being colonised.

bill red, powerful

lores white

breeding plumage

back of nape dense black, streaked

bill blackish

underparts white

winter plumage

underparts dark grey

Voice Scratching and raucous calls, e.g. 'krsch' or 'zeck'.

Black Tern

Chlidonias niger (terns)
22–28 cm   WSp 64–68 cm   Long distance migrant

The Black Tern builds its nest on floating plant material and among water plants. These provide good protection against predators. Usually, several pairs live together in breeding colonies. The species is even more gregarious on its migratory route to Africa and several hundred birds can quickly assemble in good feeding areas.

breeding plumage

underwing coverts whitish

tail grey, slightly forked

juvenile

back dark brown, streaked

Habitat Breeds on inland waters with floating plants. Outside breeding season on inland and coastal waters.

> **Breeding season** May–August
> 2–3 brown or green, black mottled eggs
> 1 brood per year

head black

plumage blackish-grey

all black

breeding plumage

black 'mask'

faint collar

winter plumage

Voice *Calls penetrating 'kik-kik'.*

207

White-winged Black Tern

Chlidonias leucopterus (terns)
20–23 cm   WSp 63–67 cm   Long distance migrant

Similar to the Black Tern, this tern mostly hunts in curving flight patterns. It picks up insects or small water-borne animals en route. In recent years, the eastern European species has appeared more frequently in central Europe and breeds here in some areas. This is possibly due to measures to drain its breeding territory.

underwing coverts black-white

breeding plumage

back dark brown, streaked

tail white, slightly forked

juvenile

bill black

Habitat Breeds on calm lake shores or flooded meadows; in winter on calm inland and coastal waters.

> **Breeding season** May–August
> 2–3 brown or green, black mottled eggs
> 1 brood per year

breeding plumage

plumage black

crown striped

black patch behind eye

wings white

winter plumage

Voice *Calls rasping 'cherr' or 'kerr'.*

Puffin

Fratercula arctica (auks)
L 26–29 cm   WSp 47–63 cm   Short distance migrant

winter plumage

underwing coverts dark grey

compact build

black collar

breeding plumage

silvery-white around face

Habitat Breeds on cliffs with grassy covering along sea coasts; otherwise always on open seas.

> **Breeding season April–August**
> 1 whitish egg with faint marking
> 1 brood per year

The Puffin's scientific name translates as something like 'Arctic younger brother'. The bird mostly breeds in large colonies along steep sea coastal areas where it digs holes up to one metre deep in the ground or uses existing hollows. It feeds on small fish that it catches on dives and can reach up to depths of 60 m.

powerful, colourful bill

round head profile

juvenile (winter)

bill smaller than adult

blackish around face

breeding plumage

legs red

Voice At breeding sites, low growling or chattering sounds.

Little Auk

Alle alle (auks)
L 17–19 cm   WSp 40–48 cm   Short/Medium distance migrant

winter plumage

tail short

neck short and thick

underwing coverts pale

breeding plumage

Habitat Breeds on rocky coasts and coastal cliff faces. Outside the breeding season on open seas.

> **Breeding season June–September**
> 1 bluish or greenish egg
> 1 brood per year

The smallest of the auks, the Little Auk is one of the world's most common birds. It breeds in many millions in vast colonies on islands in the Arctic. Only a few birds reach Europe in winter. Except for in the Skagerak straits, the Little Auk usually has difficulty finding an adequate supply of the small crabs it feeds on.

throat black

breeding plumage

bill small and thick

Voice Usually silent. Trilling, chattering and barking calls at breeding site.

tail short, slightly cocked

winter plumage

throat white

Guillemot

ria aalge (auks)

38–43 cm   WSp 64–71 cm   Short distance migrant

uillemots jostle for position, since they are packed shoulder
shoulder on narrow cliff ledges. They lay their eggs on the
are rock and these are pear-shaped, so they do not roll over
e cliff edge. Due to its fin-like wings and blunt rear end with
quat legs, the Guillemot makes an excellent diver. It catches
        fish at depths of up to 100 m, though on land it
               moves rather clumsily. The similar
                  Brünnich's Guillemot (*U. lomvia*)
                     often breeds in the same
                        colonies on Iceland
                        and in Norway.

wings narrow, underparts pale

inter
umage

breeding
plumage

face white with
black streak

winter
plumage

bill long and pointed

head, neck and upperparts
blackish-brown
(in summer often paler)

reeding
umage

thick bill with
white streak

ünnich's Guil-
mot

face black

winter plumage

breeding
plumage

legs black, with
webbed feet

Did you know?

*Bringing food to the nest
is very laborious for the
Guillemot. Therefore the
three-week old chicks,
which are still unable
to fly, jump down from
their steep cliff ledges.
The adults then escort
the chicks out onto the
open seas where they are
fed until they can fend
for themselves.*

Habitat *Breeds along
steep rocky coastlines.
Otherwise lives on
open seas.*

> **Breeding season
> April–July**
> 1 white to turquoise-
> coloured egg
> 1 brood per year

209

Voice *At breeding
site, long, muffled to
cooing cries ('arrr');
chicks call weakly
'pili–pili'.*

Razorbill

Alca torda (auks)
L 37–39 cm   WSp 63–68 cm   Short distance migrant

build more squat than Guillemot

winter plumage
breeding plumage

underwing coverts with more contrast than Guillemot

Habitat *Breeds on steep coastal cliffs, otherwise only on open seas.*

> **Breeding season April–August**
> **1 whitish, slightly mottled egg**
> **1 brood per year**

The Razorbill often forms joint breeding colonies with the Guillemot, although it prefers slightly more protected cliff areas in niches or small holes. It performs a curious mating flight with delayed wingbeats. The chick leaps into the sea while still unable to fly and its parents escort it to feeding grounds.

head, neck and upperparts deep black

breeding plumage

thicker, more angled bill with white bar

tail longer than Guillemot, often slightly cocked

face white

winter plumage

Voice *Penetrating, squawking 'arrr' call.*

winter plumage

underwing coverts white

Black Guillemot

Cepphus grylle (auks)
L 30–32 cm   WSp 52–58 cm   Resident bird/Short distance migrant

breeding plumage

white wing panel

appears slightly tubby

Habitat *On sea near coastlines and breeds on step cliffs or sandy shores.*

> **Breeding season May–August**
> **1–2 white to brownish mottled eggs**
> **1 brood per year**

The Black Guillemot remains within range of the coastline while searching for food and catches small fish and crabs. Its breeding behaviour is also different to other auks as it only forms loose colonies, often breeding alone. The eggs are incubated either in cliff holes or hollows in sandy steep cliff faces.

bill lon and po

plumag black

white wing panel

breeding plumage

legs red

juvenile (winter)

winter plumage

back streaked

wing panel streaked

head, neck and underparts white

Voice *Whistling and chattering calls.*

Great Northern Diver

Gavia immer (divers)

69–91 cm   WSp 127–147 cm   Short/Medium distance migrant

The Great Northern Diver needs a clear stretch of water of at least
–10 m in order to take off. It can therefore only breed on larger
trips of water. Close by the water's
dge it constructs a large pile
f plant material that serves
s a nest. After they have
ledged the youngsters
re supervised by their
arents for about up to
hree months. The White-billed Diver
G. adamsii), which is native to Siberia,
pends winter on Scandinavian coasts and
an be distinguished from the Great Northern
Diver by its yellowish, upturned bill.

large feet

Habitat *Breeds on
large, deep lakes,
mostly near sea coasts
in winter.*

> **Breeding season
> May–September**
> **1–3 brownish, dark
> brown mottled eggs**
> **1 brood per year**

211

Voice *Short deep
'kwuk' in flight.
Laughing call series at
breeding site and pro-
tracted, wailing calls.*

Did you know?

*You will frequently
spot Great Northern
Divers (there called
Common Loons) on
North America's larger
lakes. The laughing
and wailing calls are
part of the scenery and
frequently feature as
acoustic backdrops in
American films.*

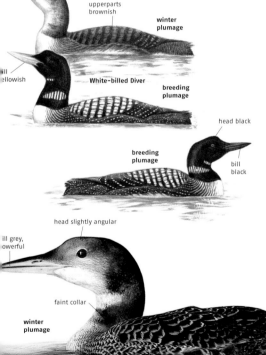

upperparts
brownish

**winter
plumage**

ill
ellowish

White-billed Diver

**breeding
plumage**

**breeding
plumage**

head black

bill
black

ill grey,
owerful

head slightly angular

faint collar

**winter
plumage**

Red-throated Diver

Gavia stellata (divers)
L 53–69 cm WSp 106–116 cm Short/Medium distance migrant

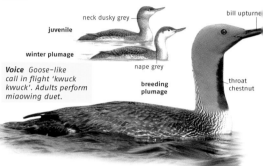

head heavily lowered

A slender body and squat legs at the rear distinguish the Red-throated Diver as an adept diver. However, on land it is rather clumsy. It therefore only leaves the water to climb onto the nest that is right by the water. From its smaller breeding areas on lakes it flies out to the nearby coastline to catch fish out at sea.

Habitat Breeds in pools and lakes in the tundra. Especially at sea near coastlines in winter and also on larger lakes.

> **Breeding season May–August**
> **1–3 brownish, dark brown mottled eggs**
> **1 brood per year**

neck dusky grey

juvenile

winter plumage

nape grey

bill upturned

throat chestnut

breeding plumage

Voice *Goose-like call in flight 'kwuck kwuck'. Adults perform miaowing duet.*

Black-throated Diver

Gavia arctica (divers)
L 58–73 cm WSp 110–130 cm Short/Medium distance migrant

The Black-throated Diver lowers its head into the water to search for fish and dives as soon as it spots its prey. Thanks to the webbed toes, it is a fast swimmer. Dives last for one or two minutes and at depths of up to 40 m. Unfortunately some birds are entangled in fishing nets and drown.

Habitat Breeds in tundra and on moorland. In sea coastal regions and on lakes during migration and in winter.

> **Breeding season April–September**
> **1–3 brownish, dark brown mottled eggs**
> **1 brood per year**

rear nape black

winter plumage

white panel

head grey

breeding plumage

throat black

Voice *Goose-like call in flight 'kwow'. Plaintive rising wailing calls in breeding season.*

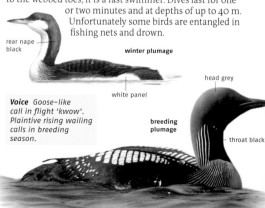

Great Crested Grebe

Podiceps cristatus (grebes)
46–61 cm   WSp 85–90 cm   Resident bird/Short distance migrant

The Great Crested Grebe builds floating nest platforms that it anchors to water plants. Juveniles ride on their parents' backs for up to three weeks and are fed for 10 weeks – at first with insects, later on with small fish. The adults catch the fish on dives up to 30 m deep. If there is insufficient food at the breeding site, the Great Crested Grebe flies to neighbouring lakes. However, it never leaves the water apart from when in flight.

Habitat Breeds on stagnant waters, mostly with reedbeds. Winters on larger lakes and along coastlines.

> **Breeding season** March–October
> **2–6 whitish unmarked eggs**
> **1–2 broods per year**

neck long, pale

noticeable white wing panel

bill long, pink

winter plumage

Voice Penetrating calls only uttered in breeding season: short 'kar-arr' or longer 'er-wick'.

213

Birder's tip
Great Crested Grebes are not shy birds and also appear at busy lakes. From March to June, you can stand at the shore and watch the ceremonial mating ritual, for instance, the shaking of the head, presenting nesting material, splashing and standing upright.

juvenile

head streaked

black-red-brown feathery crest

breeding plumage

Little Grebe

Tachybaptus ruficollis (grebes)
L 25–29 cm   WSp 40–45 cm   Resident bird/Short distance migrant

adult with chick

Habitat *Stagnant, often very small inland freshwater lakes. Outside breeding season also on rivers.*

> **Breeding season April–October**
> **5–6 whitish, unmarked eggs**
> **2 broods per year**

If the Little Grebe feels disturbed, it immediately dives into the water. It only raises its head above water under cover of dense vegetation by the shore. In its breeding territory it is therefore often only noticed due to its trilling mating calls. Although the chicks can dive from day one, they prefer to remain on their parents' backs for a week or so.

bill pale

nec brownis

winter plumage

yellow patch at bill base

head chestnut

Voice *Mating trills a series of rapid single notes, often in duet with both partners.*

breeding plumage

214

Red-necked Grebe

Podiceps grisegena (grebes)
L 40–50 cm   WSp 77–85 cm   Short distance migrant

head streaked

juvenile

Habitat *Breeds on small, calm lakes and ponds. In winter on larger lakes and along sea coasts.*

> **Breeding season April–September**
> **2–6 whitish, unmarked eggs**
> **1–2 broods per year**

The Red-necked Grebe is unmistakeable in summer time. Its winter plumage is similar to the Great Crested Grebe (p. 213). For breeding, the Red-necked Grebe prefers smaller lakes and in winter the expanse of the sea. Here it mainly dives for small fish. In summer, it also catches insects, shellfish and frogs.

winter plumage

bill yellow

front of nape grey

face silvery

breeding plumage

Voice *In early breeding season, a series of abrupt 'cherk' calls, also wailing calls individually or as duet.*

neck red-brown, shorter than Great Crested Grebe

Slavonian Grebe

...odiceps auritus (grebes)
...1–38 cm WSp 59–65 cm Short distance migrant

forehead flat
bill thick, straight
cheek white

winter plumage

breeding plumage

...ales and females get together in
...eir winter quarters and move on
...o their breeding territory as a pair.
...ere they build their floating nest out of
...ater plants. After fledging, the chicks initially
remain on their parents' backs. The Slavonian
Grebe prefers to feed on small fish and insects
that it also picks off the water's surface.

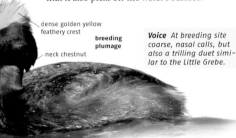

dense golden yellow feathery crest

breeding plumage

neck chestnut

Voice *At breeding site coarse, nasal calls, but also a trilling duet similar to the Little Grebe.*

Habitat *Breeds on lakes and ponds; winters primarily in coastal sea areas and larger lakes.*

> ***Breeding season*** *May–September*
> *3–6 whitish, unmarked eggs*
> *1 brood per year*

Black-necked Grebe

...odiceps nigricollis (grebes)
...8–34 cm WSp 56–60 cm Middle distance migrant

forehead high
bill slender
lores blackish

winter plumage

...he Black-necked Grebe is the most
...regarious of the European grebes.
...ou often spot it in groups. It preferably
...so breeds in colonies. It often seeks the
...ompany of Black-headed Gulls to benefit from their defensive
...ehaviour against predators. In spite of similar colouring, Black-
...eaded and Slavonian Grebes can be clearly distinguished by
...eir head and bill shape, regardless of the plumage.

drooping spray of plumes

breeding plumage

neck black

Voice *Silent in winter. Short rising calls and high-pitched trills in breeding season.*

Habitat *Breeds preferably on lakes and ponds with plenty of water plants. Large lakes as winter quarters.*

> ***Breeding season*** *April–August*
> *3–4 white eggs*
> *1–2 broods per year*

Whooper Swan
Cygnus cygnus (swans)
L 140–165 cm WSp 205–235 cm Short/Medium distance migrant

neck long

Habitat *Breeds on lakes. In winter both on lakes and flat coastal waters as well as on arable fields and meadows.*

> **Breeding season April–October**
> **4–6 yellowish-white eggs**
> **1 brood per year**

The Whooper Swan requires lots of time for breeding. After building the nest, about 10 days pass before the female has laid all her eggs. These have to be incubated for five to six weeks and the first cygnet is not ready to fly for three months. Parents and juveniles then depart together for their winter quarters and remain together until springtime.

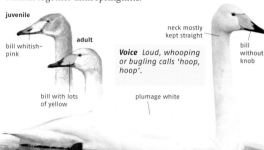

juvenile

bill whitish-pink

adult

bill with lots of yellow

neck mostly kept straight

bill without knob

Voice *Loud, whooping or bugling calls 'hoop, hoop'.*

plumage white

216

Bewick's Swan
Cygnus bewickii (swans)
L 115–140 cm WSp 170–195 cm Long distance migrant

neck relatively sho

Habitat *Breeds on lakes in the tundra; in winter on wetland meadows and arable land as well as lakes.*

> **Breeding season May–September**
> **3–5 yellowish-white eggs**
> **1 brood per year**

Due to the short Arctic summer, Bewick's Swan has to restrict its breeding season to the shortest possible period. The juveniles can already fly at the age of two months and shortly afterwards, in September, they begin their migratory flight to milder winter quarters. In May, they break their return flight at the White Sea, where they feed on plant roots to store energy for the flight to Siberia.

juvenile

adult

bill whitish-pink

bill with less yellow than Whooper Swan

Voice *Loud, but gentle and quiet calls ('oop-oop').*

plumage white

Mute Swan
ygnus olor (swans)
125–160 cm   WSp 208–240 cm   Resident bird

he Mute
wan was
nce seriously
unted and
00 years ago it
ad disappeared
rom many
arts of Europe.
However birds roaming parks in
the wild have ensured the increase of
the population and reclaimed lost breeding grounds. This swan
uffers in winter when many birds starve, as food is covered by
ce and snow. The male defends the nest at the breeding site and
protects feeding sites from predators. When the juveniles are
eady to fly after four or five months, they are also
hrown out of the nest.

**black bill
with knob**

Habitat *Lakes, gently
flowing rivers and
dikes, also coastal
lagoons; also forages
on arable land.*

> **Breeding season
April–October**
> **5–8 greenish-grey eggs**
> **1 brood per year**

Voice *Nasal honking
at enemies and also
hissing, whistling
sounds in flight.*

bill grey

plumage brownish

juvenile

217

constructs massive nest stacks

Birder's tip

*The Mute Swan is a
vegetarian. In the
water it uses its long
neck to reach plants
from the water's bed.
Especially in winter,
you can watch the
swan on land as it
eats grass blades and
rapeseed leaves in
meadows and fields.*

plumage white

**bill dark
orange**

Bean Goose

Anser fabalis (geese)
L 66–84 cm   WSp 142–176 cm   Medium/Long distance migrant

wings dark

belly unstreaked

Habitat Breeds in taiga and tundra. In winter on meadows and fields, at nighttime on lakes.

> Breeding season May–September
> 4–6 whitish eggs
> 1 brood per year

Two subspecies of the Bean Goose spend winter in central Europe. You can distinguish the species by their shape and black area on their bill. The Taiga Bean Goose is native to Scandinavia and western Siberia, whereas the Tundra Bean Goose breeds in northern Siberia. The Tundra Bean is more widespread in winter. In addition to green plant fragments, it also feeds on grain.

Taiga Bean Goose

head dark

bill bla orange

Tundra Bean Goose

Voice In flight nasal calls ('ung-unk').

legs orange

Pink-footed Goose

Anser brachyrhynchus (geese)
L 60–75 cm   WSp 135–170 cm   Long distance migrant

upperwir cover pa

belly unstreaked

Habitat Breeds in tundra on cliffs and marshes. In winter on meadows and fields.

> Breeding season May–September
> 3–6 whitish eggs
> 1 brood per year

The Pink-footed Goose replaces the very similar Bean Goose on Spitsbergen, Iceland and Greenland. Depending on winter weather conditions, it commutes back and forth from Denmark to Holland. Before the long flight to its breeding territory, it stocks up on energy reserves in northern Norway.

bill short, black to pink

head dark

often migrates in flocks, frequently in arrow-shaped formation

legs pink

Voice In flight slightly higher-pitched calls than Bean Goose ('ang-ank').

Greylag Goose

Anser anser (geese)

76–89 cm   WSp 147–180 cm   Resident bird/Short distance migrant

In recent years, Greylag Geese have increased in number. This is due to conservation measures, although the UK also has a large feral population. The Greylag Goose is the first bird to breed on water and you can already spot the bird on its nest by the end of the winter. The first chicks already emerge in April and both parents supervise them.

bill powerful

upperwing coverts pale

belly lightly streaked

Habitat Breeds on a variety of waters providing cover, also in parks. In winter on meadows and fields.

> **Breeding season March–July**
> **4–6 white eggs**
> **1 brood per year**

Voice Mostly a musical 'ang-ang' call, slightly lower and coarser than other grey geese.

Greater White-fronted Goose

adult

wings dark

belly black streaked

Anser albifrons (geese)

65–86 cm   WSp 135–165 cm   Long distance migrant

Although this species does not breed in Europe, it spends the winter here in flocks. Orange-billed birds from Greenland remain on the British Isles and pink-billed birds from Siberia stay in central Europe. The rounder-headed Lesser White-fronted Goose (*A. erythropus*) travels from northern Eurasia to south-eastern Europe.

Lesser White-fronted Goose

forehead white

eye-ring yellow

juvenile

not white at base of bill

belly unstreaked

white around base of bill

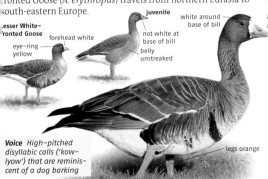

legs orange

Habitat Breeds in tundra. In winter on fields and meadows, at night-time on lakes.

> **Breeding season May–September**
> **5–6 yellowish-white eggs**
> **1 brood per year**

Voice High-pitched disyllabic calls ('kow-lyow') that are reminiscent of a dog barking

Canada Goose

elongated neck

Branta canadensis (geese)
L 90–100 cm WSp 160–183 cm Resident bird/Short distance migrant

Habitat *Breeds on lakes and ponds; forages on fields and meadows. In winter also on shallow coastal waters.*

> **Breeding season March–August**
> **5–6 yellowish eggs**
> **1 brood per year**

This species, native to North America, was introduced to England over 300 years ago. In the last century, the geese were initially released in Sweden and later also in Germany and other northern European countries. The Canada Goose, as with many other species of goose, feeds mostly on land on plants and also reaches water plants, like a swan, stretching out its long neck.

white patch on throat and cheek

neck long, black

adult with chicks

upperparts brown

Voice Calls resonant, trumpeting 'a-honk'.

Barnacle Goose

upperwing coverts pale grey

Branta leucopsis (geese)
L 58–71 cm WSp 132–145 cm Short/Long distance migrant

belly white

Habitat *Breeds on cliffs in tundra and along rocky coastlines. In winter on saline meadows and other grassland.*

> **Breeding season May–September**
> **4–5 whitish eggs**
> **1 brood per year**

You can watch Barnacle Geese on saline meadows as they graze in winter. However, to breed they search for a place on cliff faces. The newly hatched chicks leap down from a great height. The parents quickly lead them to the nearest stretch of water where they are finally safe from Arctic Foxes lurking about and ready to attack the colony.

grazing flock

face white

neck short, black

Voice Yapping call ('gnuk') higher than Brent Goose (p. 221).

Brent Goose

Branta bernicla (geese)

55–66 cm   WSp 110–120 cm   Long distance migrant

After a short breeding season in northern Siberia, the dark-bellied Brent Goose arrives in Europe in autumn. However, breeding is not successful every year. If there are no lemmings in the tundra, Arctic Foxes eat Brent Geese eggs instead and may wipe out the entire brood. The pale-bellied Brent Goose breeds from Greenland to Spitsbergen and spends winter in the British Isles. You occasionally also spot a Red-breasted Goose (*B. ruficollis*) in a flock of Brent Geese, as they actually travel from Siberia en route for the Black Sea.

Habitat Breeds in tundra in coastal areas. In winter on saline meadows, mudflats, also fields and meadows.

> **Breeding season June–September**
> **3–5 greenish-white eggs**
> **1 brood per year**

wings dark

head and neck black

pale-bellied Brent Goose

belly whitish

Dark-bellied Brent Goose

white patch

Red-breasted Goose

neck and cheek chestnut

belly blackish

221

Voice Low, throaty mostly repeated calls ('rruk or rronk').

Birder's tip
An ideal time to watch the Brent Goose is in April or May when large flocks are out on tidal mudflats. They stock up on fat reserves needed for the flight to the White Sea, their only stop en route to Siberia.

Shelduck
Tadorna tadorna (ducks)
L 58–67 cm   WSp 110–133 cm   Short distance migrant

wings black and white

Habitat *Coastlines as well as lakes and rivers near coasts.*

> **Breeding season**
> **April–August**
> 8–10 yellowish eggs
> 1 brood per year

The Shelduck breeds in holes and prefers to nest in rabbit burrows. Shortly after hatching, both parents lead their chicks to the water, where they immediately dive for snails and small crabs. Soon afterwards, many adults depart for their moulting grounds, while juveniles of several pairs congregate in 'nurseries'.

red, knob-billed

♂

head greenish-black

chest ring orange

head grey-brown

juvenile

bill pale

♀

no knob on bill

Voice *In its breeding territory, you can hear a rapid, low quacking and light twanging call.*

Egyptian Goose
Alopochen aegyptiacus (geese)
L 71–73 cm   WSp134–154 cm   Resident bird

wings black-white-green

plumage orange-brown

Ruddy Shelduck

eye patch dark

Habitat *Breeds by lakes and other inland water, also in parks.*

> **Breeding season**
> **March–September**
> 6–10 whitish eggs
> 1–3 broods per year

This African species was established in England in the 17th century and recently arrived in Holland and Germany. Now over 5,000 pairs nest here on the ground, in earth holes or trees. The similar Ruddy Shelduck (*Tadorna ferruginea*) is native to south-eastern Europe.

wings black-white-green

legs long, reddish

Voice *Various husky gabbling and trumpeting calls.*

Mandarin Duck

Aix galericulata (ducks)
L 41–51 cm   WSp 65–75 cm   Resident bird

In its eastern Asian native territory, the Mandarin Duck has become very rare due to hunting. In the British Isles and central Europe, escapees and feral birds form large populations. The North American Carolina Duck (*A. sponsa*) can also be spotted in the wild in Europe, however, it breeds less frequently than the Mandarin Duck.

flanks with small light patches
bill dark
♀
Carolina Duck
♂

white supercilium
bill with light tip
♀
flanks with large light patches

bright mane
♂
orange coloured 'sail'

Habitat Along inland waters with glades of trees, frequently in parks.

> *Breeding season April–August*
> *9–12 cream coloured eggs*
> *1 brood per year*

Voice *Different calls during mating, otherwise silent.*

White-headed Duck

Oxyura leucocephala (ducks)
L 43–48 cm   WSp 58–69 cm   Resident bird

This White-headed Duck suffered a dramatic decline in population due to loss of habitat. The remaining European population is especially under threat today because of interbreeding with the Ruddy Duck (*O. jamaicensis*). This North American species was introduced into England and is reaching central and southern Europe.

bill blue, concave
head black–white
♂
faint dark stripe on upper neck
♀
Ruddy Duck

Habitat Breeds by saltwater lakes with reedbeds; in winter also on more open lakes with calm water.

> *Breeding season May–September*
> *5–6 grey to greenish eggs*
> *1 brood per year*

bill blue, swollen at base
head white
strong dark stripe on upper neck
♀
♂
tail vertically cocked

Voice *Various calls when mating, otherwise mostly silent.*

Wigeon
Anas penelope (geese)
L 45–51 cm WSp 75–86 cm Medium/Long distance migrant

white wing panel ♂

head roundish

♀

Habitat *Breeds by lakes; outside breeding season on inland water and meadows, especially along coast.*

> **Breeding season April–September**
> **7–9 creamy coloured eggs**
> **1 brood per year**

Like the Brent and Barnacle Goose, the Wigeon frequently grazes on saline meadows. As its relatively small body loses a lot of heat in winter, it rarely takes rests and has to feed day and night. In springtime, this routine does not change, as it has to store enough energy for the migration flight to Siberia.

high forehead
eye area dark
♀

head rust red with brown crown
♂

flanks reddish-brown

back and flanks grey

Voice *Characteristic, high-pitched and descending whistling call ('whee-oo').*

Shoveler
Anas clypeata (ducks)
L 44–52 cm WSp 70–85 cm Medium/Long distance migrant

belly rusty brown ♂

fore-wings pale blue

♀

Habitat *Breeds by lakes and in marshes; in winter on inland water, only occasionally along sea coasts.*

> **Breeding season April–August**
> **8–12 greenish to yellowish eggs**
> **1 brood per year**

The special shape of its bill means that the Shoveler can filter plant fragments and animals from the water's surface. While doing so, you can observe the Shoveler stretching out its neck over the water's surface. The breeding pair gets together in winter and the male leaves the female to rear the chicks on her own.

bill long and broadly spoon-shaped
♀

Voice *Apart from hoarse calls in mating season, infrequent calls.*

head metallic green
♂

chest white

Mallard

Anas platyrhynchos (ducks)

L 50–65 cm   WSp 81–99 cm   Resident bird/Medium distance migrant

From autumn onwards, the male duck has an impressive breeding plumage that is important later on in the mating season. The male's contribution to the breeding process, as with all other ducks, ends after mating. Afterwards, the magnificent plumage is shed and replaced by a simpler, winter plumage for summer. The female depends on her camouflaged plumage when hatching the chicks on the ground and only leaves the nest at times of acute danger.

♂

♀

blue panel at outer wing edge

Did you know?

Mallards can build their nests on pollarded willows, but they also nest on the ground or in cities in the most curious places, for example, in flower containers or on rooftops of houses.

Habitat *All types of water, from large lakes to small ponds; mostly only on calm sea stretches.*

> **Breeding season February–September**
> **7–13 greenish to brownish eggs**
> **1 brood per year**

female with chicks

225

orange

♀

blue wing panel

head metallic green

bill yellow

♂

belly and back grey

Voice *Various quacking and whistling calls.*

Gadwall

Anas strepera (ducks)
L 46–58 cm WSp 84–95 cm Medium/Long distance migrant

white wing patch

Habitat *Stagnant and inland rivers and lakes with gentle currents.*

> **Breeding season**
> *April–August*
> *8–12 yellowish-brown eggs*
> *1 brood per year*

Although it is inconspicuously coloured, the male Gadwall performs a striking mating display with dancing, upright strutting and head-nodding. In the mating season, you can watch the typical chasing flights with the female accompanied and pursued by one or two males with great persistence.

bill dark grey

♀
bill orange
white wing patch

♂
body grey

white wing patch

Voice *Occasional hollow or wheezy quacking; other calls similar to Mallard.*

Pintail

Anas acuta (ducks)
L 50–66 cm WSp 80–95 cm Medium/Long distance migrant

neck long and thin
♂
♀

Habitat *Breeds by lakes; during migration and winter especially in coastal waters.*

> **Breeding season**
> *April–August*
> *7–11 greenish-yellow eggs*
> *1 brood per year*

With its long neck, the Pintail is one of the ducks best at dredging and dabbling for food. The entire front body is immersed under water while the rear points to the sky. The duck holds position with powerful movements of its feet, while pulling up floating plants from the water in its bill and reaching a depth of 50 cm.

bill grey

♀

head chocolate brown

♂

long pointed tail

Voice *Various soft, penetrating and quacking calls.*

Teal

nas crecca (ducks)

34–43 cm   WSp 53–59 cm   Short/Long distance migrant

he Teal prefers to congregate in groups outside
he breeding season. During the day, you can often
ee the birds resting, as they mainly forage for food at night-time.
mall plant parts and water-borne animals are picked out of the
water (also with head completely immersed), and on
mudflats the Teal scoops up edible tit-bits from the
surface with outstretched neck.

green
wing panel

ead faintly
reaked

♀

head
brown-green

white side streak

♂

Voice *High-pitch
call 'krrit'.*

llow patch on rear body

Garganey

nas querquedula (ducks)

37–41 cm   WSp 60–63 cm   Long distance migrant

♂

♀

pale
fore-wing

he Garganey is the only species of duck to leave
urope in autumn. It spends winter in Africa,
vhere it prefers to stay in rice fields. Due to the disappearance of
uitable wetlands in breeding sites and long periods of drought in
ts winter quarters, numbers of this species are in heavy decline.

Voice *Flight call a nasal quack; during mat-
ing, prolonged, hollow
sounding crooning.*

head pale streaked

♀

white streak from eye
to nape

head and chest
reddish

flanks grey

♂

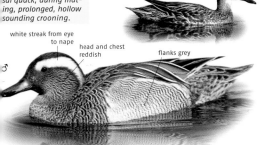

Red-crested Pochard

Netta rufina (ducks)
L 53–57 cm WSp 84–88 cm Resident bird/Short distance migrant

broad, whit
wing-ba

Habitat Calm inland waters, preferably with reedbeds along banks.

> **Breeding season**
> **April–August**
> 8–10 grey eggs
> 1 brood per year

The Red-crested Pochard has a strikingly large, round head. The male is not interested in hatching the brood, although keeps watch when the female leads the youngsters out of the nest. As the nest is located close to the water's edge and on the ground, it is prone to flooding at high tide.

pale head area

bill red
winter plumage

bill dark gre

bill red

head orange

♂

Voice *Various short calls, only rarely heard.*

Pochard

Aythya ferina (ducks)
L 42–58 cm WSp 72–82 cm Short/Medium distance migrant

wings pale
poor i
contras

Habitat Breeds by lakes and ponds with dense, overgrown banks; in winter also on slow moving rivers.

> **Breeding season**
> **April–September**
> 7–11 greenish to brownish eggs
> 1 brood per year

Although the Pochard's rounded rear end causes little resistance in the water, this duck can only dive at best up to 2 m deep. However its food sources are varied and include small plant fragments and insect larvae as well as mussels. The smaller, almost entirely brown Ferruginous Duck (*A. nyroca*) is native to eastern Europe.

eye white

under tail are
white

Ferruginous Duck

♂

♀

head rufous red

back and flanks brownish–grey

light patch by eye

♀

Voice *Usually silent, only different short calls in mating season.*

back and flanks pale grey

♂

Tufted Duck

Aythya fuligula (ducks)

40–47 cm WSp 67–73 cm Short/Medium distance migrant

fore-wing black ♂

♀

broad white wing-bar

The Tufted Duck is very good at diving. It picks up food, mainly mussels, from the water's bed. It mainly feeds during the dark and spends the daytime digesting its meals and resting. In winter large assemblies of Tufted Ducks gather in sheltered inlets and bays.

Voice Usually silent, only different short calls in mating season.

Habitat By lakes, ponds and coastal lagoons.

> **Breeding season May–September**
> 6–11 grey-green eggs
> 1 brood per year

♀ faint crest

back brown

black crest

eye yellow

back black

♂

Scaup

Aythya marila (ducks)

40–51 cm WSp 72–84 cm Medium distance migrant

fore-wings grey ♂

♀

In winter the Scaup often rests in large flocks in coastal inlets and bays or on lakes near the coast. At night-time it flies out on the open seas and dives for mussels and shellfish. Most of the birds seen inland are juveniles, which are distinguished from the smaller Tufted Duck by the shape of their head and white patch at the base of their bill.

Voice Mostly silent, only different short calls in mating season.

Habitat Breeds in tundra and along sea coasts; in winter preferably in coastal waters and by large lakes.

> **Breeding season May–September**
> 6–11 olive grey eggs
> 1 brood per year

large white area round base of bill

back grey-brown

♀

greenish glossy shimmer

back pale grey

♂

Eider

Somateria mollissima (ducks)
L 50–71 cm   WSp80–108 cm   Short distance migrant

Habitat Breeds along sea coasts; spends winter on calm coastal waters, occasionally also inland.

> **Breeding season April–August**
> **4–6 greenish to brownish eggs**
> **1 brood per year**

Voice In the mating season, the males utter a soft croon ('coo-roo-uh') and females a low gabbling.

The Eider catches a variety of different shellfish on its diving trips. It shakes its bill to dismember large crabs before swallowing legs and claws. In many places blue mussels are the main source of food and the Eider swallows them whole, only digesting and breaking them down afterwards when resting and using its powerful stomach muscles. The similar King Eider (*S. spectabilis*), which can be distinguished by the shape of the head, breeds on the northern coast of Siberia and arrives at the Norwegian coastline in winter.

♂
wing black-white
♀

bluish patch at nape
♂
orange-coloured notched bill
King Eider
rounder head shape than Eider
♀
upperparts and flanks with angular bars

upperparts and flanks streaked
♀

Did you know?

The soft down that the female uses to line her nest is used in Scandinavian countries and elsewhere as filling material for cushions. The Eider duck is highly valued due to this commercial usage.

head shape triangular

♂

nape green

Long-tailed Duck

angula hyemalis (ducks)

36–47 cm   WSp 73–79 cm   Short distance migrant

The Long-tailed Duck is less restricted to shallow and calm water than other duck species as it can dive up to 50 m deep. On the water or sea bed it mainly searches for mussels. In springtime it prefers to feed on herring spawn in the Baltic Sea and searches in large groups, as the spawn is easier to spot. While the Long-tailed Duck often stays far away from the coastline Steller's Eider (*Polystica stelleri*), which commonly breeds in Siberia and overwinters in Scandinavia, prefers to remain near coasts by the water's edge.

Voice In late winter and early springtime, male utters nasal, yodelling musical calls.

Habitat Breeds by coasts and small lakes; in winter on calm coastal waters, occasionally inland.

> *Breeding season May–August*
> *5–9 yellowish to greenish eggs*
> *1 brood per year*

wings dark monochrome

♂

♀

dark eye patch   ♂

angular head shape

Steller's Eider
♀

231

Birder's tip

In the mating season, Long-tailed Ducks often come quite close by the coastline. An ideal place to watch the display in March is by the Baltic Sea, where the flight display is emphasised by different head movements and flight circuits.

white from ...e to nape   ♀

back brown

very long pointed tail

♂

bill with pink stripe

Common Scoter
Melanitta nigra (ducks)
L 44–54 cm WSp 79–90 cm Short/Medium distance migrant

wings dark uniform ♂

♀

head and nape pale coloured ♀

Habitat Breeds by lakes; in winter almost exclusively on calm coastal waters, rarely on large inland lakes.

> **Breeding season**
> **May–September**
> 6–9 brown eggs
> 1 brood per year

The Common Scoter dives after certain types of mussels and digs them out of the sand with its bill. In calm coastal areas where mussels are in plentiful supply, several thousand birds gather in late summer where they moult and spend the winter. On its migratory route to these regions, the Common Scoter flies in long chains along coastlines.

upper bill orange

plumage uniform black

♂

Voice Nocturnal cooing on migration, otherwise a few calls in mating season.

Velvet Scoter
Melanitta fusca (ducks)
L 51–58 cm WSp 90–99 cm Short/Medium distance migrant

brilliant white wing panel ♂

♀

legs red

Habitat Breeds by lakes in the tundra and along sea coasts; in winter on calm coastal waters, rarer on inland lakes.

> **Breeding season**
> **May–September**
> 7–9 pale brown eggs
> 1 brood per year

In mixed flocks, the Velvet Scoter is immediately noticeable because of its white wing panel. As their diet is similar, the Velvet Scoter can often be spotted in the same winter quarters as the slightly smaller Common Scoter. The female rears the young alone, although she leaves them only after four weeks and before they are able to fly.

♀

pale patches before and behind eye

Voice Whistling and hoarse calls during mating.

white eye patch

bill ti orang

♂

Goldeneye

ucephala clangula (ducks)

42–50 cm   WSp 65–80 cm   Short distance migrant

The Goldeneye dives after insect larvae, shellfish and mussels that it stabs with its pincer-like bill.
This requires plenty of light so that the Goldeneye tends to feed only during the daytime and gather in assemblies at collective sleeping places at night. The female hatches the eggs in a tree hole.

eye yellow

head dark brown

ll ort

white patch at base of bill ♂

chest white

Habitat *Breeds in woodland glades by lakes and rivers; in winter by lakes, rivers and calm coastal waters.*

> *Breeding season March–August*
> *8–11 blue-green eggs*
> *1 brood per year*

Voice The male throws its head back when mating and utters a harsh nasal call.

Smew

ergellus albellus (ducks)

38–44 cm WSp 55–69 cm Short/Medium distance migrant

white wing panel

n summertime the Smew, a tree-hole nester, rimarily feeds on insects. In winter, however, s food is mainly small fish. Then thousands pon thousands of Smews collect at the IJsselmeer in central etherlands and by the Polish-German Szczecin lagoon and nly a few birds visit other lakes.

Voice Crooning and quacking calls in mating season.

high forehead ♀

lower head area white

hite head with crest

black 'mask' ♂

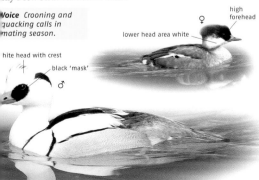

Habitat *Breeds on waters with woodland glades; in winter by lakes, rivers and calm coastal waters.*

> *Breeding season May–September*
> *7–9 buff coloured eggs*
> *1 brood per year*

Goosander

Mergus merganser (ducks)

L 58–66 cm   WSp 82–97 cm   Short distance migrant

white wing panel

long neck

Habitat Breeds on waters with woodland glades (also coasts); in winter by lakes, rivers and calm coastal waters.

> **Breeding season March–September**
> **8–12 cream coloured eggs**
> **1 brood per year**

When it is time to breed the female searches for a tree hole or even a cliff crevice. Broods have even been found in church towers. When they are only one or two days old, the Goosander chicks jump down to the ground from a considerable height and the female leads them to the nearest stretch of water. Here they immediately begin to dive for waterborne insects and small fish.

mane downwards-facing

sharp demarcation of the brown head

bill long and thin

head greenish–black

chest and belly salmon coloured

Voice In flight, a harsh 'karr' is audible, also different calls in mating season.

234

Red-breasted Merganser

Mergus serrator (ducks)

L 52–58 cm WSp 70–86 cm Resident bird/Short distance migrant

white wing panel, divided

Habitat Breeds on coastlines, lakes and rivers; in winter primarily on calm coastal waters.

> **Breeding season April–September**
> **8–10 brownish to greenish eggs**
> **1 brood per year**

The Red-breasted Merganser has a bill with serrated teeth, as do all its relatives. Using its bill, it specialises in catching small fish. It spots its food while under water and dives, if necessary, to catch it. The Red-breasted Merganser breeds on the ground, mostly under shrubs or protected by tall clusters of long grass.

ragged mane, downwards facing and towards rear

brown head, faintly demarked

head greenish–black

bill lon and thi

chest brown

Voice Hoarse calls in mating season and 'prrak' in flight.

Fulmar

Fulmarus glacialis (fulmars)

45–50 cm   WSp102–112 cm   Resident bird/Long distance migrant

Fulmar can live for over 40 years and only begins to breed at the age of nine years. However, before this it begins its search for a mate and a nesting place on a cliff ledge and remains faithful to both for many years. Like albatrosses, the Fulmar uses updrafts between the waves and can fly like this for hundreds of kilometres, almost without beating its wings. This means that it can search for food for its chicks over a vast area.

Habitat *Always on the high seas and only on rocky coasts for breeding.*

> **Breeding season May–September**
> **1 white, unspeckled egg**
> **1 brood per year**

235

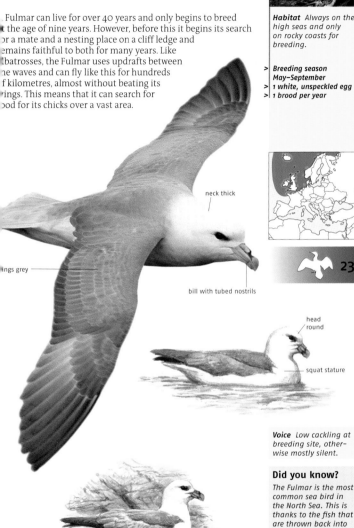

neck thick

wings grey

bill with tubed nostrils

head round

squat stature

breeds on cliff ledges

Voice *Low cackling at breeding site, otherwise mostly silent.*

Did you know?

The Fulmar is the most common sea bird in the North Sea. This is thanks to the fish that are thrown back into the sea and provide a plentiful food supply. Often several thousand Fulmars and shearwaters trail a single trawler.

Sooty Shearwater
Puffinus griseus (shearwaters)
L 40–51 cm   WSp94–109 cm   Long distance migrant

body underparts
uniform blackish

wing under
parts wi
whitish par

tubular nostri

Habitat Breeds on sea
coasts in the southern
hemisphere, otherwise
only on open seas.

> **Breeding season**
> **October–May**
> 1 white egg
> 1 brood per year

After the breeding season, the Sooty Shearwater
flies tens of thousands of kilometres several times
over. From its breeding sites on the islands near the
Antarctic it reaches as far as the North Atlantic. From
July to November it arrives at the
coastlines of western Europe and
also crosses the North Sea. In strong
winds, especially, its flight continues
in a constant up and down motion
as it is buffeted above the waves.

upperparts uniform blackish

wings narrow

Voice At sea only
occasionally hoarse
or screeching calls,
mostly silent.

Cory's Shearwater
Puffinus diomedea (shearwaters)
L 45–48 cm   WSp100–125 cm   Long distance migrant

Habitat Breeds on
rocky islands in the sea,
otherwise preferably on
open sea or near sea
coasts.

> **Breeding season**
> **May–October**
> 1 white egg
> 1 brood per year

Cory's Shearwater breeds on many small
Mediterranean islands in large colonies.
Although it only visits the breeding site at
night-time, you can watch it gathering in flocks
on nearby waters. Its characteristic flight is
noticeable and consists of a flat gliding motion
with few wingbeats, then a steep, soaring climb
for several metres and rapid descent.

wings lon
narrow

upperpa
dark gre
brown

bill pale

underparts white

wing edged black

Voice Nasal, moaning
calls audible in
breeding colonies.

Manx Shearwater

Puffinus puffinus (shearwaters)
30–38 cm   WSp 76–89 cm   Long distance migrant

The migratory behaviour of the Manx Shearwater is very unusual for a European bird. From its breeding areas it crosses the Atlantic and arrives at the eastern coast of South America. In early spring it returns to Europe again. During this journey it searches the water's surface for shellfish and occasionally dives in to catch them.

Habitat Breeds on rocky, grass-covered islands, otherwise only on open seas.

> *Breeding season April–October*
> *1 white egg*
> *1 brood per year*

bill black

upperparts uniform blackish-brown

Voice Cackling and quacking calls at breeding site, silent out at sea.

underparts brilliant white

Mediterranean Shearwater

Puffinus yelkouan (shearwaters)
30–40 cm   WSp 76–93 cm   Short distance migrant

As the name suggests, the Mediterranean Shearwater is a resident of Mediterranean waters. It breeds in colonies and is also very gregarious when searching for food. You can regularly watch groups of Mediterranean shearwaters at the Black Sea. The Balearic Shearwater (*P. mauretanicus*), which is slightly paler on the upper part of its body, breeds in the western Mediterranean.

Habitat Breeds on rocky islands in the sea, otherwise preferably near sea coasts.

> *Breeding season April–September*
> *1 white egg*
> *1 brood per year*

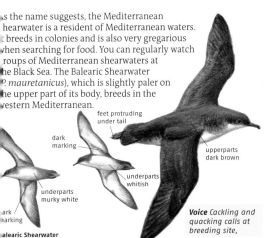

feet protruding under tail

dark marking

upperparts dark brown

underparts whitish

dark marking

underparts murky white

Balearic Shearwater

Voice Cackling and quacking calls at breeding site,

Storm Petrel
Hydrobates pelagicus (storm petrels)
L 14–18 cm   WSp 36–39 cm   Long distance migrant

Habitat *Breeds on rocky islands at sea, otherwise exclusively on open seas.*

> **Breeding season May–September**
> **1 white egg, occasionally with brownish speckles**
> **1 brood per year**

The Storm Petrel only feeds its young at night-time, when it comes to land to its nest hidden in a rock crevice. Its breeding colonies are therefore notoriously difficult to find, and are most easily located by listening for calls at night. The Storm Petrel spends most of the time at sea where it picks up small shellfish from the water's surface and constantly dances about in fluttering flight.

rump white

tail-end straight

white bar on underwing coverts

Voice Hoarse croons at breeding site, ending with nasal sound.

Leach's Storm Petrel
Oceanodroma leucorhoa (storm petrels)
L 19–22 cm   WSp 45–48 cm   Long distance migrant

Habitat *Breeds on rocky islands at sea; otherwise exclusively on open sea.*

> **Breeding season May–August**
> **1 white, faintly speckled egg**
> **1 brood per year**

The Leach's Storm Petrel skilfully flies between high waves searching for small fish or crabs. It trails its legs on the water's surface. This bird mostly breeds in North America. If it is surprised by storms en route to its tropical winter quarters it may arrive at the North Sea coast.

rump V-shaped white

wing underside blackish

forked tail

Voice Hoarse cooing and nasal cackling at breeding site.

Gannet

Morus bassana (gannets)

87–100 cm   WSp 165–180 cm   Short/Long distance migrant

The Gannet is an impressive sight when it is hunting for fish. From its search flight at a height of 30–40 m, it makes an almost vertical dive and by flattening its wings against its body adopts an arrow-like shape to dive and plunge up to 3 m deep into the water. With the aid of wingbeats it can even reach depths of 20 m in pursuit of fish. Gannets tend to hunt in groups of large shoals of fish are available, although search flights of up to 100 km are necessary in order to spot these hunting grounds.

breeds in giant colonies

plumage mottled brown

juvenile
(few weeks old)

wings long and
narrow with
black tip

adult

juvenile (1 year old)

head
yellow

bill long,
powerful

juvenile
(2 years old)

adult
in vertical
dive

upper- and
underparts
white

Habitat Breeds on steep coasts and rocky islands; mostly hunts on open seas.

> **Breeding season April–September**
> 1 bluish egg
> 1 brood per year

239

Voice Loud and low call at breeding site 'arrah' or repeated calls.

Birder's tip

Gannets are not shy at their breeding sites. You can watch them close up in different colonies on the British Isles, in France and on Helgoland as they build their nest, mate and rear the young.

White Pelican

Pelecanus onocrotalus (pelicans)
L 140–175 cm WSp270–360 cm Medium/Long distance migrant

underwing coverts black-white

head retracted, ne appears very thick

Habitat *Breeds on various lakes, also searches for food near sea coasts.*

> *Breeding season April–September*
> *2 white eggs*
> *1 brood per year*

The White Pelican breeds in colonies and also prefers to hunt in communities. Shoals of fish are encircled and driven together until every bird can scoop up its prey from the water with its enlarged pouch-bill. The Dalmatian Pelican (*P. crispus*), which is very rare, also breeds in south-eastern Europe.

Dalmatian Pelican

underwing coverts pale

often congregates in a group

pouch-bill orange

Voice Silent except during the breeding season.

eye region bare pink

bill long

pouch-bill yellow

Shag

Phalacrocorax aristotelis (cormorants)
L 65–80 cm WSp 90–115 cm Resident bird/Short distance migrant

neck thin

Habitat *Almost exclusively on rocky sea coasts; only occasionally in inland waters.*

> *Breeding season March–August*
> *1–6 pale blue eggs*
> *1 brood per year*

The Shag builds its nest out of seaweed or other floating plants and anchors this structure to cliffs or crevices in cliff faces. It only leaves the boundaries of its breeding territory if it cannot find enough fish as its basic food source. Generally, a juvenile aged three years will settle in the colony where it was born.

bill thinner than Cormorant

crest

plumage black with greenish glow

breeding plumage

high-crowned head

juvenile

throat white

under-parts brown

winter plumage

underparts white

Voice At breeding site, gurgling and clicking calls.

Mediterranean   **Atlantic**

Cormorant

Phalacrocorax carbo (cormorants)

L 80–100 cm   WSp 130–160 cm   Resident bird/Medium distance migrant

Cormorants breed in large colonies. They fish together and their evening assemblies in large, collective sleeping communities characterize this bird as gregarious. In central Europe, the Cormorant constructs its nest from twigs in a tree that is often near herons. To conserve energy during its migration flight to winter quarters, groups of Cormorants fly in an arrow-shaped formation with each bird profiting from the slipstream of the bird ahead. The Pygmy Cormorant (*P. pygmeus*), a smaller version of the Cormorant, lives on inland waters in south-eastern Europe.

neck kinked

Habitat Breeds on cliffs along coasts and in lakeside coppices; forages by rivers, coasts and lakes.

> *Breeding season March–August*
> 3–4 light blue eggs
> 1 brood per year

241

Voice Loud and low guttural cackling in breeding and sleeping places.

Birder's tip

You can often see Cormorants resting with wings outstretched. Unlike most other water birds, it cannot coat its plumage in an oily covering. This means it can dive better, but must dry out its feathers afterwards.

breeding plumage

face white

plumage shimmering black

winter plumage

breeding plumage

throat light

head brown

tail long

Pygmy Cormorant

in breeding season white patch

neck and upperparts brown

juvenile

belly light

Index of Species

Index of Species

Index of Species

Illustrations
All bird illustrations by **Paschalis Dougalis/Kosmos**, except for three bird topography drawings on pages 6 and 7 by **Steffen Walentowitz**. Distribution maps and silhouettes by **Wolfgang Lang**.

Photographs
Adam 29m, 32br, 53tl, 59b, 64b, 73mc, 73b, 84mr, 86bc, 89tr, 96b, 101ml, 101lce, 105ml, 107b, 113b, 122mr, 125mr, 125mc, 126bc, 161mc, 162tl, 163tr, 174tl, 175mc, 175lce, 177tr, 194br, 199ml, 201b, 208mr, 218tl, 219mr, 219b, 220mc, 221tr, 221b, 224tc, 225ml, 234br, 241lce; **Angermayer** 25tr, 66tl, 97b, 131tr, 240tl; **Aquila/Lankinen** 104br; **Aquila/Thomas** 238ml; **Bethge** 110tl; **Bethge/Hecker** 25mc; **Buchhorn/Silvestris** 48mc, 160bc; **Buchner/Limbrunner** 191b; **Danegger Blm,** 3 2.byt, 19m, 43mc, 75lce, 83mle, 94tle, 113tr, 129lce, 141tr, 143lce, 154mle, 157mc, 159tc, 161mle, 164mr, 213tr, 223mle, 226bc, 227lce, 225mc, 229mc; **Delpho** 136mc, 140tr; **Diedrich** 21m, 148mle, 148mr, 154mr, 156mr, 179tr, 183ml, 206mc, 220ml, 232ml; **J. Dierschke** 207mr, 218br; **V. Dierschke** 135mr, 156br, 178bc, 196ml, 200tc, 220bc; **Diemer** 155mc; **FLPA/Silvestris** 112tl, 138ml, 150tl, 156tl; **Fünfstück** 21tc, 40tl, 53tr, 54b, 68tl, 76m, 83tr, 85mr, 93mr, 93tr, 128bc, 141tc, 180tl, 196lce, 204ml, 216tr, 226br, 228tl, 228br, 233tl, 240mc; **Fürst** 1m, 3. 4byt, 16, 22b, 44tr, 46mr, 64m, 65b, 72br, 75ml, 81tr, 92mr, 122ml, 129tr, 162mr, 164tl, 168br, 186ml; **Gensbol** 104tr; **Gottschling** 55mc, 196mi, 196br, 196bc; **Groß** Blt, 3t, 27tr, 33b, 38tl, 44mr, 49tr, 57b, 61tr, 62tl, 65tr, 66b, 75mr, 82ml, 85tc, 86ml, 86tr, 87tr, 104ml, 107tr, 115ml, 119b, 121ml, 121tr, 123b, 132ml, 143mr, 143bc, 146mc, 151tr, 157mr, 163mr, 165lce, 167tr, 182br, 197tr, 222b, 228lce; **Gross/Silvestris** 54tl; **Grüner** 1b, 3b, 25mr, 26tr, 31br, 35b, 36br, 39b, 41tr, 42tl, 46tl, 53mr, 53b, 54ml, 67tm, 72mc, 78b, 82b, 85lce, 90tl, 91b, 93ml, 93lce, 97mr, 114tl, 115mr, 116tc, 120tl, 123mc, 128ml, 128mr, 140tl, 141ml, 147ml, 150ml, 150br, 160ml, 160tl, 161br, 162ml, 164ml, 169b, 170ml, 170tr, 176bc, 184br, 189tc, 190mr, 190br, 195mr, 195tc, 195bc, 198tr, 199tr, 201tr, 204b, 206ml, 206tl, 214mc, 215mr, 220mr, 223mr, 225tr, 227mr, 232mc, 232b, 235mc, 235tr; **Haag** 69lce, 176mr, 194tl, 202b, 214bc; **Halley** 24br, 26b, 36tl, 37b, 38mr, 45mc, 53tc, 63mc, 70ml, 95tr, 98tl, 100br, 102mr, 110ml, 116tl, 130br, 133tl, 134bc, 137ml, 137bc, 138br, 139mc, 139tl, 140ml, 144mr, 145tr, 157lce, 169tr, 175tr, 179mr, 185ml, 186tr, 194mc, 195lce, 198mr, 202ml, 208b, 210ml, 211tr, 211b, 236ml, 238tr; **Harrop** 20mr; **Hautala** 110mr; **Hecker** 20tl, 24mc, 24tl, 25b, 28tl, 39tr, 40ml, 42b, 46b, 50tl, 51b, 52m, 52tl, 57tr, 60b, 66ml, 67tr, 69ml, 76b, 78mr, 78tl, 84ml, 84bc, 86tl, 87mr, 88tl, 88b, 92br, 96tl, 97tr, 105tc, 106mc, 111tr, 117tr, 118br, 122bc, 131bc, 132bc, 162br, 165tr, 170mc, 177mr, 177lce, 188mr, 192ml, 193tr, 196mc, 196tl, 200mr, 205tr, 210br, 212tl, 214br, 216mr, 224bc, 225b, 230b, 233ml; **Heintzenberg** 26ml, 56ml, 102tl, 130ml, 133tl, 143tr, 194lce, 229ml, 231lce; **Heinzelmann** 62ml; **Hinze** 90ml, 90bc, 141lce, 217b; **Höfer** Blb, 2, 3 3.byt, 19tr, 23b, 28ml, 30m, 30tl, 34tr, 38ml, 38b, 41ml, 47b, 66tr, 72mc, 76tl, 77b, 79tl, 86mc, 95b, 97mc, 98mr, 98br, 99b, 122br, 124tl, 126mr, 126tl, 134ml, 145lce, 146tl, 149tr, 154tl, 159mc, 165mc, 173tr, 173b, 177mc, 180tr, 180bc, 184ml, 186br, 189mr, 191tr, 195tr, 197b, 199mr, 199mc, 208ml, 216mr, 218bc, 220tl, 222tl, 239tr, 239b, 241br; **Hoskin/Silvestris** 170br, 72tr; **Hüttenmoser** 158br; **Jachmann** 28br, 55bc, 120ml, 120br; **Kalden/Silvestris** 163ml; **Kattlás** 41bc; **Klees** 1t, 3 4.byt, 34ml, 34mr, 34tl, 48tr, 54tr, 67b, 73tc, 94b, 127lce, 136bc, 159tr, 161tr, 168tl, 193ml, 194ml, 239tc; **Lacz/Silvestris** 152tl, 49b, 142mc, 183mr; **Lange/Angermayer** 166mc; **Lenz/Silvestris** 230mc; **Lembrunner** 20ml, 20b, 24ml, 39ml, 41mr, 63tc, 64tl, 69mr, 69bc, 73mr, 73tr, 79tr, 82tl, 85ml, 90br, 92tl, 98ml, 112b, 114ml, 114br, 115lce, 120mc, 125tr, 127tr, 131br, 132mr, 132tl, 132br, 136tl, 139bc, 140br, 142tl, 144ml, 146ml, 148tl, 148bc, 153tr, 165mr, 168mr, 168bc, 171b, 173mc, 179mc, 180ml, 181ml, 182ml, 185mr, 187tr, 187b, 188ml, 195ml, 196tr, 200ml, 203ml, 207tr, 212tr, 215mc, 224ml, 224br, 226ml, 227bc, 229bc,233tr, 234mc, 237tr, 240tr; **Marquez/Silvestris** 137tr; **McElroy** 198mc; **Mestel/Hecker** 27mc, 109b, 170tl, 171tc, 216b, 220tr, 226tl, 229tr, 234tl; **Moosrainer** 23tr, 27lce, 36ml, 39mr, 43tr, 43lce, 44tl, 48ml, 48br, 60tl, 61b, 63tr, 66mr, 70mr, 70tl, 72ml, 89b, 99tr, 100mr, 105mr, 105b, 106br, 111b, 115tr, 118ml, 118mc, 135tr, 135bc, 136mr, 144br, 149b, 154bc, 157ml, 157tr, 158tl, 161mr, 161lce, 163lce, 164bc, 166tl, 166br, 172mr, 172br, 174br, 176mc, 178mr, 178br, 181tr, 182mr, 192tl, 198b, 203b, 204tl, 213b, 215ml, 220br, 224mc, 228mc, 233lce, 233bc; **Newell** 236tr; **Nill** 18b, 22tl, 36bc, 58ml, 71ml, 71tr, 75mc, 80tl, 91tr, 101mr, 118tl, 119tr, 124ml, 125lce, 133mr, 133lce, 134mr, 138tl, 142ml, 143mc, 146br, 147lce, 151ml, 158ml, 189mc, 190tl, 206b, 208ml, 212b, 234ml, 240br; Pforr 31tr, 47m, 56b, 78mc, 80b, 103tr, 109tr, 137mr, 160mr, 163mc, 192b, 202tl; **Pfützke** 104bc; **Pollen** 223b; **Pölting/Angermayer** 219tr; **Reinhard** 100ml; **Reinhard/**

Angermayer 60mr; **Reszeter** 44ml, 44br, 45mr, 45Ice, 55mr, 74ml, 74br, 236mr, 238tl;
chmid/Angermayer 56tl, 62mr, 168ml, 169mc; **Schmidt** 27mr, 40mr, 40b, 43mr, 58tl, 70b,
8ml, 92ml, 92tr, 118mr, 122tl, 126ml, 155b, 172ml, 172tl, 174ml; **Silvestris/Schiersmann** 104tl;
ohns/Silvestris 114tc, 115mc; **Sprank/Silvestris** 176tl, 210tl; **SWAN Buckingham**, 205mc;
ynatzschke 18tl, 32tl, 37ml, 79tc, 129br, 130tr, 134tl, 158tr, 167br, 183b, 200br, 202mr; **Tepke**
11tc, 236tl, 236tr; **Thielscher/Silvestris** 46ml, 123tr, 185tr; **Tuschel/Willner** 18tr, 26tl, 32mr,
2tc, 36mc, 74mc, 110b, 140mc, 147tr, 178ml, 193Ice, 198ml, 234tr, 121Ice; **Varsvuo** 55tr, 63mr,
3bc, 102ml, 102br, 102bc, 229mr, 232tl; **Volmer** 240mr; **Wendl/Angermayer** 50mc; **Wendl/**
eininger 135ml; **K. Wernicke** 155tr, 167ml, 174mr, 176ml, 176br, 182tl, 183tr, 186mr, 186mc,
86tl, 186Ice, 188tl, 189Ice, 189bc, 190ml, 193mr, 199b, 203mr, 203tr, 204mr, 209tr, 209b,
10mr, 212ml, 212mc, 214tl, 215tr, 217mc, 217tr, 218ml, 219ml, 222mr, 226tc, 230tl, 233mr,
34bc, 241tr; **P. Wernicke** 88mc, 139tr, 141mr, 141mc, 141tc, 143tl; **Wernicke/Silvestris** 175mc;
Vilhelmshurst/Silvestris 116ml, 223tr, 50br, 51ml, 87b, 179Ice, 218mr, 229Ice, 231br; **Willner**
4tr, 171tr, 180mr, 227tr, 228ml, 228tr, 240ml; **Wisniewski/Silvestris** 152b, 216ml; **Wöhler/**
ilvestris 56mc; **Wothe** 150mr, 150tr, 156bc, 188bc, 237mr; **Zeininger** 21tr, 28mc, 29tr, 31m,
2mle, 33m, 33tr, 34b, 35tr, 37tr, 43tc, 45tr, 47tr, 48tl, 50ml, 51mr, 51tr, 54mr, 58mc, 58b, 59tr,
2b, 65m, 68b, 69tr, 71mc, 72tl, 74tl, 75tr, 77tr, 79mr, 79bc, 81b, 82mr, 84tl, 85mr, 87mc, 90mc,
oootl, 101tr, 103b, 105tr, 106ml, 106tl, 106bc, 108tl, 108b, 114bc, 116br, 117b, 124mr, 128tl, 130tl,
36ml, 138mr, 142br, 144tl, 151mr, 151Ice, 153b, 156ml, 158mc, 159Ice, 163bc, 164br, 166ml, 168tc,
78tl, 181b, 184mr, 184tl, 184Ice, 185Ice, 189tr, 192mr, 198tl, 200tl, 205b, 207ml, 207b, 214ml,
14tr, 215Ice, 216tl, 224tl, 226mr, 227ml, 227mc, 231tr; **Ziesler/Angermayer** 222ml

ey
= top; m = horizontal central; b = bottom; l = left; c = vertical central; r = right; BI = inside
overs; by = by

BLACK'S **NATURE GUIDE**

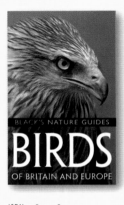

ISBN 978 1 4081 0155 1

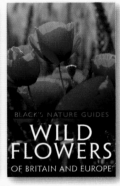

ISBN 978 1 4081 0153 7

ISBN 978 1 4081 0154 4

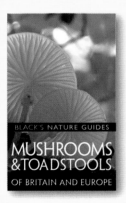

ISBN 978 1 4081 0156 8

ISBN 978 1 4081 0152 0

The new Black's nature guides – compact, concise and comprehe

www.acblack.com

Discover nature
with A&C Black

ISBN 978 07136 8666 1

ISBN 978 07136 7237 4

ISBN 978 07136 7560 3

ISBN 978 07136 8666 1

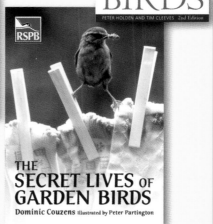

ISBN 978 07136 6616 8

www.acblack.com

Observing Birds

Birdwatching is an increasingly popular hobby. No matter where you live, be it town or countryside, birding is an activity open to everybody. Here are a few pointers for beginners who would like to learn more about birds and birdwatching.

The importance of binoculars

Even when a bird is very close it can be difficult to see the finer details of its plumage, and it is only from a distance that a bird can be watched behaving naturally. This is why binoculars are an essential part of the birdwatcher's kit.

There are two types of binoculars. One has porro prisms, in which the eye-pieces are closer together than the large lenses toward the front; the other has a roof prism, in which the eye-pieces and large lenses are in line, which generally makes these types of binoculars less bulky. The characteristics of a pair of binoculars are denoted by two figures (separated by an x). The first corresponds to the magnification, the second the diameter of the large lens in millimetres (thus 10 x 42 binoculars have a ten times magnification and a 42 mm-diameter large lens). As a general rule, the higher the magnification of a pair of binoculars the bigger and heavier they are, and the less stable the image. Likewise, the larger the coefficient between the two figures the brighter the image (thus a 10 x 42 pair – coefficient of 4.2 – is slightly brighter than an 8 x 32 (coefficient 4) but far less than an 8 x 42 (coefficient 5.25).

Binoculars come in all sorts of shapes and sizes, with prices varying between £15 and £1000 a pair. So which is the best to buy? First, it's worth bearing in mind that an 8x magnification is ideal for birdwatching, with the maximum for this being 10x. Any magnification greater than this (12x, 16x or even 20x) is too high – finding a bird through the binoculars will be very difficult and the image will be very unsteady. So 8 x 32, 8 x 42, 10 x 40 or 10 x 42 binoculars are the best for birding. Porro prism binoculars are usually the least expensive, but they tend to be more fragile, and generally their optics are inferior. The cheapest models (between £15 and £30) are only really of very occasional use. They are certainly not recommended for regular or intensive use as they may be tiring for the eyes and cause headaches. However, there are porro prism binoculars available at £35–£60 of that are of reasonable quality; these can be recommended for beginners. More expensive porro prism models are stronger with good optics; they compare favourably with the lower priced roof-prism binoculars. For anyone thinking of taking up birdwatching more seriously, roof-prism binoculars are the way to go. They are compact, are water- and dust-tight, and have better optical quality. Again there is a wide range of prices, though they are generally more expensive than porro prism binoculars. There are compact models that cost between £100 and £200 which not only have good optics but have the added advantage of being relatively light to carry. However, they do not generally give a bright image and can be difficult to use in low-light conditions, at dusk, for example. Roof-prism binoculars of £300 or more include the best models that money can buy, by well-known optics companies such as Swarovski, Leica, Zeiss and Nikon

In summary:
• for occasional use choose porro prism 8 x 30 or 8 x 32 binoculars, at the top end of the market (about £40);
• for regular use choose a good quality 8 x 42 or 10 x 42 binocular, preferably roof-prism; price £70 or more;
• for more serious birding invest in a high-end pair of roof-prism binoculars (8 x 32 or 10 x 42), from £200 upwards.

Adjusting your binoculars

Many people fail to adjust their binoculars properly prior to use. It is essential to have the lenses in line with your eyes. If the eye-pieces are too far apart, then a dark area appears in the centre of the image; if they are too close together the dark area appears at the edges of the image. Don't hesitate in changing the width between eye-pieces in borrowed binoculars, it can easily be changed back. All binoculars have a means of dioptric correction. It helps account for differences in the vision of each eye. This adjustment is easy and only needs to be done once.

1. Shut the right eye and focus on a stationary object in the middle distance with the use of the focus wheel.

2. Now shut the left eye and open the right one; if the image isn't clear then put it into focus using the adjustment around the right-hand eye-piece (or on the central axis in roof-prism models).

3. Now look at the object with both eyes; the image should be perfect. If not try the process again.

Once this pre-focusing has been accomplished, normal focusing is done using the central focusing wheel only.

Binoculars are an essential piece of birding equipment.

Other equipment

A pair of binoculars is the basic tool for birding, but other equipment is also important.

Clothing

It is not necessary to be dressed in camouflage gear to get near to birds, though duller rather than brightly coloured clothing can help. Much more important is comfort. A birder needs to be at ease with their environment, to be able to move easily and not to be too hot or too cold. Birds have such keen sight and are so sensitive to movement that it is very difficult not to have been seen; better to be discreet, be silent and to keep calm when close. Pay particular attention in choice of footwear; rubber boots in wet areas, hiking boots on long walks or rocky terrain, comfortable trainers elsewhere.

Notebook

It is important to keep a notebook when out in the field. You can list species seen, the day's weather, information on the site visited, notes on behaviour and also on the plumage of any birds you haven't been able to identify.

Telescopes

Serious birders spend serious money on telescopes. Of course, a telescope allows better views of distant birds, and can make identification much easier. However, they are expensive, hard to carry around, and probably not for the beginner. It is best to use binoculars to start with, then move on to working with both binoculars and telescope later.

A good guide

No matter what level of birding you have reached, there will be times when you are stumped by a bird and need back up. For this you will need a decent bird identification guide. Even the most experienced birders carry a guide around with them! This book will help you identify all of the common birds you will see, as well as most of the rarer ones. It often pays to do a little research beforehand; memorising the shapes, colours and calls of species you are expecting to come across in a given habitat can make locating the birds much easier. There are numerous guides to the birds of Britain and Europe which can be used in conjunction with this book.

Getting the most out of birding

There are some simple rules that birdwatchers should follow to help them get the most out of their birding

Be discreet

Birds have very good eyesight and will often fly when humans come too close. To see these birds and to avoid startling them, a birder needs to move slowly without making sudden movements, without speaking loudly and while making as little noise underfoot as possible. By keeping elatively quiet and by moving slowly nd deliberately, you can scan more asily for small movements or quiet, hin calls; birds are often first located y their calls, especially in woodland. n the countryside it is best to walk long a woodland edge or hedgerow ather than along the middle of a field, nd to walk in the shade rather than in he sun to help you blend in to the ackground. In addition, quiet, and iscreet behaviour will be appreciated y birders and other visitors.

eep your distance

t is always best to keep some way way from a bird to avoid disturbing it nd causing it to fly away. Try to keep till as much as possible. Binoculars hould be raised slowly and any novements kept slow. Bear in mind hat you should avoid disturbing the ird at all costs. The energy a bird vastes escaping from a clumsy birder ould mean the difference between life nd death. It is important to keep calm or this reason – indicating a bird's osition to others by waving, esticulating or calling out is almost uaranteed to end with the bird flying way, never to be seen again.

e patient

good birder must be a patient birder. inding a bird can take a long time, eeing it well even longer. Those who ake up photography and digiscoping eed even greater reserves of patience. irdwatching for beginners can be a ource of frustration, as there may be

times when few birds are seen, and conditions may be poor. Experience helps you deal with this, and the eventual reward is worth it! The only remedy is to spend as much time looking at birds as you can, learn to enjoy watching and testing your identification skills on common birds, and don't despair if you struggle at first – remember, all birdwatchers have to learn the ropes!

Choose your location carefully

Although they occur more or less everywhere, birds concentrate in rather few places. Most species occupy a definite habitat, outside of which they are rarely seen. it is therefore important to know which species occur in which habitats. The best places for beginners are wetlands, forest edges and open spaces with copses. An RSPB reserve is a great place to start, where you'll have the added bonus of hides, helpful guides and, in some of the larger ones, the use of telescopes and a visitor centre.

While relatively common, Kingfishers are shy, wary birds. However, with patience and luck you may be able to see one resting on a streamside perch.

Author

Volker Dierschke has been a keen birder since his childhood. His grandfather, who was an ornithologist in his spare time, inspired him. After graduating in biology from Göttingen University, Dierschke continued his research on the migratory behaviour of birds at ornithologica field stations on Helgoland and at Hiddensee. His doctoral thesis investigated the migratory behaviour of waders and he also studied the distribution of seabirds in German coastal areas. Today, Volker Dierschke is one of Germany's best-known ornithologists. He is editor of the magazine *Die Vogelwelt* and works as a freelance biologist and author.

With 958 photographs (see index of illustrations pp. 248/249) and 747 colour drawings of birds by Paschalis Dougalis/Kosmos, 3 bird topography drawings on pages 6 and 7 by Steffen Walentowitz and 368 distribution maps and 13 insets by Wolfgang Land.

The photograph on page 2 shows a Nuthatch. The photographs on page 3 show (from top to bottom): Yellowhammer, Wood Pigeon, Kestrel, Grey Heron, Redshank and a Black-necked Grebe Pages 16 and 17 show a pair of Bee-eaters.

Published 2008 by A&C Black Publishers Ltd, 38 Soho Square, London W1D 3HB

www.acblack.com

First published 2007 by Franckh-Kosmos Verlags GmbH & Co. KG, Stuttgart, Germany

Copyright © 2008 by Franckh-Kosmos Verlags GmbH & Co. KG

ISBN 978-1-4081-0155-1

A CIP catalogue record for this book is available from the British Library

This book is produced using paper that is made from wood grown in managed sustainable forests. It is natural, renewable and recyclable. The logging and manufacturing processes conform to the environmental regulations of the country of origin.

Author: Volker Dierschke
Commissioning Editor: Nigel Redman
Project editor: Jim Martin

Translation by Heide Kunzelmann (in association with Artes Translations)
Design by Fluke Art, Cornwall

Printed in Italy

10 9 8 7 6 5 4 3 2 1

Cover photograph: Red Kite © tbkmedia.de/Alamy